28 4/0/04

FROM
WEIMAR
TO
WALL STREET

VOLUME 3
1918-1929

FROM
WEIMAR
TO
WALL STREET

INTRODUCTION BY

ASA BRIGGS

Project editor Peter Furtado

Project art editor Ayala Kingsley

Text editors Louise Jones, Mike March, Sue Martin, Robert Peberdy

Designers Frankie Wood, Janet McCallum, Wolfgang Mezger, Gill Mouqué, Niki Overy, Linda Reed, Nicholas Rous, Tony de Saulles, Dave Sumner, Rita Wütrych

Cartographic manager Olive Pearson

Cartographic editor Zoë Goodwin

Picture research manager Alison Renney

Picture research Jan Croot, Diane Hamilton, Rebecca Hirsh, Angela Murphy, Diana Phillips, Linda Proud, Christine Vincent, Charlotte Ward-Perkins

Editorial assistants Monica Byles, Elaine Welsh

 AN EQUINOX BOOK

© Andromeda Oxford Ltd 1993

Devised and produced by Andromeda Oxford Ltd 11–15 The Vineyard Abingdon Oxfordshire OX14 3PX England

This edition published by Hamlyn, part of Reed Consumer Books Ltd, Michelin House, 81 Fulham Road, London SW3 6RB

ISBN 0-600-57991-3

Printed in Germany by Mohndruck Graphische Betriebe GmbH. Gutersloh.

CONTENTS

James Foreman-Peck
University of Hull
Brian Foss
Freelance writer
Michael Geyer
University of Chicago, USA
Robert Gildea
Merton College, Oxford
Anthony Glees
Brunel University
Roger Griffin
Oxford Polytechnic
Jennifer Hargreaves
Roehampton Institute,
London
Nathaniel Harris
Freelance writer
Nigel Harris
University College, London
Gundi Harriss
Birkbeck College, London
David Horn
University of Liverpool

Julian Jackson
University College of
Swansea
Keith Jeffrey
University of Ulster
Matthew Jones
St Antony's College, Oxford
Paul Kennedy
Yale University, USA
Ghislaine Lawrence
National Museum of Science
and Industry, London
Peter Lowe
University of Manchester
Keith Lyons
London School of Economics
Dermott MacCann
Brunel University
Peter Martland
Corpus Christi College,
Cambridge
Roger Morgan
London School of Economics

Lucy Newton
Leicester University
A. J. Nicholls
St Antony's College, Oxford
David Penn
Imperial War Museum,
London
Brian Holden Reid
King's College, London
Catherine Reilly
Freelance writer
Denis Ridgeway
Formerly of Royal Navy
Scientific Service
Gowher Rizvi
University of Warwick
Keith Sainsbury
University of Reading
Harry Shukman
St Antony's College, Oxford
Penny Sparke
Royal College of Art, London
Jill Stephenson
University of Edinburgh

Stanley Trapido
Lincoln College, Oxford
T.H.E. Travers
University of Calgary,
Canada
S.B. Whitmore
Formerly British Army of the
Rhine, Germany
Paul Wilkinson
University of Aberdeen
Elizabeth Wilson
North London Polytechnic
Roger Zetter
Oxford Polytechnic

CARTOGRAPHIC
ADVISORS
Colin Bruce
Imperial Collge, London
John Pimlott
Royal Military Academy,
Sandhurst

INTRODUCTION

The main legacy of World War I was not the victors' peace, a peace imposed on Germany that clearly could not last, but revolution that swept first across the plains and mountains of Russia, an empire which until 1917 had been ranged under its czar on the other side. Revolution in Germany did not succeed. Yet the Russian Revolution, which began as a wide-ranging revolt against czarism but was captured by Lenin's Bolsheviks, had consolidated its gains by 1929. By then it had already gone through many phases, military, political, economic and cultural. After bitter debates between the leading Bolsheviks, Stalin emerged as a wily and ruthless leader, and from 1927 onward he maintained supreme command of a bureaucratically controlled Communist party that condemned any "deviation from the general party line" as he formulated it. His rival Leon Trotsky, a brilliant writer and orator who demanded "permanent worldwide revolution", was expelled from the party and driven into exile in 1929. Stalin's slogan "socialism in one country" was implemented coercively through Five Year Plans, the first of which, launched in 1928, concentrated on heavy industry and on the forced collectivization of the peasantry. It was designed, at incalculable human cost, to transform the whole economy of the Soviet Union.

The capitalist economies of the different Western European countries faltered and fluctuated during the 1920s while that of the United States boomed. Britain never recaptured the position of international economic leadership that it had secured before 1914, although it clung to its free-trade policy and in 1925 controversially restored the gold standard. Its industrial problems multiplied under the pressure of foreign competition. France, which in 1919 had been awarded substantial financial reparations from defeated Germany, four years later occupied Germany's industrial heartland, the Ruhr, when the Germans whose currency had been made worthless after spiraling inflation, paid neither in hard cash nor in gold. Yet three years later the French franc had fallen to one tenth of its prewar value and there was a domestic political crisis.

Defeated Germany, which never met any of its reparation obligations out of its own economic resources, alienated many citizens in its period of catastrophic inflation. Although its economy seemed strong between 1925 and 1928 – far stronger than it had been in 1913 – its working class was sharply divided between Social Democrats and Communists, the latter looking to Moscow for guidance. Sections of the middle classes were already being attracted to Hitler's National Socialist party, which in 1928 had 100,000 members, although it had only 12 seats in the National Parliament.

A substantial share of Germany's reparations debt was held in the United States, and these and other war debts inexorably drew the United States, where isolationism was strong, into complex international negotiations. Yet the American economy seemed in especially good shape during the 1920s. These were golden years of prosperity, when industrial production, based on substantial entrepreneurial investment and relatively well-paid assembly-line labor, increased in ten years by 60 percent. Wages rose, too, if at a far less rapid rate, and above all consumption, raising American standards of living to what, even to Americans, seemed dazzling heights. In March 1929 Herbert Hoover, the new Republican president, claimed in his inaugural address to the nation that man was in sight of triumphing over poverty. The ironic dimension of this claim was to appear only later, for the American stock market boomed more than any other kind of market as stock prices doubled between January 1928 and September 1929.

There had also been a brief period during the 1920s when it had not seemed ironical to talk of man triumphing over war as well as want. The United States had chosen not to join the League of Nations, the new international organization to pursue peace, which had been set up in 1919 – with the American Democratic president Woodrow Wilson as one of its chief instigators. In 1928, however, 15 countries signed the Kellogg-Briand Pact, drafted by the American secretary of state, Frank B. Kellogg, and the French foreign secretary, Aristide Briand. They "condemned and renounced war as an instrument of national policy" and agreed to settle peacefully all international disputes.

Three years earlier, the Locarno Pact, signed in London, had pointed the way. Briand was one of its signatories. Others were the German chancellor Gustav Stresemann, who was to die in 1928, and the British foreign secretary, Sir Austen Chamberlain, brother of Neville Chamberlain, who was to be British prime minister when World War II broke out in 1939. Germany, Belgium, France, Great Britain and Italy – now Fascist Italy under the control of a dictator, Benito Mussolini – mutually guaranteed peace in Western Europe, and Germany undertook to submit to arbitration disputes involving Belgium, France, Czechoslovakia and Poland.

Czechoslovakia and Poland were two of the new nation states created at Versailles in 1919 with Wilson once again as their chief advocate. Untroubled by doubts, he believed in national self-determination as the key to a policy of peace. It proved difficult to translate principle into practice. Moreover, the relevance of the fact that the new nations, carved out of the prewar autocratic empires of Austria-Hungary, Russia and Turkey and given a place on the map at Versailles, all contained other national minorities was not clearly appreciated by him or by others. Nor was the fact that aggressive nationalism is seldom a force for peace.

Far away from Europe, Japan, developing rapidly despite a great earthquake in Tokyo in 1923 which killed 140,000 people, drew on traditional roots in the formation of its own brand of nationalism, expanding economically. In 1929 its population was more than double that at the time of the Meiji restoration in 1868, and its leaders were looking outside for markets and materials. China, too, Japan's greatest potential market, had its own strong nationalist movement, the Guomindang, although the Chinese Communist party, launched in 1921, gained ground before 1928 and, by appealing to peasants, mobilized its own independent armies.

Broadcasting and communications

News of what was happening in distant parts of the world reached Europe and the United States far more quickly than ever before during the 1920s, not only as a result of the rise of the press and of international press agencies but because of the

▶ New York's financial district c. 1917.

development of radio broadcasting. Before 1920 Marconi's radio devices and those of his competitors were largely associated with the transmission of private or business messages of the kind that might have been sent by wire. Now they became associated with broadcast programs, listened to by ever-larger audiences. Singing from London in 1920, the Australian soprano Nellie Melba was heard simultaneously all over Europe. Meanwhile, in the United States so many radio stations were created, each dependent for its income on advertising revenues, that there was "chaos on the ether".

Britain found a halfway house for the organization of sound broadcasting. It was not backed by business, as it was in the United States, nor propaganda broadcasting, as it was in the Soviet Union. Programs were paid for out of license fees that were collected by the Post Office. The British Broadcasting Company of 1922, the creation of a radio manufacturers' business consortium, gave way in 1927 to a British Broadcasting Corporation, governed by Royal Charter. The initials, BBC, did not need to be changed. And the same man, John Reith, managed both, imposing his own philosophy.

Broadcasting provided not only news but information, education and entertainment, and like many other inventions of the 1920s – particularly the gramophone – it gave new life to the home. There was new one form of entertainment, however, which took people out of the home: the cinema. Huge audiences were attracted to the "movies", many of them made in the United States which, drawing on talents from different countries, had become the dominant force in the film industry

An age of contrasts

There was highly sophisticated jazz just as there was highly sophisticated cinema – the latter associated less with the United States, however, than with France and with Germany. The Atlantic, now crossable in a single bound by an aircraft, or in modernist splendor and comfort on a luxury liner, was now less of a cultural divide. Paris was a Mecca for Americans committed to literature and the arts. The Berlin of the late 1920s had a culture of its own, the culture of the smoky cabaret. It was obviously ironical at the time that in the United States there was prohibition of the manufacture and sale of alcohol, introduced in 1920. It did not lead to the disappearance of nightclubs: alcohol became more attractive rather than less. Mainstream America spotlit what was happening to marginal America: the attempted enforcement of virtue made possible the rise of bootleggers and the booty of the gangster. Chicago underworld king Al Capone became one of the best-known men in the United States.

In Britain, too, there were contrasts. In London cocktails could be bought freely, as well as gin, whisky and other alcoholic drinks of all kinds, including English beer, yet for all the glitter and self-conscious modernity of Mayfair the countryside remained traditionalist. This was essentially the "age of Baldwin", a pipe-smoking Conservative prime minister who was born in a small Midlands town and preferred the country to the city. This preference was shared by many Englishmen, not least those who worked in the City of London. The increase in the number of automobiles – made for and bought by the masses in the United States, though still not yet in Britain – made it possible to escape to the wilderness in the United States and to the countryside in Britain. It also made possible, however, on both sides of the Atlantic, the unplanned spread of suburbia, notionally bringing the country into the city but in fact causing the outlying regions of the city to sprawl chaotically over miles of farmland.

Meanwhile, more people were beginning to plan the size of their families through birth control, a practice which despite continuing criticism, particularly on religious grounds, was beginning to become respectable. As the size of families fell, women enjoyed a greater measure of freedom, expressed also in dress. More women found fulfilment in the workplace, particularly in the office where machines such as typewriters were increasingly sold as essential accessories for the smart young secretary. Women were also beginning to enjoy a greater measure of political influence. Britain gave them the vote in two instalments, the first in 1918 for women over 30, the second in 1928, for those over 21, the so-called "flapper vote". Norway, Denmark, Finland, the Soviet Union, Australia and New Zealand had already led the way before 1918. In Germany women were enfranchised in 1919 and in 1920 in the United States (though some states had enfranchised them earlier). France lagged behind. As in some other Western countries, there was more fear there of a declining population – which meant an aging population – than of a population explosion.

An English novelist, Aldous Huxley, dealt with some of these themes when he wrote pessimistically in 1932 of a "brave new world". An American, two years younger, F. Scott Fitzgerald, who had made his mark in 1920 with his rallying cry to youth, *This Side of Paradise*, wrote his revealing novel *The Great Gatsby* five years later. It was a fable of American life. American society could raise you up and force you down, and what happened to the individual could happen to the whole of society.

during World War I. Hollywood stars of the 1920s included the comedian tramp Charlie Chaplin, born in London's East End, and Pola Negri, an attractive actress born in Poland. Both made their names in silent films.

It was a revolutionary change when "talkies" took over in the late 1920s, much as television (already dreamed of) was to take over from sound broadcasting a generation later. One of the first batch of novelty films featuring sound was a part-talkie, *The Jazz Singer* (1927), with Al Jolson as the voice of the singer. It was an appropriate choice, for jazz rhythms provided the beat of the age. Jazz drew on the cultural inheritance both of America and of Africa. Many people did not like it: others felt liberated by it. They expressed themselves too in dancing. This was the age of the Charleston and of Tin Pan Alley.

THE
REVOLUTIONARY
FLOOD

"Germany accepts responsibility for causing all the loss and damage to which the Allied and Associated Governments and their nationals have been subjected as a consequence of the war imposed upon them by the aggression of Germany and her Allies."

TREATY OF VERSAILLES, 1919

"The murder of prominent Zionists in various parts of the Holy Land, gives some indication of the real and imminent peril of an Arab revolt."

PALESTINE NEWS, 1922

"Our interests for peace are far greater than our interests in creating a machinery of defense. A machinery of defense is easy to create, but beware lest in creating it you destroy the chance of peace."

RAMSEY MACDONALD, 1924

"Let each one of us first be a citizen of Europe linked together by the great concept of civilization which imbues our Continent... we have the right to speak of a European Idea."

GUSTAV STRESEMANN on the Treaty of Locarno, 1925

"The Soviet Union is carried on by a reign of terror more complete and horrifying than ever existed under the Romanoffs. Democracy in Russia is a complete farce – a tragic farce – for the illusion that the people rule is maintained by the imprisonment and death of all who disagree."

EMMA GOLDMAN, 1925

"...if I had been an Italian I am sure I would have been wholeheartedly with you from the start...your movement has rendered service to the whole world."

W. CHURCHILL to Mussolini, 1927

"...we have passed from the policy of restricting *the exploiting tendencies of the kulaks to the policy of* eliminating *the kulaks as a class."*

JOSEF STALIN, 1929

Time Chart

		1919	1920	1921
Europe/Mediterranean		• 12 Jan: Socialist uprising, Berlin (Ger) • Jan: Irish Republic declared, Dublin; start of Anglo–Irish War • 18 Jan: Opening of Paris Peace Conference (PPC) • 23 Mar: Formation of Italian fascist party • 28 Jun: Germany signed Treaty of Versailles • 31 Jul: German Weimar Republic established • 10 Sep: Treaty of St Germain: Austrian republic and Allies • 27 Nov: Treaty of Neuilly: Bulgaria and Allies	• Foundation of UK Communist Party • Mar: UK parliament's Home Rule Act passed, dividing Ireland into N (6 counties) and S (26 counties) • 1 Mar: Miklós Horthy became regent of Hungary (ruling for 24 years) • 4 Jun: Hungary cut to ⅓ pre-war size by Treaty of Trianon • Nov: Defeat of White armies in Crimea ended Russian civil war	• Italian Communist Party founded by Antonio Gramsci • Feb: UK unemployment exceeded 1,000,000 • Apr: German war reparations fixed at £6600 million plus interest • 14 May: Fascists gained 29 seats in Italian parliament • 16 Dec: UK parliament ratified peace agreement ending Anglo–Irish war and recognizing Irish Free State (S Ire) as a dominion within Commonwealth
The Middle East		• 13 Apr: Unarmed protesters massacred by UK troops at Amritsar (Ind) • May: Mustafa Kemal (Atatürk) began nationalist revolution in Turkey • 10 Aug: Turkish empire dismembered by Treaty of Sèvres • Nov: Egypt granted constitution by UK • Dec: UK's India Act set up elected bicameral parliament	• Apr: Syria and Lebanon became French mandates; Mesopotamia (Irq) and Palestine, UK mandates • 23 Apr: In Turkey, Mustafa Kemal (Atatürk) became 1st president of provisional republican government • Sep: Indian Congress Party adopted Gandhi's program of non-violent noncooperation (satyagraha)	• Coup in Persia led by Colonel Reza Khan • May: Nationalist riots in Egypt suppressed by UK troops • Jul: Start of rebellion in Spanish Morocco; Riff Arabs led by nationalist Abdel Krim • 23 Aug: Emir Faisal crowned king of Iraq (Faisal I)
Africa		• Anglo–French partition of Cameroons and Togoland (former German W African protectorates); mandates later issued by League of Nations • SW Africa mandated to Union of S Africa	• League of Nations mandate divided German E Africa between UK and Belgium, creating Tanganyika and Ruanda-Urundi • Jul: Kenya (E Afr) made a UK crown colony	• Formation of Kikuyu Association in Kenya (E Afr)
The Americas		• Founding of US Communist Party, under William Foster • 29 Jan: Prohibition constituted in US (to 1933), by 18th Amendment • 19 Nov: US Senate voted against ratifying Treaty of Versailles, thereby excluding US from League of Nations	• Jan: 1000s arrested in US Communist scare • 26 Aug: US women enfranchised, by 19th Amendment • 1 Dec: Alvaro Obregón elected president of Mexico	• 18 Oct: US Senate ratified peace treaties with Germany, Austria and Hungary
Asia and Pacific		• By Treaty of Versailles, control of Shandong province (Chn) officially transferred from Germany to Japan	• Australian Communist and Country parties founded	• Jul: Foundation of Chinese Communist Party by Chen Tu-hsiu and Li Ta-chao • 5 Nov: Crown Prince Hirohito became regent of Japan
World		• International Labor Organization formed • Feb: League of Nations pledged support at PPC • Mar: Founding of 3rd International (Komintern)	• Dec: 1st full meeting of League of Nations Assembly, in Geneva (Sui), attended by 41 nations	• 12 Nov (to Feb 1922): Washington Conference on naval disarmament and the Pacific (US, UK, Fr, Ita, Neth, Bel, Port, Chn, Jap)

1922	1923	1924	1925	1926	1927	1928	1929
• 6 Apr: Treaty Rapallo between Germany and USSR, establishing diplomatic and economic relations • 4 Jun: assassination of German foreign minister Walther Rathenau, a Jew, by rightwing nationalists • 0 Oct: Mussolini ited to become me minister by tor Emmanuel III • 0 Dec: Russia came Union of viet Socialist publics (USSR)	• 11 Jan: Occupation of Ruhr (Ger) by French and Belgian troops • Apr: Josef Stalin became head of USSR Communist Party • 10 Jul: All nonfascist parties abolished (Ita) • 13 Sep: General Miguel Primo de Rivera became dictator of Spain • 8–9 Nov, Munich Putsch: Hitler's failure to overthrow Bavarian state government (Ger) • 20 Nov: Introduction of *Rentenmark*, to curb inflation (Ger)	• Republican Party founded in Spain by Manuel Azaña • Jan–Oct: UK's 1st Labour goverment, under Ramsay MacDonald • 21 Jan: Death of Lenin (USSR) • 25 Mar: Greek republic proclaimed • Apr: Fascist party victory in Italian general election • 16 Aug: Dawes Plan on reparation payments agreed by Germany and Allies • 30 Aug: Introduction of *Reichsmark* (Ger)	• 25 Apr: Field Marshal von Hindenburg became Germany's 1st elected president • Oct: Arrests after police raid on UK Communist Party HQ • Nov: Foundation of SS by Nazis (Ger) • 1 Dec, Locarno Pact: Treaties signed by European powers (Ger, Bel, Fr, UK, Ita); French and Belgian borders with Germany confirmed; Rhineland made a demilitarized zone	• Jan: Mussolini assumed power to rule by decree (Ita) • Jan–Aug: Theodoros Pangalos ruled Greece as a dictator • May: UK's 1st General Strike, in support of coal miners' dispute • May: Military coup in Poland, led by Józef Pilsudski (effective dictator to 1935)	• UK Trades Disputes Act outlawed general strikes and compulsory political levying by trade unions • Jan: End of Allied military control of Germany • Jul: Clashes between *Heimwehr* (fascist) and *Schutzbund* (socialist) private armies in Vienna (Aut) • Oct: Norway's 1st Labor government elected • Dec: Trotsky expelled from Communist Party (USSR)	• Launch of Stalin's 1st Five–year Plan in USSR; beginning of land collectivization • Italian Communist Party leader, Antonio Gramsci, sentenced to 20 years' imprisonment • May: In UK, suffrage extended to women over 21	• Liquidation of *kulaks* (farmers) ordered by Stalin (USSR) • Jan: Alexander I of the Serbo-Croat-Slovenes (3 Oct, Yugoslavia) set up a royal dictatorship • Jan: 7-hour working day introduced (USSR) • 11 Feb: Lateran Treaty established Vatican as City State, ruled by Pope • May: Little Entente signed (Tch, Yugo, Rom) • Aug: Germany accepted Young Plan for war reparations
JK protectorate gypt ended eb: Suppression 6-month Muslim ellion in Indian vince of Malabar; ginning of renewed du–Muslim tension Mar: Gandhi sen-ced to 6 years in son for sedition (Ind) iep: Turkish capture Smyrna ended Greek sence in Asia Minor	• Tangier (Mor) declared an international free port • 15 Mar: Sultan Ahmed Fuad proclaimed King Fuad I of Egypt • 24 Jul: Treaty of Lausanne between Turkey and Allies, renegotiating 1920 Treaty of Sèvres • 29 Oct: Turkish republic proclaimed, with Mustafa Kemal (Atatürk) as president	• Mecca (Arabia) captured by forces of Emir Ibn Saud • Feb: Gandhi released from prison (Ind) • Mar: Caliphate (spiritual leadership of Islam) abolished in Turkey • 15 Mar: Opening of 1st Egyptian parliament	• Riff rebels under Abdel Krim pushed south into French Morocco, having expelled Spanish from north • Jul: Opening of Iraq's 1st parliament, in Baghdad • Druse uprising began in Syria, against French military presence (to Jun 1927)	• Lebanon proclaimed a republic • 8 Jan: Ibn Saud declared himself king of Hejaz and Nejd (Arabia), overthrowing King Hussein • Apr: Pahlevi dynasty founded in Persia, as Reza Khan crowned shah in Tehran • May: Moroccan nationalist Abdel Krim surrendered to Franco–Spanish army led by Marshal Pétain	• May: King Ibn Saud of Hejaz and Nejd (Arabia) recognized by UK		• Jan–Oct: Civil war in Afghanistan, led by Habibullah, resulted in election of Nadir Khan as king • Aug: Arab–Jewish clashes in Jerusalem (Pal) led to 250 deaths • Dec: Turkish women enfranchised
2 Sep: UK formally nexed S Rhodesia as elf-governing colony	• Segregationalist Nationalist Party in coalition government with Labor Party; James Hertzog as prime minister (S Afr) • N Rhodesia formally made a UK protectorate	• Afrikaans made official language of Union of S Africa	• Joint Front set up between ANC and Indian community (S Afr)	• Friendship and arbitration treaty signed by Ethiopia (Abyssinia) and Italy			
American nference met, in shington (US); merican Court of stice reinstituted	• 3 Aug: Calvin Coolidge sworn in as US president, on death of Warren Harding • Dec: US support for President Obregón of Mexico against right-wing military uprising	• Johnson–Reed Act set US immigration at 2% of each nationality as 1890 census • General Plutarcho Calles elected Mexican president • Jul: End of US military occupation of Dominican Republic; constitutional government set up under Pres. Horacio Vázquez	• 170-day miners' strike in US • 5 Mar – 3 May: 5th Pan-American Conference, Santiago (Chi); Gondra Treaty on prevention of conflict • Aug: 1st national congress of Ku Klux Klan (US)	• 31 Jul: Mexican priests began a strike (to 1929), after enforcement of anti-clerical clauses of 1917 constitution	• Canadian autonomy within Commonwealth reaffirmed by opening of embassy in Washington, DC (US) • Escalation of dispute between Paraguay and Bolivia over Chaco Boreal • Beginning of guerrilla resistance to US inter-vention in Nicaragua	• Jun: US Agricultural Marketing Act encouraged establishment of farming cooperative associations • 7 Nov: Republican Herbert Hoover elected US president	• May: Revised US tariff legislation increased duties payable; led to retaliation by overseas nations • Aug: League of Nations arbitration convention rejected by Paraguay and Bolivia
		• Vietnamese Nation-alist (1931, Indochinese Communist) Party founded by Nguyen Ai Quoc (Ho Chi Minh) • 12 Mar: In China, death of Sun Yat-sen; Jiang Jieshi made leader of Kuomintang		• Start of Communist-led nationalist uprising in Dutch E Indies (until 1927) • 25 Dec: Hirohito became emperor of Japan on death of father	• Mar: US/UK shelling of Nanking (Chn) after Nationalist capture • 12 Apr: Communist purge in Shanghai (Chn) • Jun: Indonesian Nationalist Party (PNI) founded	• Apr: Japanese troops began year-long occupation of China's Shandong province • Oct: Jiang Jieshi established Nationalist government at Nanking, claiming control of unified China	• Indonesian nationalist leaders, including Achmed Sukarno, gaoled (Dutch E Indies)
5 Feb: 1st sitting Permanent Inter-onal Court of tice, at The gue (Neth)	• Sep: Dominions' right to make foreign treaties recognized by UK at Imperial conference in London			• Germany joined League of Nations		• 27 Aug: Kellogg–Briand Pact (renouncing war as an instrument of national policy) signed by 15 nations in Paris (Fr)	• 24 Oct, Black Thursday: Depression ushered in by panic selling of 13 million shares on Wall Street (US)

Datafile

The Great War was a vast struggle of attrition in which industrial and military mobilization held the key to success. The major combatants maintained mass armies in the field for four years, supplying them with thousands of tonnes of shells, food and other supplies. The naval powers also maintained large battlefleets, with extensive requirements for fuel, ammunition and manpower. And as the war developed, every combatant was forced to devote resources to the development of a third arm, capable of taking the war to the enemy by air. The human and material cost of this effort was immense. Mass war produces mass casualties, and advances in military technology – particularly in the form of the high explosive shell and the machine-gun – reduced land warfare to a grim struggle of attrition in which victory went to the army which could sustain huge losses the longest. The human slaughter was underpinned by an equally great economic effort. The highly developed industrial economies of the Great Powers were mobilized to produce vast quantities of military equipment.

German gunpowder production

(Tonnes per month, millions — April 1914, Oct 1914, Oct 1915, April 1917, April 1918, Oct 1918)

◄ **The economies of the combatant powers were restructured to meet the increasing demands of the war. Factories and workers were switched away from their normal peacetime activities to produce the materials of war. The effects are made clear by statistics for German gunpowder production which increased fourteenfold in four years.**

► **Nowhere was industrial mobilization more impressive than in Britain. UK munitions production increased by factors varying between 500 and 1000 percent – an achievement which allowed Britain to expand its volunteer army to match the much larger conscript forces of its continental allies and enemies.**

UK munitions production

- Guns
- Tanks
- Aircraft
- Machine guns

(Thousands — 1914, 1915, 1916, 1917, 1918; values shown: 91, 300, 3,390, 4,314, 33,500, 79,700)

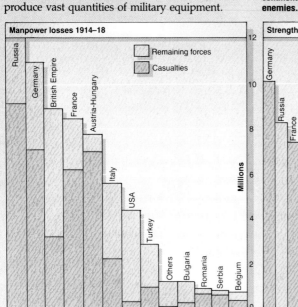

Manpower losses 1914–18

- Remaining forces
- Casualties

(Russia, Germany, British Empire, France, Austria-Hungary, Italy, USA, Turkey, Others, Bulgaria, Romania, Serbia, Belgium — Millions)

Strength of armies 1914

(Germany, Russia, France, Italy, Austria-Hungary, Turkey, UK, Serbia, Belgium, Montenegro — Millions)

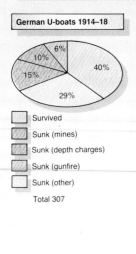

German U-boats 1914–18

- 40% Survived
- 29%
- 15%
- 10%
- 6%

- Survived
- Sunk (mines)
- Sunk (depth charges)
- Sunk (gunfire)
- Sunk (other)

Total 307

▲ **Europe became a continent in arms, with millions of young men donning the uniforms of their countries and serving in the trenches. The scale and duration of the fighting produced an inevitably heavy toll in casualties – the dead, wounded and prisoners were also numbered in millions, accounting in many cases for over half the total mobilized.**

◄ **The failure of Germany's surface fleet to make an impact on the war placed the U-boats (submarines) in the forefront of the naval struggle. While German submarines sank millions of tonnes of Allied merchantmen, the cost was high – well over half the U-boats deployed were lost to mines, marine hazard and anti-submarine weapons.**

▲ **Superior German organization and economic mobilization produced the largest army to take the field in 1914 with 5 million men marching to the guns. Only Russia and France fielded forces on the same scale. Of the other original combatants, only Britain had the capacity to produce a force of equivalent size under wartime conditions.**

► **The large battles fought on the Western and Eastern Fronts were bloody, sprawling engagements which dragged on for weeks and sometimes months, drawing in millions of men. Verdun, the epic battle for the strategic center of France's defenses, dwarfed all others in scale, but everywhere the scale of the fighting was immense.**

Forces at major campaigns

- France
- Germany
- UK
- Russia
- USA
- Turkey
- Anzac

(Verdun, Marne, Somme, Chemin des Dames, Spring offensive, Gallipoli, Meuse-Argonne, Champagne, 1st Battle of Masuria, 3rd Battle of Ypres, 2nd Battle of Masuria, Tannenberg — Millions)

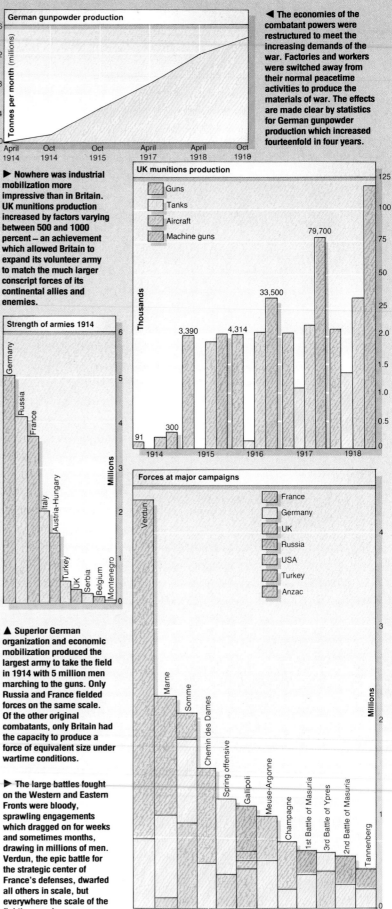

THE IMPACT OF THE GREAT WAR

The effect of total war
The coming of peace
The democratic tide
after the war

In 1914, according to British prime minister David Lloyd George, the Great Powers of Europe had "slithered over the edge into war", none of them apparently driven by a powerful aggressive motive. Four years later, Europe had been transformed in a hideously profligate war. Over nine million soldiers had died, and an international army of disabled veterans was a permanent reminder of the horrors of the war. Even after 1918 men continued to succumb to their war wounds or complications of war-related conditions. Ex-soldiers themselves spoke of a "burnt-out" generation. In this war, moreover, truth had been a major casualty.

The impact of total war

World War I had changed the nature of political life in the 20th century irrevocably. It had both expanded the public domain at the expense of the private, and raised the level of tolerance of "civilized people" toward political violence and brutality. There were three major elements in this

▼ French reservists on their way to join the colors in 1914. Postwar, survivors from the millions of Allied working-class conscripts found their horizons expanded and their economic power bitterly curtailed.

chilling process. First, propaganda, preparing the ground for the suppression of dissent and the vilification of the enemy. Propaganda became simply government-sponsored lies, put out to stop people from thinking for themselves in wartime. Hatred was preferable to thought. One of the worst repercussions of this kind of thought control was that later, in World War II, accurate stories of German atrocities in concentration camps were consistently and tragically disbelieved. After all, it was said, governments always make up such stories. But not always: just from 1914 onward.

Second, the war had created conditions which made internal subversion and its suppression key aspects of the waging of war. Undermining the war effort of the enemy by means of subversion was not new, but it had now taken on a new, imperialist form, as each side sought to prize the other's colonies away from the mother country by covert means. Minorities had become potential enemies, and had been treated as such.

World War I in Europe

1914	1915	1916	1917	1918
August 3 Germany invades Belgium, intending to march on Paris.	**February 8–22** Russians are forced to retreat on the Eastern Front.	**February 21–December 18** Germans launch a massive but unsuccessful attack on Verdun.	**April 6** USA enters war on Allied side.	**March 21** Germany launches Spring offensive on Western Front.
August 26–30 Germany defeats a Russian advance at Tannenberg.	**March 10–13** Battle of Neuve Chapelle.	**May 31–June 1** Decisive sea battle at Jutland.	**April 16–29** French offensive on Western Front bringing little gain.	**July 18–November 10** Allied counteroffensive drives Western Front eastwards, and
September 5–10 Westward German advance halted by French and British in early September, leading to trench warfare.	**April 25** Allied offensive at Gallipoli, abandoned January 1916. **September 25–October 6** French offensive on Western Front, with limited results.	**June 4–October 10** Brusilov offensive by Russia drives back Austria-Hungary. **July 1–November 19** Little gain after costly British offensive on Western Front.	**July 31–November 10** Allies make minor advance at Third Battle of Ypres. **October 24–November 10** Central Powers defeat Italy at Caporetto.	peace initiatives by Germany lead to the signing of the Armistice on November 11.

▲ **The Great War had involved continuous military operations on four fronts around the Central Powers alliance of Germany and Austria-Hungary. On the Western Front, stretching from Switzerland north to the English Channel, the Germans had confronted the British, French and Belgians, while on the Eastern Front the two Central Powers had stood together against Russia until revolution had taken Russia out of the war. Italy had entered the war on the Allied side in 1915. In the Balkans, Bulgaria had joined the Central Powers in 1915 and Romania had briefly joined the Allies in 1916.**

Third, whatever the pious words of the combatants, all civilians had become legitimate targets of hostilities. One conspicuous example was the German submarine campaign against Allied merchant shipping, which was intended to cut off essential supplies from the United Kingdom and bring about a negotiated settlement. A second example was the continuation of the Allied blockade of German ports after November 1918, the primary result of which was to increase death among noncombatants, infants, the infirm and the elderly. After four years of war and staggering losses of human life, a kind of numbing of sensibilities had set in among political leaders and the populations they led, to the point where they could convince themselves that killing civilians by starvation was a legitimate tactic of warfare.

The Allied blockade may have been a war crime, but even this act pales into insignificance in comparison with the policy of genocide which the Turks executed upon defenseless Armenians in May 1915. With little or no justification, and under the cover of the war, the Turks forcibly deported from their traditional homes over one million Armenians, of whom perhaps 500,000 died of torture or disease. It was a massacre on a scale previously unknown.

The Nazis were to take a special interest in the Armenian massacres. Whatever the sources of Hitler's policy of exterminating the Jewish people during World War II, his mad project, like so many other abominable features of 20th-century life, was prefigured a generation earlier during World War I. This terrible cruelty was a dreadful legacy to the postwar world.

The end of the conflict and start of the peace

On 11 November 1918, the war ended in victory for the Allies. Though no Allied army had set foot on German soil, Germany's will to resist had collapsed, the Kaiser had abdicated two days earlier and the country's institutions were in disarray.

But had the war really ended with the Armistice? On one level it clearly had, now that the political struggle which had been carried out in military terms over the previous four years had effectively been decided. But putting the decision into practice was an intricate matter: beyond the activities of the military on the Western front, there was the business of diplomacy and peacemaking to attend to, which meant that military pressure had to be kept up, at least until Germany accepted the Allies' peace terms, as they were to do at Versailles on 28 June 1919. The other losers accepted defeat in five separate treaties signed over the following 14 months, until 20 August 1920, when Turkey and the Allies signed the Treaty of Sèvres.

Such precision in defining the end of a war is necessary under international law. But what lawyers and diplomats say rarely describes the world in which ordinary people live. There are several reasons to consider World War I as an upheaval that continued well beyond the formal end of the conflict: indeed, it has sometimes been argued that World War II was an extension of the same conflict, with the intervening years witnessing a break in hostilities rather than a genuine peace.

Despite the armistice, hostile action against the Central Powers continued until the diplomats had concluded their work. The armistice was, even in strict legal terms, only a truce rather than a formal end to hostilities. To prevent Germany from using this breathing space to reconstitute its armies – a hopeless enterprise in any event – the Allied blockade continued until July 1919. This meant that food and other goods were in short supply during the difficult winter of 1918–19 throughout Central Europe. It was even more difficult to distinguish between war and peace in Eastern Europe, where the Russian Revolution and consequent civil war brought continued hostilities until 1921, as far west as Warsaw.

These upheavals were both a continuation of the conflict between Europe's Great Powers, and

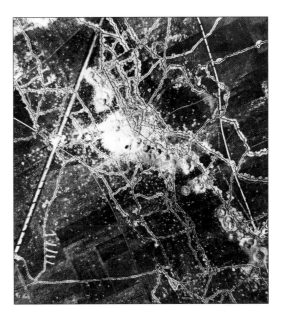

◄ The spider's web of stalemate – an aerial view of trench networks on the Western Front. These entrenchments were continuous defensive lines, supported by a network of trenches and strongpoints over several miles and protected by thick barbed wire barriers. For four years, the effectiveness of these lines of defense limited the area of conflict to a narrow zone, subject to constant ferocious bombardment from artillery and infantry; the cost, counted after the war, was millions of human lives.

▼ A British tank with supporting infantry. Introduced by the British in 1916, early tanks were slow, unreliable and vulnerable to artillery fire, and often they operated over terrain that was so waterlogged that their cross-country performance was of little benefit. These deficiencies were remedied in succeeding years and tanks, like the equally erratic mines, used against them by the Germans in World War I, were hugely important in the conduct of World War II and subsequent conflicts.

an extension of the social upheaval that began to shake many of the combatant nations as the war entered its final phase. From 1916 a mixture of war-weariness and xenophobic nationalism was widely apparent. In Britain Lloyd George, and in France Clemenceau, had taken over leadership of governments dedicated to the pursuit of victory at almost any price. Field Marshal Hindenburg and General Ludendorff effectively ran Germany after the summer of 1916, and set their faces against any form of compromise peace. In the autumn of 1917 government-sponsored the Fatherland party was set up to mobilize public opinion behind the policy of German annexation of surrounding territories, particularly those with substantial German minorities. National hatred was deliberately stirred up, not only between the warring states but within them. In Austria-Hungary the Croats, Czechs, Romanians, Poles and Ukrainians sought independence, creating bitterness among their former German and Magyar masters. The subject peoples of the Russian Empire, too, were hoping for freedom. It was inevitable that many national enmities would be unleashed.

The fomer ruling elites of Germany, Austria-Hungary and Russia were defeated and bewildered, and looked for scapegoats. White Russians fled to the west, and brought with them fears of an international Jewish plot to overthrow Western civilization. Before Germany was forced to sue for peace in October 1918, those who sought to expand Germany's frontiers were already blaming those they called defeatists or

pacifists, behind the lines. Antisemites did not hesitate to claim that Jews were responsible for Germany's ills. These irrational hatreds were masked in the autumn of 1918 by relief at the end of hostilities and by hopes that political changes in Europe might bring greater freedom for the people of all countries. When such hopes began to fade the darker emotions that had been stirred up in the war manifested themselves once again.

The democratic tide after the war

By the time the war ended it was being acclaimed as a victory for democracy over dynastic authoritarianism. This explanation was given credibility by the fact that czarist Russia had been replaced, in the anti-German alliance, by the republican United States. When the Germans dismembered Russia under the Treaty of Brest-Litovsk, they envisaged German royal families obtaining fiefdoms in the east. By contrast, the vast majority of new states created by the Treaty of Versailles – following the principles of the United States president Wilson's 14 Points – were republics.

Monarchism proved to be a dying principle in Europe; although German nationalists professed nostalgia for their old emperor and the crowned heads of the German states, the possibility of their restoration was never a popular issue. In Austria there was more interest in unification with Germany than in putting the Habsburgs back on the throne. Ironically, it was only in Hungary, which had previously been hostile to the reactionary Habsburg monarchy, that the ruling

▼ Military planning in the Great War was often uninspired and out of touch with the real situation at the front. Many commanders were unaware of the daily horrors that their men had to face and could not summon the technological or administrative support required for such a massive operation. Interwar scientific development was hastened by the specter of military requirements, and the face of war was to change in the course of the century, though hardly for the better.

elites seemed to support restoration, creating an anomalous "regency" under Admiral Horthy in March 1920. This curious state of affairs has been descibed as a regency without a monarch led by an admiral without a navy.

Elsewhere the end of the war commonly brought a wideranging democratization of political institutions, at both national and local level. This occurred in the victorious powers, the defeated states and in the new nations set up after the war. Full male suffrage, proportional representation and even votes for women were introduced in many countries. In Belgium, for example, where proportional representation had existed since 1899, full suffrage for men was promulgated in 1919. Holland adopted a similar system in 1918, and introduced universal suf-

frage, including votes for women, two years later. The new German republic elected its constituent assembly on proportional representation and universal suffrage. Even in Britain, where democracy was slow to arive, votes were granted to certain categories of women in 1918, and true universal suffrage was established in 1928. There appeared to be no obstacles anywhere to the establishment of truly responsible, democratic government based on parliamentary consitutions. Even the Roman Catholic Church, which had traditionally opposed political liberalism, seemed to be modifying its attitudes. The war had reconciled many French Catholics with the republican system in France, and legitimist monarchism lost all political credibility. In Italy the Vatican allowed Roman Catholics to vote for the first time in 1919.

▲ The grim reality of trench warfare, portrayed by the German artist Otto Dix. "Shell shock" was a term coined in this war to describe the hugely traumatic after-effect on totally unprepared human beings of remaining for days on end in muddy trenches and airless dugouts surrounded by the dead, tormented by rats and lice, assailed by a constant barrage of noise and exposed to random danger from exploding shells, snipers' bullets and sometimes even the waterlogged terrain itself. Those who escaped death or mutilation were often scarred mentally for the rest of their lives.

Datafile

The war efforts of the European combatants were only sustained by the mass mobilization of industry and the civilian population. At the beginning of the war, tension and political protest were submerged by patriotic fervor, but as the war dragged on, economies began to show signs of strain and the sacrifices demanded of the people increased. The result was that the fighting nations faced rises in leftwing political opposition – some faced revolution as well.

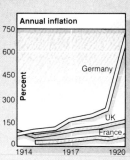

Socialist representation 1914

▶ One sign of economic strain was a rising inflation rate. By the middle of the war inflation was moving steadily upwards all over Europe, and in Germany, in particular, the problem was beginning to reach disastrous proportions. Defeat dealt the final blow to the German economy, and by 1920 inflation was running out of control.

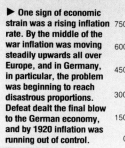

Annual inflation

▲ Socialism had made steady progress in Europe prior to 1914. Although patriotism stifled political protest in the early years of the conflict, the presence of many leftwing representatives in Europe's parliaments provided a focus for a radical challenge to authority when the economic and social costs of the fighting began to bite.

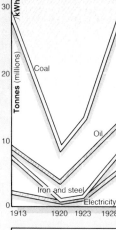

Soviet industry

▶ While levels of labor unrest fluctuated in different fashions, the general trend in all the major combatants was upwards, with the workforce increasingly resorting to strike action in response to the demands of war. Continuing economic problems pushed the trend up even more steeply after peace came in 1918.

Labour unrest

◀ Gradual wearing down under the strain of the war effort, and widespread socio-political disruption after the shock of revolution, combined to push the Russian economy into crisis. Industrial production fell sharply until 1920 – after that, the corner was turned by state coercion, at heavy cost to the workforce.

▼ Russian industrial workers were politically aware and made a clearer identification between economic and political grievances than elsewhere in Europe. As the crisis of 1917 approached, huge rises in political strikes showed that the Russian industrial worker no longer considered his rulers fit to rule.

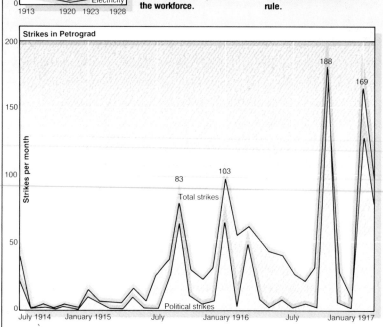

Strikes in Petrograd

The outbreak of World War I was greeted with rapturous enthusiasm in the belligerent states and with horror elsewhere. In Berlin, Paris and other cities, soldiers rushed to the colors to the accompaniment of cheering crowds. Britain sent a small expeditionary force to France and volunteers hastened to enlist. War also suppressed internal political conflicts such as Britain's problems over Ireland.

At the same time, it had a divisive effect on the international labor movement. At its congress in Stuttgart in 1907 the International had condemned war and committed itself to opposing it. Yet during the first week of war in August 1914 the Belgian, French and German social democrats agreed to support their countries' war efforts. The German Social Democrats saw their country threatened by czarist autocracy. The French were afraid of Prussian militarism. Fear of defeat at the hands of a tyrannical foreign power outweighed any feelings of solidarity with workers abroad, while socialist leaders were afraid of alienating their own rank-and-file membership who had been carried away by patriotism when the war broke out. There were socialist demonstrations for peace in Germany and elsewhere, but socialist leaders who tried to resist the war were overwhelmed by nationalist fervor. In France the socialist leader Jean Jaurès was assassinated on 3 July 1914 and in Germany Hugo Haase, the antiwar parliamentary spokesman of the Social Democrats, was forced by weight of numbers to support the voting of German war credits in the Reichstag on 4 August 1914. In the belligerent countries only two socialist parties – the Serbian Social Democrats and Lenin's Bolsheviks – rejected outright any participation in the war.

Disillusion in Europe

As the war dragged on, and its privations increased, the working classes of Germany became more skeptical about their government's attempts to blame Russia for everything. Among the parties of the left a struggle ensued between those socialists who refused to continue to support the war effort and those who, like Friedrich Ebert and Philipp Scheidemann, believed it was in the best interests of their party to do so. In April 1917 the antiwar dissidents, having been expelled from their own party, set up the new and more radical Independent Social Democratic party (USPD) dedicated to opposing the war. Some radical elements within it, such as the Spartacists led by Rosa Luxemburg and Karl Liebknecht, were actively trying to foment revolution.

The Italian social democrats had traditionally been radical and Italy's neutrality in 1914 made it easy for most of them to assert their commitment to peace. Even so, a minority were impressed by

WAR AND REVOLUTION

the power of nationalism, among them Benito Mussolini, then a socialist newspaper editor in Milan, who became committed to Italian intervention in the war. August 1914 proved that international working-class solidarity was a myth and that tribal loyalties were the real force in world affairs.

When Italy joined the war on the Entente side on 24 May 1915 it was clearly for territorial gain, and met with bitter opposition from the left. The "maximalist" or revolutionary wing of the Italian socialist party gained in strength. Defeats and hardships during the war deepened the cleavage in Italian politics between its supporters and opponents. The political system came under particular strain at a time when it was having to adjust to a broadening of the franchise in 1911 which gave organized labor and the Roman Catholic peasantry greater political opportunities. Before 1915, a skilful liberal politician such as Giovanni Giolitti might have been able to integrate these disparate elements into the parliamentary system, but the conflicts over the war made that almost impossible.

▼ A people's war – women workers in a British aircraft factory. During the Great War, with so many young men in uniform, industry could only reach the high targets it was set by bringing thousands of women into the factories.

In Austria-Hungary too, the appalling levels of casualties at the front, as well as shortages of food and consumer goods at home, damaged civilian morale. The hardships further exacerbated the relationships between the different nationalities within the empire. Hungary was fairly able to provide for itself, but was not generous to other areas. In the German-speaking provinces, and especially the large towns such as Vienna, food was very scarce.

Politically, the empire was on the verge of breakdown. The Reichsrat (imperial parliament) was suspended and all criticism muzzled. On 21 October 1916 the Austrian head of government, Count Carl Stürgkh, was assassinated by a young socialist, and on 21 November the aged Emperor of Austria-Hungary, Franz-Josef, died. His successor, Charles, lacked the prestige to halt the impending disintegration. The United States' entry into the war in April 1917 further encouraged those political groups – such as the Czechoslovakian National Committee in Paris – who were working for the liberation of the subject nationalities. President Wilson was known to

The Partition of Ireland

◄ The Irish republican flag raised above the Dublin post office during the Easter rebellion of 1916. With British attention concentrated on the Great War, several thousand armed Irish insurgents surprised the authorities by seizing strategic buildings in Dublin. After some considerable confusion, the British recovered to surround the isolated rebel outposts with forces greatly superior in number. The Irish leaders were executed.

In 1912, after pressure from the Irish parliamentary party, a British Liberal government introduced a Home Rule bill, involving the ceding of power, in almost everything except foreign affairs and defense, to a parliament in Ireland, which became law in 1914, though it was never implemented. The bill was fiercely opposed by the Unionist (and predominantly Protestant) minority, concentrated in the six industrialized northeastern counties of Ireland.

As it was, the intervention of World War I delayed the bill's implementation, during which time the character of the nationalists' demands changed. In the first postwar election, in 1918, Sinn Fein, the party of separatist nationalists, supplanted the Irish parliamentary party as the major nationalist party. Negotiations began in the autumn of 1921 between the British government under pressure from the United States and international opinion and Sinn Fein, culminating in the establishment of an independent Irish state within the framework of the British Commonwealth. Ireland was partitioned so the northern six counties with their Protestant majority remained within the United Kingdom. While the Unionists reluctantly accepted the settlement, it divided the nationalists into pro- and antitreaty factions of Sinn Fein and started a civil war.

▼ A makeshift barricade erected during the 1916 rebellion. A lack of public support for the uprising allowed the British to restore order and force the outnumbered rebel garrisons to surrender. Harsh repressive action, including the execution of many of the insurgent leaders, hardened public opinion and, transformed the rebels into martyrs for the cause of Irish independence.

favor self-determination for national minorities, while the length and severity of the war gave them hope, in that, if both the Russian and the Habsburg empires collapsed, nationalities like the Czechs or Poles would not have to choose between them.

The last of the Russian czars

By 1917 the situation in Russia was dire. Despite some notable victories, particularly against the Austrians in eastern Galicia in September 1914 and General Brusilov's offensive at Bukovina in 1916, the czar's armies were largely defeated. They had been forced back out of Russian Poland and suffered enormous casualties. The logistical support for the Russian army at the front was lacking, and the severe losses of manpower and horses were damaging agriculture. Privation and war-weariness became widespread.

On 10 March 1917 bread riots in Petrograd (renamed from "St Petersburg" after the outbreak of war) led to a mutiny amongst garrison troops. The government proved powerless to act. A soviet of workers and soldiers was established, while at the same time politicians in the Duma assumed that the authority in the state had passed to them. On 15 March (old style, 2 March) Czar Nicholas II was persuaded to abdicate and a Provisional Government of Duma politicians was established, led at first by Prince Lvov and later by Alexander Kerensky, a liberal lawyer and member of the Socialist Revolutionary party.

Everywhere the "February revolution" was hailed as a great act of liberation. In Germany the newly formed Independent Socialists welcomed it at their founding congress. In France and Britain concern over Russian instability mingled with hope that the new liberal regime might wage war against Germany more effectively (a hope shared by many of the Duma politicians). Even inside Russia revolutionary parties (like the Marxist Mensheviks and populist Socialist Revolutionaries who wanted a socialist society based on the peasantry) agreed not to oppose the new Provisional Government for fear of provoking counterrevolution.

This consensus was shattered by Lenin, who arrived from Switzerland on 15 April 1917. He announced that the Bolshevik party would attack the new regime root and branch and demanded an immediate end to the war, land for the peasants, and bread for the people. The Germans welcomed Lenin's agitation because it damaged Russia's war effort. Indeed they had allowed Lenin's party to travel through their territory and even provided the Bolsheviks with funds to develop their organization.

By contrast the Russian Provisional Government led by Kerensky and his colleagues was committed to national defence and constitutional reform. No major steps towards social change would be taken, however, until a constituent assembly had been elected. Already in the villages peasant communes were seizing landlords' land while the relaxation of harsh military discipline in the army after the czar's abdication encouraged desertion and sometimes mutinies. Agitation by the soviets and mistrust of the

government by the officers at the front, many of whom regarded Kerensky as the embodiment of treason, undermined troop morale.

After a further military setback in early July 1917, General Kornilov, the commander of the troops at the front, staged an unsuccessful coup in Petrograd in September, with the intention of establishing a military regime. This led to the arming of workers' militias or Red Guards loyal to the Petrograd soviet, which increasingly came under the influence of the Bolshevik party. On 4 October 1917 Leon Trotsky became chairman of the soviet as the Bolsheviks made final plans to seize power. By then the administrative system and military command structure in Russia were beginning to disintegrate.

The Bolshevik revolution

The Petrograd soviet established a military revolutionary committee whose stated purpose was to resist counterrevolution. Dominated by Bolsheviks, this body gained the support of most of the soldiers in the city's garrison. Despite the nervousness of Zinoviev, Kamenev and others among his colleagues, Lenin pressed ahead and seized power in Petrograd on 7 November 1917 (old style, 27 October). The provisional government offered little resistance. Kerensky fled. The Bolsheviks set up a Council of People's Commissars to run the revolution and in December established the Cheka, a security police force headed by a Pole, Felix Dzerdzhinsky.

The democratically elected constituent assembly in which the Socialist Revolutionaries, not the Bolsheviks, were the largest party met on 5 January 1918 but was prevented from continuing by Bolshevik soldiers. Liberals and other "enemies of the people" were arrested by the Cheka. Although there was resistance to the Bolshevik seizure of power in many parts of Russia, often the opposition was patchy and uncoordinated. The Socialist Revolutionaries split and their left wing worked for a time with the Bolshevik government. Meanwhile the provisional government's supporters who wanted to overthrow Lenin often found they could not easily cooperate with reactionary army officers to achieve their objective. Only in areas where there were non-Russian nationalities such as Finland and the Ukraine were the Bolsheviks checked.

One of the first measures taken by the Bolsheviks, on 8 November 1917, was to abolish the

▲ Massacre on the streets of Petrograd in July 1917. During the overthrow of the czarist regime and the prolonged power struggle that followed such scenes were repeated all over the country. The toppling of the statue of Alexander III in Moscow symbolized the end of czarism. Economic and social problems bequeathed by the feudal autocracy were not so easily solved.

◀ Russian peasants starving by their hut. Torn by revolution and war, the new Soviet regime was also beset by famine.

▶ Lenin addressing troops in Sverdlov Square, Moscow, in 1920. Lenin and Trotsky (standing beside rostrum) were chiefly responsible for the Bolshevik rise to power and the successful defence of the party's position in the subsequent civil war. A brilliant theorist and persuasive orator, Lenin was also a master of political tactics. He was ably supported by Trotsky, one of the most brilliant military organizers of modern times.

▲ Revolutionary art – the new Soviet state often used posters to spread its message – the appeal to the work ethic was a common theme. Here the message is, "We destroyed our enemy with weapons, we'll earn our bread with labor – comrades, roll up your sleeves for work!"

private ownership of land and to redistribute it amongst the peasantry. Although the Bolsheviks' authority was not established in the countryside this land policy and the fact that they were not associated with the landlords in the eyes of the peasants gave them an advantage over their "white" opponents in the civil war that followed.

Civil war and intervention in Russia

Against the wishes of the left Socialist Revolutionaries and many of his own party Lenin made a separate peace with the Germans. Under the treaty of Brest-Litovsk, signed on 3 March 1918, the Bolsheviks conceded large areas of western Russia, with the creation of puppet states in the Baltic, in Poland and in the rich wheat-growing region of the Ukraine. The treaty gave the Bolsheviks breathing-space from German pressure but encouraged intervention against them by the western powers after a variety of White forces sought aid from the allies of the former provisional government. For three years a bitter civil war raged across Russia, bringing with it famine, economic dislocation and refugee problems.

Allied support for the Whites was substantial but sporadic and ill-organized. Early in March 1918 the British landed near Murmansk, hoping to prevent arms dumps and enemy prisoners-of-war falling into the hands of the Germans. US, British and Italian troops were sent to the Archangel area for the same purposes, though once established it was clear that they were also engaged in a political war to help overthrow the Bolsheviks. In southern Russia British forces invaded the Baku oilfields on the Caspian Sea and established themselves in the western Caucasus, while the French occupied part of the northern coast of the Black Sea around Odessa.

In Siberia the Japanese sent more than 70,000 troops to Siberia to occupy the area from Lake Baikal to Vladivostok. President Wilson had grave inhibitions about this extension of Japanese power although the Japanese forces were joined in the area by over 10,000 British and Canadian troops, 7,000 Americans and token forces from France and Italy.

As the civil war progressed the dictatorship of the Bolshevik party under Lenin became more repressive. The Red Army, which was organized by Leon Trotsky, used former czarist officers closely supervised by Bolshevik party commissars. Sometimes those who proved disloyal or laggardly were shot. In July 1918 an attempted rising against Lenin's regime by Socialist Revolutionaries was suppressed with great ferocity. Terror became commonplace, and news of Red atrocities was played up in the Western press. Particularly shocking to many was the murder of Czar Nicholas II and his family at Ekaterinburg on 16 July 1918.

Until the autumn of 1918 the aim of the intervention was to keep the Russian front alive against the Germans despite the Bolshevik–German peace treaty of earlier that year. But as the German threat receded, Allied leaders became more concerned with the politics of intervention. The French were anxious to chastise a Bolshevik government that had repudiated czarist debts while some, like Foch and Churchill, regarded Lenin's doctrines as a menace to civilization itself. Britain was interested in the control of Russia's oil supplies and some of the Japanese military were attracted by the possibility of dominating Siberia.

Disagreements over these objectives, fatigue among the troops and the public's reluctance to

The Russian Revolution and Civil War

1917

November
Bolsheviks seize power in Petrograd and Moscow.

December
Armistice signed by Germans and Bolsheviks.

1918

January–February
Cossack armies defeated by Red Guard.

February–May
Germans occupy the Causasus and Crimea.

March 3
Treaty of Brest-Litovsk signed between Germany and Russia.

March 5
British forces disembark at Murmansk to support Whites.

April 6
Japanese forces disembark at Vladivostok; the Whites set up a government there in July.

June
White governments are set up in Samara and Omsk.

August
The British set up a White government in Archangel. Allied forces land at Vladivostok.

November 28
French troops land at Odessa; the British occupy Baku and Georgia

1919

April
Red Army expels Allies from Ukraine and enters Crimea.

September–October
Allies evacuate Archangel and Murmansk.

October 22
White attack on Petrograd is repulsed.

1920

May 6
Kiev occupied by Poles and Ukrainian nationalists.

June 11
Kiev retaken by Red Army, who then advance into Poland, only to be repulsed in August by Poles near Warsaw.

1921

March 1
Sailors mutiny at Kronstadt, but are quelled two weeks later.

March 18
Treaty of Riga defines the frontier with Poland.

Scale 1: 20 000 000

Boundary of Russian Empire 1914

● Center of Bolshevik influence July–Sept 1917

○ Principal town where Bolsheviks seized power Nov–Dec 1917

Eastern Front Nov 1917

Area controlled by Bolsheviks Aug 1918

Advance of anti-Bolshevik armies

Boundary of Bolshevik territory Oct 1919

Front line of anti-Bolshevik armies May 1920

Soviet territory 1921

–·–·– International boundary 1921

▲ After withdrawing from World War I in March 1918, the Bolshevik state faced a grave new challenge in the form of Western intervention. Together White and Allied forces make deep incursions all round Russia's borders. Drastic action by Lenin and Trotsky created a new Red Army, which repelled these invaders and launched a brief invasion of Poland. The Bolshevik cause was aided by lack of coordination or agreement among the White forces and the war-weariness of Allied governments.

continue intervention in Russia once the war with Germany had come to an end brought the campaign to a halt. By the spring of 1920 Allied forces had been withdrawn from European Russia. The Americans left Siberia in January 1920, quickly followed by the European contingents. The Japanese continued to occupy the area but came under strong American pressure to evacuate it. In 1922 they complied and Soviet control was established over the whole of Siberia. Only northern Sakhalin remained under Japanese occupation until 1925 by which time the Union of Soviet Socialist Republics (a name that had been adopted two years earlier) had established itself in a new Europe.

Russo-Polish war

At the end of the Russian civil war in May 1920, Polish forces had advanced into Russia and taken Kiev. However the Red Army counterattacked so successfully that by the end of July they were nearly at the gates of Warsaw. Aided by French arms and advisers the Poles managed to fight back and the war ended in September with the Poles obtaining a generous frontier in the Pripet marshes east of Pinsk. This was several hundred kilometers to the east of a demarcation settlement proposed by Britain as Poland's eastern boundary in December 1919, and that frontier remained a bone of contention between Poles and Russians until the end of World War II.

ART AND REVOLUTION

The upheavals of the early decades of the 20th century left no sphere of human activity untouched. The art of the period both reflected the demise of the old order and in its own way contributed to it. Cubism and Futurism were, according to the Russian artist Kasimir Malevich, the "revolutionary form of art that foreshadowed the revolution in political and economic life in 1917". To Lenin, Russia was the weakest link of the capitalist chain; once that link broke, capitalism would collapse, leaving the world ready for socialism. Likewise, to contemporary Russian artists Cubism signaled the end of the bourgeois era in art: an era which, they believed, Russia would – uniquely – be able to bypass as a stage in its own development.

Foremost among the movements that grew out of Russian Cubo-Futurism in the post-Revolutionary period were the Constructivists. They and others sought to eliminate the differences between art and engineering, between painting and music, between poetry and design and between fine art and propaganda. Rejecting the world of nature and false nostalgia, they championed urban culture, the machine and the language of the street. Artists now aspired to change reality rather than simply mirror it. Traditional easel painting was abandoned in favor of utilitarian design (of everything from boiler suits to the abortive Monument to the Third International by Vladimir Tatlin) and public spectacles such as the reenactment of the Bolshevik revolution on the occasion of its first anniversary. "The streets our brushes, the squares our palettes", proclaimed the Futurist poet Vladimir Mayakovsky.

One of the earliest post-Revolutionary art forms was poster design. Often, but not always, political, the posters featured combinations of abstract shapes (showing the influence of Malevich's Suprematist movement), bold experimental typography (Lissitsky's contribution) and photomontage (Rodchenko's innovation). During the Russian civil war "agitprop" (agitational propaganda) trains and ships, brightly decorated with political slogans, carried artists, poets and politicians around the battlefronts to reinforce the revolutionary message among the troops. Artists at this time were under no compulsion to produce or agitate for the state; many genuinely believed in the revolution and the possibilities it offered for the future.

This period, one of the most creative in the history of art, also had an impact outside Russia, giving the world, among other things, Vsevolod Meyerhold's "theater in the round", the films of Sergei Eisenstein, and the German Bauhaus school, in which the Russian painter Vassili Kandinsky was a major force. In Mexico the ideals of the Bolshevik revolution inspired artists to produce art for the public, in the form of murals. This "great Renaissance" in Mexican art began around 1920, a decade after the national revolution that deposed the Diaz dictatorship, and lasted until the fall of the Obregon government in 1925.

◄ The Soviet artist El Lissitzky's poster *Beat the Whites with the Red Wedge* (1919–20) combines an urgent political message with realistic exploration. Designed in the Constructivist style which sought a new art for the revolutionary and machine age. By the early 1930s the Communist party rejected Constructivism in favor of an esthetically more conservative style.

► The Agitprop trains, covered in revolutionary imagery and spreading revolutionary leaflets, were an important element in bringing the Bolshevik revolution from its urban heartlands to the Russian country as a whole. On a larger scale, the dramatist Nathan Altman had staged a futurist reconstruction of the storming of the Winter Palace in Petrograd itself on the first anniversary of the October Revolution.

◄ Lenin was closely associated with the new art, appearing here on a plate of 1921. Stalin, on the other hand, was no friend of the avant garde, seeing its work as decadent and bourgeois; it was firmly repressed under Zhdanov.

◄ The theater director Vsevolod Meyerhold (1874–1940) developed another revolutionary version of an old art form, putting Constructivism on the stage, as in this production of "The Bathhouse", put on in Moscow in collaboration with Mayakovsky. It was a satirical work attacking the lifestyle of the bourgeois.

▲ The heroic art of Socialist Realism was adopted not only by the Soviet Union after its initial years, but in Communist China too. The official "art of the state" maintained an educative role – celebrating the ideals of work and community service, while the figures on posters always marched to the left.

◄ The art of rival artists such as Diego Rivera and José Clemente Orozco formed an important element in the popularization of the Mexican Revolution. Although each approached the concept of "socialized art" differently, they were untied by a "native tradition" of the Aztecs and Mayans.

Datafile

The Paris peace conference was spoiled from the outset by the distrust between the Allied leaders that had built up over the course of the war. Though there was a pressing need to redraw the map of Europe to prevent future disputes, the French and the British had each felt that they had had to shoulder too high a proportion of the burden of the war effort, and neither wished to see the United States take over a leading role in world affairs. For his part, President Wilson disliked all power politics and was determined not to be a tool of European imperialism. He pressed for the establishment of the League of Nations to help replace the old world of secret diplomacy, which he saw as a major contributing factor to the outbreak of war.

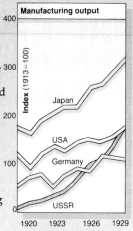

Manufacturing output

▲ The economy of Japan, barely affected by the war, grew more significantly between 1913 and 1920 than that of any other Power. By 1920, Russian output, ravaged by revolution and civil war, was only 12 percent of the 1913 figure.

The Treaty of Versailles 28 June 1919

1. The signatories accept the Covenant of the League of Nations, which includes guarantees of their territories.

2. Germany to lose certain territories. Provisions include the return of Alsace-Lorraine to France and the loss of German colonies to Allied powers as mandated territories of the League of Nations. The Rhineland is to be demilitarized.

3. Limits are imposed on German military power: army limited to 100,000 men (all volunteers); navy limited to 36 major ships, 15,000 men and 1,500 officers (no submarines and replacements capital ships); no air services allowed.

4. Former Kaiser and German military leaders to be tried for violations of laws of war.

5. Germany accepts responsibility for damage caused by war and will pay reparations (to be determined by Allies).

6. Allied forces to occupy the Rhineland for 15 years.

7. Germany abrogates the Treaty of Brest-Litovsk.

◀ Of all the clauses in the Versailles treaty, clause 5, in which the Germans were forced to accept blame for the war and pay reparations for the damage done, proved the most unacceptable to the German people.

Covenant of the League of Nations

1. Original members are Allied signatories of the postwar peace treaties.

2. Assembly to contain representatives of all members; Council to consist of representatives of permanent members (USA, UK, France, Italy and Japan) and of four others elected by the Assembly.

3. All members to reduce armaments to lowest possible levels.

4. Principles of collective security. Each member to respect the security of all others. All disputes to be referred to the Council. No member to go to war until the Council's procedures have been implemented.

5. Procedures for arbitration, including the establishment of a permanent Court of International Justice.

6. All members to join action against a member who violated the Covenant. First course would be economic sanctions, then military intervention. Provision made for nonmembers to join action.

7. Colonies of defeated powers to become mandates of the League and administered by selected powers.

8. Members to cooperate on other matters, such as transport, commerce, labor. Other international organizations to be brought under League direction. Red Cross to be encouraged.

9. Provisions for amending the Covenant.

◀ The covenant of the League of Nations was the first major attempt to set up an international organization for dealing with political conflict between nations by rational and public means. Although it proved ineffectual in the face of irrational forces such as fascism, and was disbanded in 1946, its agencies did much useful work, including in the collection of international data such as the manufacturing output statistics (top).

▼ Energy consumption statistics bear out the great predominance of the United States economy through the 1920s, as the main European Powers struggled to make up for the losses incurred during the war.

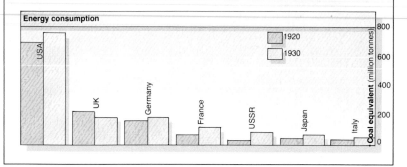

Energy consumption

The end of World War I came suddenly and left the victors with enormous problems. Germany as defeated, Austria-Hungary was disintegrating, the Ottoman Empire was in ruins and the future of Russia was uncertain. Had the western Powers been united in purpose and coordinated in their actions, the peacemakers would still have faced a daunting task. In fact they were badly organized and mistrusted one another.

The Paris Peace Conference

France's major problem was security against its more powerful German neighbor. Before the war its safety had rested on the alliance with Russia, but the Bolshevik revolution of 1917 had replaced a friendly regime with a hostile one. Even if Bolshevik rule was shortlived – and in November 1917 there were few who thought it would last long – its successor was an unknown quantity. The British wanted a peace that would establish their empire as the leading world Power while preserving Germany as a sound trading partner and a useful counterweight to France. President Wilson of the United States pressed for a new system of international relations. His Fourteen Points declaration called for a peace based on national self-determination, an end to old-style secret diplomacy; and the establishment of a League of Nations to help to resolve international conflicts. The Germans claimed that Wilson's principles implied a settlement based on self-determination, no punitive indemnities and an international system in which they would be permitted to play a full part.

The peace conference met in Paris for the first time on 18 January 1919, with the most important decisions taken by the "big four" representing Britain, France, Italy and the United States. The Italians soon realized that they were to be denied the territories promised to them under the 1915 Treaty of London, and their premier, Vittorio Orlando, withdrew in protest on 24 April 1919, thus leaving matters firmly in the hands of Clemenceau (the French premier), Lloyd George (prime minister of Britain) and President Wilson.

Founding of the League of Nations

France's security problem with her German neighbor was to be overcome by a guarantee of protection from Britain and the United States. The League of Nations organization was to be set up and its covenant adopted on 14 February 1919. The left bank of the Rhine was not to be annexed by France, as Clemenceau had demanded but, occupied by allied forces for 15 years and then demilitarized permanently.

However the Germans were forced to concede the provinces of Alsace and Lorraine to France, as well as surrendering frontier districts to Belgium

REBUILDING EUROPE

and Schleswig to Denmark. More serious were the substantial losses of eastern territories in Posen, West Prussia and Poland along with the port of Danzig. At the same time, the Germans were forbidden to unite with German-speaking populations of the Habsburg monarchy which would have given them control of the Danube basin making the new state of Czechoslovakia, which was crucial to the allied settlement proposed for central Europe, economically and strategically unviable. To the Germans such an application of the self-determination principle seemed grossly one-sided.

Germany also surrendered its colonies, which were parceled out among the victors under the doubtful authority of the League of Nations to whom their new proprietors were responsible for their trusteeship. Germany also lost its battle fleet and most of its mercantile marine and was ordered to reduce its army to 100,000 long-serving professional soldiers and abolish its airforce al-

▶ British troops sporting German helmets as trophies in November 1918.

▼ US president Wilson was fêted in Europe, but his own people did not support his League of Nations.

together. Most controversially of all, the Germans were required to pay compensation for all damages caused by the war including the costs of pensions for the dependents of war victims. Although this demand did not conform with Wilson's original rejection of the idea of punitive indemnities, without it Britain would have been left with almost no compensation and the French would never had been able to repay their war debts to the British and Americans.

The articles of the treaty articulating the reparations settlement held the Germans solely responsible for the war, an assertion which together with a demand for the surrender of war criminals was seen by German politicians as an affront to national honor. The Germans also resented being excluded from the League of Nations organization.

The draft treaty was presented to the Germans on 7 May 1919 and aroused immediate public outrage, fanned by the German Republican government. A list of German objections was sent to the Allies. Lloyd George, who was already uneasy over some aspects of the settlements urged conciliation. He did not want to damage Germany too much economically and was skeptical of the new Poland, which the French saw as a counterweight to both Germany and Bolshevik Russia. In common with others at Paris in 1919, Lloyd George also perceived a threat of Communist subversion in Europe.

Far from collapsing, the Bolsheviks were beginning to extend their influence outside Russia. On 4 March 1919 a new Communist International – the Comintern or Third International – was founded in Moscow, aimed at creating a worldwide and truly revolutionary socialist movement.

Under its influence Bela Kun, on 21 March, set up a Communist regime in Hungary, and on 7 April Bavaria declared itself a Soviet Republic.

Although these revolutions were abortive and soon suppressed, Austria still seemed threatened by subversion and there were disturbances in the Ruhr. The Allies, naturally, did not want to see central Europe in chaos and Lloyd George, among others, feared public reaction at home if the Germans rejected the treaty and resumed the war. They therefore agreed to make certain concessions to Germany over its eastern frontier. Upper Silesia would not go to Poland until a plebiscite had been held to decide its future and Danzig was to be a "free city" under the supervision of the League of Nations. In effect, this meant that it was administered by the Germans but the Poles could use it as a trade outlet. These concessions did not satisfy the Germans but they were given an ultimatum to accept the terms of the treaty or face invasion. They eventually agreed to sign the treaty at the Palace of Versailles on 28 June 1919.

Eastern Europe after the war

So far as Germany's major allies were concerned World War I ended in catastrophe. Austria-Hungary disintegrated and was replaced by the independent states of Austria, Czechoslovakia and Hungary. The Southern Slav element in the old monarchy joined with Serbia and Montenegro to become the new state of Yugoslavia. Galicia went to the new Polish state while Transylvania was annexed by Romania. Whereas before, the Germans and the Magyars had been the dominant nationalities in the Habsburg monarchy, their rule was now confined to rump states with substantial German and Hungarian minorities having come under Slav control. There was a significant German-speaking population in the Sudeten region of Czechoslovakia, and Magyar minorities in Czechoslovakia, Yugoslavia and Romania.

The settlement of the successor states of the Habsburg monarchy was finalized in two treaties made with Austria at St Germain on 10 September 1919 and with Hungary at Trianon on 4 June 1920. Initially the succession states were parliamentary democracies, guaranteeing individual rights, press freedom and political liberty. The Czechs, in particular, wanted to create a new balance of power in east–central Europe, and in August 1920 organized a mutual defense treaty with the Yugoslavs. In April and June 1921 Romania concluded similar treaties with Czechoslovakia and Yugoslavia. Described as the "little entente", this tripartite grouping aimed to prevent a Habsburg restoration and to defend the new states against reactionary intrigues by former elites. Despite the fanatical hostility of the Magyars and the resentment of the Austrians, the postwar settlement in Central Europe remained relatively stable until it was shattered by Hitler's aggression in 1938.

In some countries, however, a multiplicity of parties reflecting cultural, social, regional and even linguistic divisions made constructive leadership almost impossible. In 1925, the Sejm, the Polish parliament, contained 32 parties organized into 18 groups. Incapable of supporting a stable government, on 26 May 1921 it suffered a military coup launched by Josef Pilsudski. Parliament was formally retained and the press remained relatively free but the move presaged the end of Polish democracy in the longer term.

The Middle East after the Ottomans

The Ottoman empire, like Austria-Hungary, had also failed to survive the war intact. Turkey's Asian provinces, which were either under occupation or in revolt, were divided up as spheres of influence between the French and the British under the auspices of the League of Nations. The British became responsible for Palestine, Iraq and Saudi Arabia; the French for Syria and the Lebanon. Under the Treaty of Sèvres of 10 August 1920 Turkey lost western Armenia and also had to give up western Thrace and part of western Anatolia, including the important port of Smyrna, to Greece. By this time the Ottoman regime faced a serious challenge from a nationalist movement centered on Ankara. It was led by General Mustafa Kemal, who later became Turkish dictator under the name of Atatürk ("father of the Turks"). Encouraged by the British and French, the Greeks tried to suppress Atatürk's movement in 1922 but they were defeated, and in September of that year driven out of Smyrna.

With Sèvres a dead letter, the Allies contracted a new treaty with Atatürk's government at Lausanne, Switzerland, on 24 July 1923. This restored western Thrace, Smyrna and western Armenia to Turkey. So bad had relations between Turks and Greeks become, however, with massacres on both sides, that the two states agreed on a transfer of populations. In the period after the Greek defeat in 1922, 1,377,000 Greeks were expelled from Turkey and 410,000 Turks left Greece.

Formerly part of the Ottoman empire, Palestine passed to the British under the League of Nations mandate presented on 3 June 1922 which was seen as the legitimation of Zionist claims in the area. Earlier, on 2 November 1917, the British Foreign Secretary Arthur Balfour, promised Lord Rothschild that Britain would support a "national home for the Jewish people in Palestine". The "Balfour declaration", which was influenced by the Zionist Chaim Weizmann and Nahum Sokolow further stated that "nothing shall be done to prejudice the civil and religious rights of

▲ British cartoon patronizing the League of Nations' impotence in the face of war. Western democratic governments, struggling with severe economic problems and aware that their people did not want another war, were not prepared to use force to maintain peace or deter aggressive dictators.

▲ Kemal Atatürk, Turkey's most successful soldier, capitalized on his country's defeat in 1918 by mobilizing support for a national uprising. He ejected Greek occupation forces and, overturning Turkey's Islamic tradition, built a modern secular state.

◄ The signing of the Treaty of Versailles brought the Great War to its formal conclusion, but the settlement did not provide a basis for lasting peace in Europe

existing non-Jewish communities in Palestine".

The Balfour declaration formed part of the preamble of the League of Nations mandate. By 1925 there were just over 100,000 Jewish settlers in Palestine, many of whom had arrived before 1917, but their presence and the claims of the Zionists to bring in more aroused the lasting resentment of the indigenous Arab population.

Friction in Western Europe

From the beginning, the Paris peace treaties were a source of major dissatisfaction among the parties concerned. Not only the vanquished objected to them; many of the victors were also unhappy. In particular, the Italians, despite their modest military performance in the war, now complained of their "mutilated victory", for which they blamed their allies.

Most significant of all was President Wilson's failure to convince the United States Congress that it should accept the Versailles peace treaty.

The American public, suspicious of European rapacity, saw no reason why they should shoulder any more responsibilities for the Europeans. Consequently, the United States did not become a member of the League of Nations of which President Wilson had been the architect. Still more important, the United States' guarantee of France's security lapsed, leaving the French unprotected when Britain did not renew its guarantee in the light of American withdrawal. To make matters worse for France, the American presidential election produced a victory for the isolationist Republican Warren G. Harding, eliminating any further possibility of a collective security system that would involve the United States.

The League of Nations, despite the absence of the Americans, the Russians and, until 1926, the Germans, began to function in November 1920 from its headquarters in Geneva. Although it became a useful forum for international dip-

▶ The peace settlement of 1919 redrew the map of Europe and the Middle East, creating new states in the vacuum left by the collapse of the Austro-Hungarian and German empires as well as large European mandates in the former territories of the Ottoman empire. Although plebiscites were held in some regions to determine the will of the people, the new Europe was an unstable creation.

▼ French troops in the Rhineland. France was the staunchest advocate of imposing harsh peace terms on Germany. When the economically troubled Weimar Republic failed to maintain the reparation payments, France ordered the occupation of the Rhineland.

Europe in the 1920s

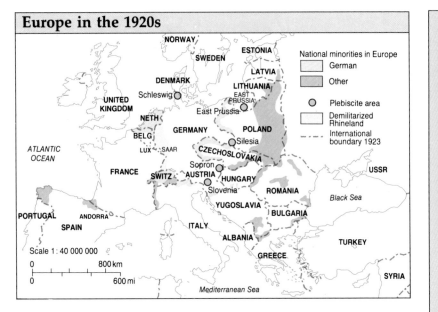

The Weimar Republic

After the flight of Kaiser Wilhelm II, a republic was proclaimed in Berlin on 9 November 1918. The following January, elections were held for a constituent national assembly. Since Berlin was insecure after an attempted leftwing uprising, the assembly met in the small town of Weimar, famous for its associations with the poet Goethe.

From the outset the Weimar Republic faced serious problems. Blamed for Germany's defeat in the war and saddled with the harsh peace settlement imposed by the Treaty of Versailles, it faced further economic dislocation caused by demobilization and labor unrest. Inflation, inherited from the Kaiser's government, worsened during the early 1920s as the result of high public spending, reparations payments and loss of confidence among foreign investors.

In 1923 the French occupied the Ruhr to force Germany to comply with reparations demands, precipitating total collapse of the currency and internal unrest. In the years that followed, the republic enjoyed something of a recovery. A new currency, the Reichsmark, was introduced, reparations payments were rescheduled under the Dawes Plan (1924), and in 1926 Germany was admitted to the League of Nations. Soon industrial production had recovered to prewar levels, and in 1928 parliamentary elections produced gains for the Social Democrats, who strongly supported the republic. However, the American stock market crash of October 1929 plunged the country into another economic crisis. The situation grew worse and by January 1932 six million Germans were out of work. Exploiting the crisis, Hitler's Nazi party became the biggest in Germany. On 30 January 1933 Hitler took up office as chancellor, replacing democracy with a Nazi dictatorship – the so-called Third Reich.

lomacy during the 1920s, the member states could not agree on how to solve the problem of disarmament themselves. In particular the French, after the United States self-imposed isolation, decided that they would have to look after themselves by adopting a rigid attitude to Germans fulfilment of the peace treaty terms.

On 27 April 1921 the Allied reparations commission set a figure of 132,000 million gold marks as Germany's debt to her former enemies. The German government finally accepted this after receiving an ultimatum on 5 May, but stressed that they believed the burden was economically impossible. The German mark, already seriously weakened by wartime government borrowing and increased postwar expenditure, declined sharply on the exchanges. On 10 January 1923 the Germans were declared in default, having failed to deliver telegraph poles which formed part of the reparations commitment. French and Belgian troops marched into the Ruhr and the German government announced a policy of passive resistance. These actions resulted in domestic German instability, increased Franco-German bitterness.

By 13 August 1923, when Gustav Stresemann took over the chancellorship in Germany at the head of a broadly based coalition, the German currency had become worthless. On 26 September the Germans called off passive resistance and the French, who had also suffered financially from the operation, expressed a willingness to negotiate. With the help of American mediation, the parties met in London and agreed a new and milder schedule of reparations payments. The new scheme, accepted on 16 August 1924, was called the Dawes Plan after its American architect General Charles G. Dawes.

The League of Nations suffered an ominous reverse when Italy seized the Greek island of Corfu on 31 August 1923 and refused to give it back. Unable to act directly, the League entrusted the matter to a conference of ambassadors who agreed that Greece should pay an indemnity for the alleged assassination of Italian officials. Only afterwards, on 27 September 1923, did the Italians evacuate Corfu. This incident illustrated the

▲ German currency in 1923 was cheaper than firewood.

fundamental weakness of the League and fore-shadowed further humiliations in the 1930s.

Following the Corfu incident the League considered the question of how to prevent war if nations were determined to embark on hostilities. The British Labour government headed by Ramsay MacDonald suggested that the acid test for responsible international behavior should be a willingness to submit disputes to arbitration. On 24 October 1924 the League assembly drew up the Geneva Protocol, committing signatories to accept arbitration in international disputes. Those who refused arbitration could expect to be regarded as aggressors and sanctions might be applied against them. Although initially received with enthusiasm, these proposals were soon rejected first and foremost by Britain and her dominions. Governments were jealous of their sovereignty and reluctant to be drawn into other peoples' disputes.

Nevertheless, by 1928 the international scene appeared more promising than for many years. The Kellogg–Briand pact, an American initiative for a general renunciation of war, further encouraged this mood of optimism. Almost all self-governing nations signed the pact in Paris on 27 August 1928.

Locarno – the era of optimism

In May 1924 the emergence of a more moderate left-wing government in France under Edouard Herriot and Aristide Briand assisted Stresemann, the German chancellor, and Austen Chamberlain, the British foreign secretary, to work towards a détente in Western Europe. The resulting Locarno pact of 15 October 1925 consisted of a number of treaties designed to prevent further frontier violations and to create an atmosphere of stability. The Germans agreed to confirm acceptance of their western frontier, which Britain and Italy said they would guarantee. This agreement furnished the French with some of the security they had been seeking since 1918 but was far from ideal. Since the guarantee was to both France and Germany, it would not be supported by military force. Instead, the French had to put their trust in the demilitarized zone on the left bank of the Rhine, which was specifically protected by the Locarno agreement. To improve relations in Western Europe, Germany was admitted to the League of Nations in September 1926. The French still had occupation troops in the area but as a further gesture of goodwill, French and British troops withdrew completely in 1930.

By comparison with the immediate postwar years the international climate had apparently undergone a remarkable change. The spirit of Locarno gave cause for optimism. Briand, Chamberlain, Dawes and Stresemann all received the Nobel Peace Prize for their achievements. However, nationalist resentments were never far beneath the surface, especially in Germany.

At Locarno the Germans had given no guarantee to accept their frontiers with Poland and Czechoslovakia though they did agree to arbitration treaties with those countries. The French for their part balanced their pact at Locarno with treaties of mutual assistance against German

aggression that they signed with the Poles and Czechs.

The Poles were uncomfortably aware that both their Soviet and their German neighbors – perhaps in concert – had designs on their territory. On 16 April 1922 the Germans had made a pact with the Soviet Union at Rapallo, whereby the two countries agreed to cooperate economically. The also began – more covertly – to engage in joint military training and armaments production. The Rapallo agreement helped the Germans to overcome some of the military restrictions that the Versailles treaty placed upon them, although militarily, they still remained very weak.

The rise of Japan

At the Paris peace conference the Japanese had insisted that they be allowed to keep the concessions in China's Shandong province that they had wrested from the Germans during the war. President Wilson opposed this plan, but unsuccessfully, and this became a focus of criticism in the US Senate when Washington rejected the peace settlement. At first China refused to be a signatory to the peace settlement, but in February 1922 the Chinese signed a treaty with Japan, Belgium, Britain, France, the Netherlands, Portugal and the United States. However, Japan and the European Powers, with the exception of Germany, retained many commercial and legal privileges in China, whose independence was largely illusory.

Japan also gained control of German islands in the Pacific under League of Nations' mandate and became a member of the League Council. However, Japan's attempt to insert a clause in the League Covenant asserting racial equality was unsuccessful. Both Australia and the United States opposed the move because they wanted to limit Japanese migration.

Further tension between the Japanese and the Americans arose over naval activity in the Pacific. However, at a naval conference held in Washington late in 1921, Japan, Britain and the United States agreed to limit the number of naval vessels in the Pacific to the satisfaction of all parties and

▲ Chinese prisoners of war during the civil war await their fate. The Chinese revolution of 1912 failed to provide viable government or answers to the country's social and political problems. By the early 1920s central power had broken down entirely and the country was ruled by a number of local warlords who competed with nationalist forces in an uneasy alliance with Chinese communities.

▲ The new Japanese emperor Hirohito photographed in 1926 in his court robes. Behind the majesty of the imperial throne, Japan had an unstable political system in which a small military elite exercised undue influence. Japanese economic growth provided the stimulus for the buildup of military power and the development of an imperialistic foreign policy. Chaos in China provided the opportunity for quick expansion.

allowed the Japanese to confirm their status as the leading naval power in the western Pacific.

When the last Chinese emperor abdicated, President Sun Yat-sen established the republic of China in 1912. However, there was no strong central Chinese government and conflicts between Sun Yat-sen's nationalist Guomindang party and former imperialist warlords ravaged the country. The nationalists established one regime in Guangzhou while a more conservative government, recognized by foreign powers, held sway in Beijing. Chinese resentment at foreign, and particularly Japanese, influence over the country grew. On 4 May 1919 students demonstrated in the streets of Beijing to protest at the failure of the Paris peace conference to guarantee China's rights in Shantung. This "May 4th movement" led to more radical anti-imperialist attitudes and in July 1921 the Chinese Communist party was established with the help of the Comintern. Moscow encouraged the Chinese Communists to collaborate with and strengthen the Guomindang as an anti-colonialist movement while building Communist influence within it. Jiang Jieshi who became the Guomindang's military leader on the death of Sun Yat-sen on 12 March 1925, began a march to the north in 1926, threatening Western colonial interests in Shanghai and Guangzhou. Initially the Communists had directed their efforts towards urban workers and intellectuals but the policy foundered and an attempt to set up a Communist regime at Guangzhou, 11–12 December 1927 was crushed with much blood-shed. Already Mao Zedong had been trying to rally peasants in the Hunan province to the communist cause and from 1927 his rural guerrilla army was a significant force. Nevertheless in 1928 Jiang's Guomindang seemed poised to take over control in China.

During World War I, China's neighbor India had supported Britain with soldiers and money and looked to Britain for some relaxation of its colonial rule in return. When Britain made no move, the Congress party put forward demands for self-government, and in March 1919 Mahatma Gandhi, a new, charismatic leader of Indian nationalism, began a campaign of civil disobedience. Widespread violence followed, culminating in the massacre at Amritsar on 13 April 1919, when British troops fired on and killed Indian demonstrators.

To try to appease nationalist opinion, the British passed the Government of India Act on 23 December 1919, giving provincial assemblies control of some areas of government and establishing a central legislature. However the British governor-general remained in overall control and the central executive was responsible to London. The legislature opened in February 1921, but failed to satisfy the Congress party which continued to press for home rule and made the provincial assemblies unworkable. In November 1927 an all-British parliamentary commission was set up in London to examine Indian grievances but it failed to meet nationalist demands for greater autonomy.

▼ A mass demonstration in Bombay in 1930 to promote a boycott of British goods. During the postwar period Indian nationalist opposition to British rule increased sharply. The movement, which was notable for its high level of female participation, found a charismatic leader in Gandhi, whose nonviolent forms of protest presented the colonial administration with insoluble problems.

ART AND POLITICS

Since the mid-19th century the French term *avant garde*, meaning "vanguard", has been applied to art that is, supposedly, ahead of its time, revolutionary. Such art has often been associated with radical – usually leftist – politics, the impulse to upset an establishment in the art-world coinciding with the need to upset a class or political establishment. But after the flourish of revolution artists and politicians have often parted company; the individualistic creative spirit is soon disillusioned with what the Surrealist painter Jean Arp called "the termite state". The cry for freedom that is often heard in revolutionary politics can be overwhelmed in the human waste that the engines of war and the machinations of politicians leave behind.

There are other kinds of politics than those of revolution, however. The Constructivist sculptor Naum Gabo, turning his art away from political statement in England during World War II, asked what he could tell people devastated by war that "they did not already know?" Instead he used his art to keep hold of memories and hopes "to remind us that the image of the world can be different."

Political commitment in artists can show itself for the right or the left, for change or conservation; but artists tend to be slightly at odds with straightforward political responses, never quite toeing the party line. The establishment can frustrate the most outrageous acts of defiance by domesticating them. As Marcel Duchamp said of his "readymades", attempts to disturb the complacency of taste, "I threw the bottle rack and the urinal in their faces and they admired them for their esthetic beauty." Protest can become chic and the artist a licensed jester, never in the driving seat. And yet occasionally, if unexpectedly, art and artists themselves become focuses for political statement and provide the ideal medium for its expression to a wider public. Poster art in the political turmoil of the interwar years had a flair which married Expressionism and Cubism with the socialist and fascist doctrines alike. Artists and writers flocked to the Spanish Civil War, and a photograph or a novel recounting the realities of the frontline could stir consciences or more simply show the world the truth of the conflict. South African freedom songs have carried a message abroad, Mexican painters expressed a revolution, German satirists like George Grosz castigated a ruling class and an entire society. Occasionally philosophers like Jean-Paul Sartre have shared picket lines with students and workers. In all these cases artists have lent their talent to the cause.

At a more personal level, artists have been as involved in political conflict as anyone else, and they have sometimes used their arts as weapons. But the power of individual artists is uncertain when dealing with political dilemmas. The works that are produced on this level are often too strident to be effective as art, too individual for the blanket certainties of political faith and too humane for the crude facts of policy.

▲ *Eclipse of the Sun* (1926) by George Grosz, whose savage indictment of the rulers of Germany after World War I helped to seal the fate of the Weimar republic.

▼ Socialist Realism, esthetically conservative and ideologically unambiguous, was universally adopted in Stalin's Russia, as in this 1930s poster celebrating Lenin.

1924-1934

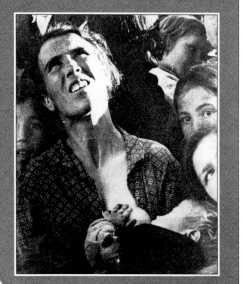

◀ The Hungarian photographer Robert Capa created modern photojournalism in the Spanish Civil War. His sympathy for the sufferings of the Spanish people and his presentation of the timeless qualities of the conflict, brought the attention of the world to the war as a struggle between good and evil. His work inspired several other photographers, including the Pole, David Seymour whose photograph of a displaced family is shown here.

◀ The Dadaist Marcel Duchamp attempted to challenge all the assumptions of the middle class. *Fountain* (1917) was a urinal, turned on its side. Here the esthetic avant-garde matched the political: though Duchamp himself took little interest in overt political statement, Dada as a whole was closely linked with the rejection of the establishment.

▲ The philosophers and novelists Jean-Paul Sartre and Simone de Beauvoir lent their support — and gave considerable prestige — to radical political movements in France in the late 1960s; Sartre supported the students' and Communist party protests on the barricades against the government in 1968 while de Beauvoir inspired the feminist movement.

37

Datafile

The political destabilization caused by the Great War exercised a profound effect for years after the last shots were fired. Victors and vanquished alike faced a decade of domestic uncertainty as the political passions aroused by the war worked their way through. In Europe, the general trend was towards increasing support for extremist solutions – in the United States, a withdrawal back into isolationism discredited those associated with the war.

French elections

10%
15%
75%

1919

▶ In Germany, the moderate leftwing Social Democratic party (SPD) retained the largest number of seats throughout the first decade of peace, but its position was weakened by more radical leftist alternatives (first the USPD and then the KPD).

24%
40%
18%
18%

1924

◀ The electoral strength of the French center-right (Rep U) remained stable between 1918 and 1928. Political realignments to its left gradually produced a more radical and effective socialist challenge.

22%
42%
20%
16%

1928

National bloc
Radical
Socialist
Republican U
Others

Italian elections

30% 31%
19% 20%

1919

◀ Italy, plagued by economic problems, disillusioned by the peace settlement and riven by instability, experienced dramatic swing towards extremism. A faction-ridden political system proved incapable of restoring confidence and the Italian public responded by handing an overwhelming mandate to Mussolini.

24% 23%
13% 20%
20%

1921

▼ In the US, the electorate dramatically repudiated Wilson and the Democratic party which had taken it to war. Despite scandal under Harding, the Republicans continued in office under Coolidge.

US presidents
1917 W Wilson   D
1921 W D Harding R
1923 C Coolidge   R
1925 C Coolidge   R

4%
4%
7%
15%
70%

1924

Socialist
Popular
Liberal democrat
National bloc
Fascist
Socialist unionist
Maximal socialist
Others

US representation

Republican   Democrat   Other

House of Representatives   Senate

Seats (percent)

100
80
60
40
20
0

1915   1917   1919   1921   1923   1925   1927

During the postwar period, Western liberal democracy was challenged by two opposing ideologies – Communism and fascism. Of the two, Communism was perceived as the greater threat. Yet, while Soviet Communism was professedly international in outlook, arousing fears in the West of world revolution, it became more isolated and introverted as the decade wore on. By contrast, fascism, as it grew in strength, became increasingly aggressive at home and expansionist abroad.

The retreat from Communist ideals

During the Russian civil war private firms were abolished and the market economy ceased to exist in all but the most primitive form. Food supplies were requisitioned from peasants, if necessary by force, to feed the starving townspeople. Many left the towns where there was no food, and returned to family villages in which the peasantry had seized what remained of the landlords' land. Between 1917 and 1927 the number of peasant farms increased from about 18 million to 25 million though the holdings decreased in size and per capita production fell.

By the end of 1920 the Bolsheviks were triumphant in the civil war but the country was economically in ruins. Discontent and hardship led to strikes in Petrograd and Moscow at the end of February 1921. A mutiny that broke out among the naval garrison at Kronstadt on 17 March was severely put down. Lenin tackled the problem of economic reform while imposing more rigorous controls on political opposition.

To encourage more food deliveries, the peasants were permitted to sell part of their produce on the free market. The government also allowed small retailers to operate again and tried to encourage the investment of foreign capital to help expand industrial output. Lenin described this New Economic Policy (NEP) as a "retreat" necessary to consolidate the Bolshevik system before pressing ahead with the realization of a socialist society. It never really succeeded because the peasants had little incentive to increase their sales. Urban production was so low that there was little for the farmers to buy with the money they earned. Arguments arose within the Communist party as to the best way to overcome these problems and foreshadowed the power struggle within the party that followed Lenin's death in January 1924.

Power struggle in the Kremlin

Leon Trotsky, the People's Commissar for War and architect of the Red Army, strongly advocated taking a tough line with the "petit bourgeois" peasants. He had emerged as the strongest Bolshevik leader besides Lenin, and

THE TRIUMPH OF IDEOLOGY

many in the party – especially Zinoviev and Kamenev – saw him as a potential Napoleon. His eventual rival, Joseph Stalin, was not a leading member of the prewar revolutionary intelligentsia like Lenin or Trotsky, but he was a more successful intriguer. Appointed General Secretary of the Communist party's Central Committee on 3 April 1922, he packed the party apparatus with men loyal to himself. When, in 1923, Trotsky complained of the high levels of bureaucracy in the party and its comparative lack of genuine workers, Stalin increased the number of 'proletarians' by 500,000, making sure that they knew whom to thank for their preferment.

At the time of Lenin's death on 21 January 1924, Trotsky still seemed to be the most likely leader. Partly in order to block Trotsky's taking power, Zinoviev, Kamenev and Stalin established a triumvirate to dominate the Politburo, the inner cabinet of the Communist party. Trotsky remained People's Commissar for war, but was otherwise isolated.

Like Lenin, Trotsky and Zinoviev, who was the first president of the Comintern's executive committee, were internationalists, who believed that socialism could not succeed in Russia unless the revolution spread to more advanced capitalist societies. However, by 1923, this prospect had receded. On 6 July 1923 the constitution of the Union of Soviet Socialist Republics was promulgated, which, while apparently giving autonomy to non-Russian areas, effectively ensured centralized control from Moscow. In December 1924 Stalin published an article claiming that it was possible to achieve "socialism in one country", even one as backward as Russia. This view was endorsed by the 14th Communist party Congress of 1925, dealing a further blow to Trotsky, who had already been deprived of his war commissariat in January of that year. Kamenev and Zinoviev, having served their purpose, were also stripped of their power bases in Moscow and Leningrad. Too late they tried to form a united opposition with Trotsky. In December 1927 Stalin denounced this group as an illegal faction and Trotsky and his colleagues were expelled from the party. Zinoviev and Kamenev recanted their "Trotskyite deviation" while Trotsky was exiled to Soviet Asia. Stalin's reign as the dictator of Russia had begun.

The Comintern and European socialism
The experience of war had radicalized many socialist movements, especially in Germany, Austria and Hungary, where defeat encouraged those on the far left to try to emulate the Bolsheviks. Even the victor countries were ripe for socialist propaganda in the postwar era, with labor unrest existing on a wide scale. Shortages of

food and capital created hardships, and often inflation made the situation still worse. Demobilized soldiers were being decanted onto a depressed labor market which had to reorient itself towards peacetime production.

At the second Congress of the Comintern in July 1920, Lenin set out 21 conditions that socialist parties would need to fulfil in order to affiliate to the new International. Among them were the acceptance of strict revolutionary discipline and the purging of so-called revisionists who had supported national defense in the war. These conditions effectively meant that the new International would be controlled by Moscow.

At its Bologna congress in October 1919 the Italian Socialist party committed itself to achieving the dictatorship of the proletariat but did not reject its parliamentary role. The general election of 16 November 1919 trebled the number of Socialists in parliament making them the largest single party. During the following months strikes and disturbances wracked the country,

▼ The writing was on the wall for Western middle classes: in the Soviet poster the name of the Third International strikes fear into the heart of a fat capitalist. But capitalism struck back – by encouraging the right wing.

"Communism is the power of the Soviets plus electricity." (Lenin)

What is Communism?

In 1848 Karl Marx published the *Communist Manifesto* in which he stressed the belief in class conflict as the central tenet of communism. Accordingly, human beings are not divided by nationality or tribal loyalty, but by to their relationship to the means of production. Those who own wealth try to exploit those who do not. Government agencies, law courts, police and even the educational system are designed, in practice if not in theory, to further the interests of the ruling classes. In a feudal, agrarian society land was "the means of production" and the ruling class was made up of landowners. As the "bourgeoisie" grew in economic power, they ousted the landowners, revolutionized production methods and, in their turn exploited the newly-created industrial proletariat. By collaborating with workers in other countries, the proletariat dispossess the wealth and create a classless society. According to Marx, the role of Communists is to take the lead in developing class consciousness among the masses in order to foment revolution when the time is ripe. Lenin developed Marx's teaching by emphasizing the importance of the party as the revolutionary vanguard. When he came to power in Russia in 1917 it was to replace a weak nascent democracy with a working-class dictatorship. Changing his party's name from Bolshevik to Communist, he proposed global revolution, with the creation, in 1919, of the Third International or Comintern.

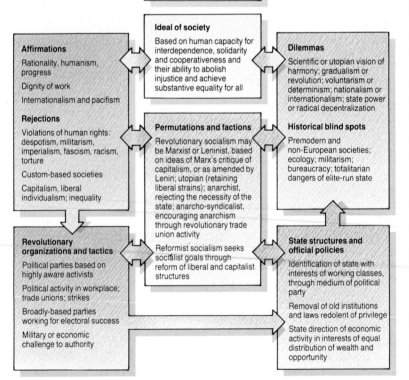

SOCIALISM

Ideal of society

Based on human capacity for interdependence, solidarity and cooperativeness and their ability to abolish injustice and achieve substantive equality for all

Affirmations

Rationality, humanism, progress

Dignity of work

Internationalism and pacifism

Rejections

Violations of human rights: despotism, militarism, imperialism, fascism, racism, torture

Custom-based societies

Capitalism, liberal individualism; inequality

Dilemmas

Scientific or utopian vision of harmony; gradualism or revolution; voluntarism or determinism; nationalism or internationalism; state power or radical decentralization

Permutations and factions

Revolutionary socialism may be Marxist or Leninist, based on ideas of Marx's critique of capitalism, or as amended by Lenin; utopian (retaining liberal strains); anarchist, rejecting the necessity of the state; anarcho-syndicalist, encouraging anarchism through revolutionary trade union activity

Reformist socialism seeks socialist goals through reform of liberal and capitalist structures

Historical blind spots

Premodern and non-European societies; ecology; militarism; bureaucracy; totalitarian dangers of elite-run state

Revolutionary organizations and tactics

Political parties based on highly aware activists

Political activity in workplace; trade unions; strikes

Broadly-based parties working for electoral success

Military or economic challenge to authority

State structures and official policies

Identification of state with interests of working classes, through medium of political party

Removal of old institutions and laws redolent of privilege

State direction of economic activity in interests of equal distribution of wealth and opportunity

◀ A Communist party reading room in 1920s Moscow with portraits of Lenin and Marx on prominent display. The Soviet state prompted universal literacy but exercised control over the press and other media. Political education, a concept inherited from earlier socialists, became a powerful propaganda weapon on the hands of the Soviets. Growth in the state-sponsored media and in education gave greater access to the public consciousness, while a strict central control of the information ensured that this consciousness reflected the values of the Soviet system.

▼ A scene from a 1925 Soviet movie evokes the Communist state's role as the bringer of progress to the huge peasant population. Behind the awe-struck peasant worthies is a picture of Mikhail Frunze who preceded Trotsky as commissar for war in 1924. In fact, the one-party state's impact on rural communities was less impressive. New peasant landholders resisted attempts to break down private production, while underinvestment in agricultural improvement led to sector-wide stagnation and profound food shortages in developing industrial centers.

culminating in workers' occupations of factories in Milan and Turin at the end of August. The unrest spread to other parts of Italy and soon affected half a million workers. The Socialist party however, instead of trying to turn these events into a political attack on the state, negotiated a compromise settlement, and the possibility of establishing a workers' state receded.

Italian socialism received another setback when the party split on the question of the Comintern. The majority of the party only accepted Lenin's 21 conditions with reservations. The sizable minority of hardliners who agreed with Lenin left the congress to form the Italian Communist party. The Italian socialist movement, increasingly torn by dissent, became an easy prey for its Fascist enemies in the years that followed.

In Germany too the split in the socialist movement begun in the war widened with the experience of revolution and the activities of the Comintern. After the collapse of the monarchy in 1918, government passed to a coalition of Majority Socialists (SPD) and Independent Socialists (USPD). However, the tendency of Friedrich Ebert, the SPD head of government, to collaborate with officers in the old Imperial army caused the coalition to break up on 27 December 1918. After elections on 19 January 1919, SPD, the largest party in the constituent assembly, shunned the USPD and collaborated with nonsocialist parties like the Roman Catholic Center and the liberal Democratic party. The government's crackdown of radical left-wing stirrings in Berlin in January 1919 and Bavaria in April and May of the same year added to the bitterness.

In the Reichstag elections of June 1920 Ebert's

SPD lost substantial ground to the much more radical Independent Socialists. At the USPD's Halle Congress in October 1920 a majority of the delegates voted to accept Lenin's 21 conditions and join the Comintern and, in effect, the small German Communist party (KPD).

The new Communist recruits were eager for revolutionary action despite the caution of more experienced comrades. Inspired by Soviet Comintern leaders, especially Trotsky, their revolutionary adventurism culminated at the end of October 1923 in attempts to seize power in Saxony and Thuringia and in an abortive coup in Hamburg. These failures made the KPD depend still more on the Comintern leadership and transformed it into an instrument of Soviet policy. The German Social Democrats – whom it described as "social fascists" – became its main target. The KPD attracted young workers, particularly those not already members of trade unions, and its representation in the Reichstag grew steadily, though it never achieved the same amount of popular support as the SPD.

In France, the postwar labor unrest and the repressive policies of rightwing governments towards labor unions encouraged a radical response amongst socialists and trade unionists, especially those who had earlier been attracted to anarcho-syndicalism. At the Congress of Tours, in December 1920, the French Socialist party voted by a large majority to join the Comintern, seting themselves up as the French Communist party and controlling both the Socialist party apparatus and its newspaper. Later, many converts who rebelled against control from Moscow, left and joined a re-established French Socialist party under Léon Blum. In France, as in Italy and Germany, the working-class socialist movement remained divided, but its class-war rhetoric still frightened the propertied classes.

Mussolini and Italian fascism

On 23 March 1919 Benito Mussolini established the Fasci Italiani di Combattimento in Milan, a movement standing for a mixture of populist extremism – demanding a capital levy, land for peasants and the confiscation of ecclesiastical property – and violent nationalism. Fascist squads, distinctive in their black shirts, stormed the headquarters of trade unions and rural co-operatives and assaulted socialist and Christian Democratic functionaries as well as German or Slav minorities in border areas. These actions were applauded by Italian middle classes, including landowners and industrial employers, who feared that a socialist revolution would overwhelm Italy, and the police often turned a blind eye to fascist excesses.

Even the veteran Liberal politician Giolitti, who headed the government from June 1920 to June 1921, regarded fascist activities with complacency and even welcomed Mussolini into an electoral alliance in May 1920. With the socialists' Roman Catholic people's party and liberal groups divided and in disarray, Italy's political crisis deepened and support for the fascists grew rapidly. After many acts of fascist violence against political opponents during the summer of 1922,

▼ Mussolini's demagogic antics made him appear ridiculous to many people, but his message of national renewal, strong government and overseas expansion struck a vibrant chord in Italy. Denied promised territorial gains by the 1919 peace settlement and demoralized by economic stagnation and the near paralysis of government, many Italians were ready to turn to a strong man with a simple message promising to restore the glory of ancient Rome.

some of the leaders of the Catholic People's party attempted to form an alliance with the socialists to oppose fascism. However, the Vatican publicly distanced itself from any such move, causing a split in the People's party.

During the night of 27/28 October 1922 Fascist squads took over most cities in northern and central Italy and thousands of "blackshirts" began to converge on Rome. Army units and police blocked the path of the insurgents, and having gained the upper hand, began preparing to recapture the provincial cities. The prime minister Luigi Facta asked the king to declare a state of siege but when Victor Emmanuel refused, Facta resigned, enabling Mussolini to demand the right to form a government, and on 31 October 1922 he did so.

At first Mussolini led his government as an orthodox prime minister, including in his government members of other parties. The chastened, but not altogether unsympathetic, parliament gave him a year's plenary powers to carry out reforms. During that time he extended fascist control over the judiciary and civil administration and intimidated working-class opposition. He appeased the business community by cutting taxes, privatizing state enterprises, dropping plans for unemployment insurance and replacing trade unions with a system of class collaboration in which industrialists were well represented.

In November 1923 Mussolini put through an electoral reform to give the largest party in parliament two-thirds of the seats. The elections of April 1924 returned an enormous Fascist majority after a violent campaign of intimidation against its political opponents. One Socialist deputy, Giacomo Matteotti, who denounced the violence was kidnapped on 10 June 1924 and murdered. A wave of popular revulsion followed and on 13 June the opposition walked out of parliament in protest in the Aventine secession. Moreover, they failed to agree on what positive action to take and Mussolini's confidence recovered. On 31 December 1924 he suppressed all opposition newspapers and arrested opponents. Two years later, in November 1926, the Fascists excluded opposition deputies from the chamber and established a one-party dictatorship.

Military takeover in Spain

The emergence of mass parties on the left, particularly the socialists and anarchists, and labor unrest troubled the Spanish parliamentary monarchy. Liberal elites too who had supported a constitution to modernize the country were dismayed by social disruption, while the army, traditionally an important factor in Spanish politics was dissatisfied by the government's neglect of military needs and by its weakness in dealing with colonial insurrection in Morocco. Matters came to a head when, in September 1923, General Primo de Rivera overthrew parliamentary government and established a military dictatorship. Like Mussolini, he retained the monarchy. De Rivera had no political party, but he shared Mussolini's contempt for conventional politics and imported Fascist rhetoric into Spain. His regime was welcomed by similar social groups to those who supported Mussolini.

Nazism and the decline of Weimar

The most virulent form of fascism characterized the Nazi movement, established in Munich in 1919 by Adolf Hitler. Hitler was born in Braunau, in Austria on 20 April 1889. Footloose art student in Vienna and Munich, he joined the German army in August 1914 and served as a front soldier throughout the war. He was also employed by the army as a propagandist against Bolshevism.

In the autumn of 1919 Hitler joined an obscure nationalist group called the German Workers' party, at that time being led by Anton Drexler. He quickly became the party's chief propagandist and spokesman, whose skills helped to win recruits to the cause. On 24 February 1920 the party changed its name to the National Socialist German Workers' party (NSDAP, or Nazis for short). Its aim was to win working people away from class war to support the cause of German nationalism. Its chief targets were Marxists, the Weimar Republic and the Jews.

Hitler inherited a virulent antisemitism, which had existed in Germany and Austria before the war, and exaggerated it to suit his own purposes. The international conspiracy of the Jews could be blamed for everything, from Germany's military defeat to the Bolshevik revolution, and from stock-exchange speculations to crippling strikes.

The Nazis established a paramilitary formation, the brown-shirted SA, (*Sturmabteilungen*), to protect their meetings and to break up those held by their opponents. As such they were not alone. In the years 1920-23 the antirepublican Bavarian government encouraged the existence of nationalist paramilitary groups, hoping that they might form the basis of an army of liberation from both the Versailles treaty and the Weimar system.

In 1923 Germany's massive inflation ruined many of the middle classes and created a crisis of confidence in the Weimar Republic. When in August of that year Chancellor Stresemann suspended passive resistance against the French occupation troops in the Ruhr, the Bavarian government encouraged a military revolt against the republican regime. However the army, headed by General Hans von Seeckt, was too cautious and the Bavarian government also wavered. Hitler, seizing the initiative, carried out a coup in Munich on the night of 8 November 1923. Although it failed, Hitler gained a personal victory, using his trial to proclaim his own responsibility for the coup, in contrast to other nationalist figures who tried to deny their complicity. A sympathetic court sentenced him to a brief period of comfortable imprisonment, during which he wrote *Mein Kampf*, a testimony to his hatred of the Jews and his geopolitical objective of expanding German "living space" (*Lebensraum*) by attacking Bolshevik Russia.

Democracy under threat

On the surface, the years that followed Hitler's putsch, 1924-28, were the most stable in the short history of the Weimar Republic. Political violence declined, the currency was stabilized and Germany's international situation improved. In the Reichstag elections of May 1928 the Nazis fared

What is Fascism?

The rise of Mussolini began a long debate into the nature of fascism as a political movement or ideology. Conventionally, fascism has been seen as a virulently destructive display of irrational politics attributable to perverse social or cultural processes at work in the evolution of particular nation states. Marxists, on the other hand, have interpreted fascism as a preemptive strike on the part of "late" capitalism to combat the threat posed by revolutionary socialism.

On a third interpretation, a highly politicized nationalism was dedicated to realizing the vision of a new order born out of the ashes of the old one. In this idea, only the rejuvenated nation can restore to human life the value and intensity eroded by "decadent" forces such as liberalism, communism, individualism, materialism, pacifism or cosmopolitanism. The urge to found a strong, healthy national community, and even create a new type of human being, is common to most forms of fascism.

Historically, fascism embraced a number of interwar movements, including the Falange (Spain), the Iron Guard (Romania), Rex (Belgium), as well as British and French Fascist parties. The most virulent forms of fascism were those of Mussolini and Hitler. The atrocities committed under Nazism were the consequence of a sustained effort to eradicate all alleged enemies of the German people so as to make way for the reborn nation the Third Reich. Following the third definition, fascism, though outlawed after World War II, has since reappeared in Latin America and in some of the new right movements in Europe.

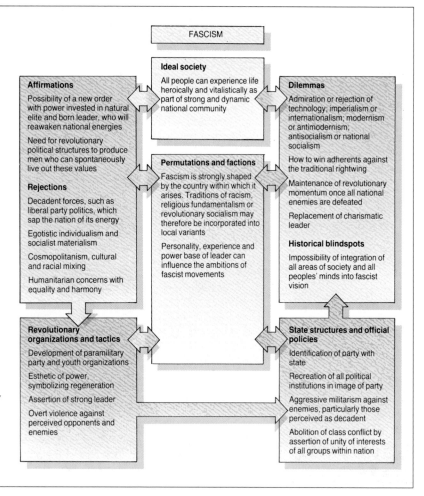

FASCISM

Ideal society
All people can experience life heroically and vitalistically as part of strong and dynamic national community

Affirmations
Possibility of a new order with power invested in natural elite and born leader, who will reawaken national energies

Need for revolutionary political structures to produce men who can spontaneously live out these values

Rejections
Decadent forces, such as liberal party politics, which sap the nation of its energy

Egotistic individualism and socialist materialism

Cosmopolitanism, cultural and racial mixing

Humanitarian concerns with equality and harmony

Permutations and factions
Fascism is strongly shaped by the country within which it arises. Traditions of racism, religious fundamentalism or revolutionary socialism may therefore be incorporated into local variants

Personality, experience and power base of leader can influence the ambitions of fascist movements

Dilemmas
Admiration or rejection of technology; imperialism or internationalism; modernism or antimodernism; antisocialism or national socialism

How to win adherents against the traditional rightwing

Maintenance of revolutionary momentum once all national enemies are defeated

Replacement of charismatic leader

Historical blindspots
Impossibility of integration of all areas of society and all peoples' minds into fascist vision

Revolutionary organizations and tactics
Development of paramilitary party and youth organizations

Esthetic of power, symbolizing regeneration

Assertion of strong leader

Overt violence against perceived opponents and enemies

State structures and official policies
Identification of party with state

Recreation of all political institutions in image of party

Aggressive militarism against enemies, particularly those perceived as decadent

Abolition of class conflict by assertion of unity of interests of all groups within nation

badly, getting only 2.1 percent of the vote and 12 parliamentary seats. They had, however, extended their organization into northern and central Germany. The party attracted the young and, though it was predominantly middle-class, it appealed to a broader social cross-section than most of the established parties.

In both Italy and Germany the enemies of democracy were helped by parliamentary systems that did not produce powerful governments able to maintain clearcut policies and generate business confidence. Any hopes of fundamental reforms in institutions such as education or the civil service evaporated and all the economic problems were blamed on the system. Even so, by 1925 fascism had only taken root in Italy and Spain. Elsewhere in Europe parliamentary government, albeit in many countries weak and often attenuated, had so far managed to survive.

In Japan, democracy was extended to give universal suffrage for men over 25 in 1925. But a wave of strikes in the economic slump experienced in Japan through the 1920s resulted in an increase in leftwing parties until Communist party leaders were arrested *en masse* in 1928. Culturally and politically, the country oscillated between an international and westernizing attitude and a militaristic and imperialist one.

However, the United States, the strongest of all the democracies, was less concerned with the state of European democracy than with domestic matters such as the prohibition of the sale of alcohol, which became law in December 1919, and laws restricting immigration passed in 1922. The alliance to defend democracy during the war ran counter to the thinking of the time.

The period between 1923 and 1929 was one of unparalleled American prosperity despite some regional backwardness and growing discrimination against the nation's black population. The wage output increased by 13 percent and manufacturing by 50 percent. As President Calvin Coolidge remarked on 4 December 1928 the country could "regard the present with satisfaction and the future with optimism".

▼ The Nazi party of the early 1920s was a small and loosely organized group of rightwing nationalists embracing several different visions of Germany's future. It grew in strength by exploiting discontent with the Versailles peace settlement and the failure of the Weimar Republic to deal with the country's severe economic problems. Only when he achieved a substantial level of electoral support did Hitler assert himself as the party's sole leader.

TRADE UNIONISM AND SOCIALISM

The task of trade unions was either to improve the conditions of the working classes within capitalist society, or to help to build a new socialist order. Within capitalist society the main aim was to bargain collectively for better wages and conditions for the whole workforce; socialism required the nationalization of industries, transport and banks. The main weapon of trade unions was strike action, its highest form the general strike of all industries. Workers tended to vote (if they had the vote) for socialist parties, but trade unions themselves were often distrustful of party politics, because even socialist politicians were seen as seeking power for themselves.

Four broad strategies were tried. The first was revolutionary. The revolutions of 1917 in Russia began as an explosion of strikes, by the mastering of which the Bolshevik party came to power. The Bolsheviks then claimed that the new state took care of workers' interests, and labor organizations lost their independence.

The second strategy prevailed in countries which remained capitalist. The war effort had obliged capitalist governments to bring labor organizations into partnership. The example of the Bolsheviks and a postwar boom in the economy provoked a wave of strikes in 1919–20, with one of its demands nationalization. But as the economic situation worsened in the 1920s employers regained the whip hand. In Britain, a strike of miners against wage-cuts in 1926 was escalated by the Trade Union Congress (TUC) into a general strike of three million workers. The political complexion of the government was all-important to the success of this strategy. A victory of the socialist-led Popular Front in France in 1936 ushered in a festival of sit-down strikes and factory occupations. The government forced employers to make major concessions.

The third option was that imposed on unions in fascist regimes. In Italy – as in Germany after 1933 – strikes were banned as only fascist trade unions were permitted, regimented into a corporative system which gave the state and employers a free hand to fix wages and conditions. Fourthly, there was the anarcho-syndicalist vision, briefly realized during the Spanish Civil War. A military coup of 1936 knocked out the government, but the unions took the argument into their own hands. They formed popular militias and collectivized farms and factories behind their lines. The anarchists saw unions as organizing cells of a new stateless society.

▶ **A meeting of factory workers in Petrograd electing members to the local soviet in 1920. The system whereby elected workers councils or soviets took responsibility for local and central government, was a theoretical high point in the translation of unionism into socialist practice, but in reality unions became mere "transmission belts" for decisions taken by the Communist party.**

▲ ▶ **One of the prime targets of unionism was to campaign against dangerous working conditions such as these boys working looms in North Carolina in the early years of the century.**

▶ **Union solidarity and political ideals were frequently promoted by colorful and graphic banners such as this British example of 1921.**

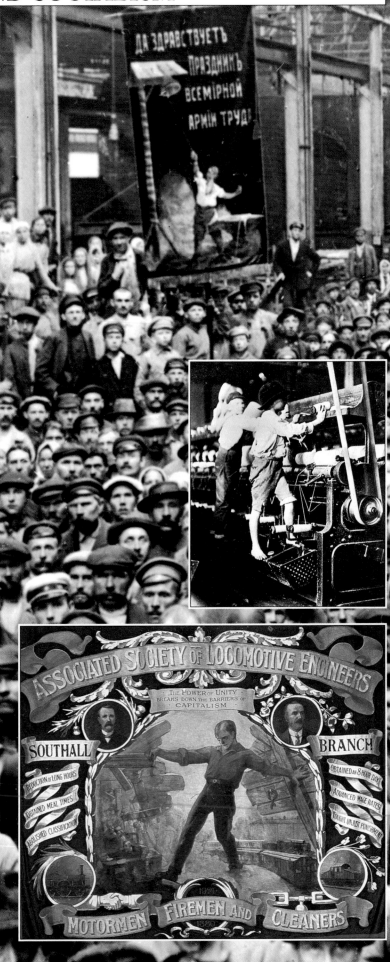

▲ Politicians such as Jean Jaurès in France campaigned democratically for socialism, opposing revolutionary socialism in the Second International. He also argued for the resolution of international conflict through arbitration and moderation.

▼◄ The clenched fist symbolised socialist opposition to capitalism and fascism in the interwar years.

▼ The socialists and communists played a major role in the defense of the Spanish republic against Franco in the 1930s. Here a republican replaces the falangist (rightist) symbol with the hammer and sickle.

ROT FRONT

THE SHADOWED WORLD

Time Chart

		1919	1920	1921	1922
Industry		• Regulations for agricultural workers put into force (Ger)	• Introduction of unemployment insurance in British and Austrian industry • German railways placed under government control	• Over 100 enterprises have to close due to lack of materials (Russ) • Rise of Venezuela as an important oil exporting country • Establishment of the Coal Council for organizing the distribution and supply of coal (Ger)	• British Broadca[st] Corporation (BBC founded (UK) • Famine in Russia due to bad harves[t] and political riots
Technology		• Introduction of the assembly line in European car production by Citroën (Fr) • Hoopes produces unalloyed aluminum (USA)	• Building of the first all-welded ship in Birkenhead (UK) • First regular radio service in Pittsburgh (USA)	• 19 Sep: Completion of the first autobahn in Germany, the AVUS	
Finance		• Mar: Support for sterling and the French franc abandoned, followed by depreciation • USA becomes main creditor nation of the world • Establishment of the Banco Central (Sp)	• Stock market collapse in London and New York • Merger among British joint stock banks • Banking legislation in Japan	• Oct: Establishment of Gosbank, the state bank of Soviet Russia • Establishment of the Caisse Centrale des Banques Populaires (Fr) • Beginning of a wave of mergers among the smaller commercial banks (USA)	• May: New law on[ ] status of autonom[y] the Reichsbank (G[er]) • Establishment o[f] Open Market Committee in the [US]
Economic Policy		• Jan: Economic crisis in the USA due to the transformation of the war economy into a peace economy • May: Nationalization of the mining industry (Ger) • Sep: German finance minister Erzberger establishes a central tax office, thus strengthening Germany's financial sovereignty • Introduction of the eight-hour day in France, Netherlands and Spain • Steelworkers' strike until 1920 (USA)	• Feb: Legislation on the establishment of works councils put into force • Feb: Rationing of food in Italy • Mar: Beginning of a general strike, especially in the Ruhr (Ger) • Jul: The Spa conference fails to settle finally German reparations	• Mar: Conference on German reparations in London. Amount fixed at 132 billion Goldmarks. • Apr: British miners' strike, demanding a reduction of hours and nationalization of the mines • 5 May: Ultimatum of London demanding a speedy fulfilment of the Treaty of Versailles, threatening Germany with the occupation of the Ruhr • Oct: Beginning of the New Economic Policy (NEP) in Soviet Russia, lasting until 1927	• Feb: Strike of German railwayme[n] • Jun: Internationa[l] high finance again[st] loan for commercializing th[e] German reparation[s] • Industrialists Sti[nnes] (Ger) and de Luber[sac] (Fr) sign an agreeme[nt] on the participatio[n of] German industriali[sts] in the regulation of reparations
International		• Jan: Peace treaty conference in Versailles. Controversy regarding German reparations • May: Establishment of the International Labor Organization (ILO) in Geneva • Foundation of the Third International	• Sep: International monetary conference in Brussels. Stabilization of currencies and a return to the gold standard discussed	• Mar: Trade relations established between the UK and Soviet Russia • May: Trade relations established between Germany and Soviet Russia	• Apr: World economic confere[nce] in Geneva. Gold exchange currenc[y] recommended • 16 Apr: Treaty of[ ] Rapallo between Germany and Sov[iet] Russia regarding economic coopera[tion] • UK imposes an import tax on all German products
Misc.		• 28 Jun: Treaty of Versailles signed by Germany (Fr)	• Jan: Founding of the League of Nations in Geneva • Beginning of the Prohibition (USA)		• Proclamation of[ ] Irish Republic lead[s to] civil war (until 1923[)] • Oct: March on R[ome] by Mussolini

1923	1924	1925	1926	1927	1928	1929
• Antitrust legislation against the misuse of economic power (Ger) • Continued export of corn after the famine (USSR)	• Foundation of Imperial Airways (UK) • Foundation of the Deutsche Rohstahlgemeinschaft as the organization of steelworks (Ger)	• Foundation of I.G. Farben (Ger) • Foundation of Chrysler Corporation (USA) • Redistribution of land in Poland at the expense of German proprietors	• Foundation of Lufthansa (Ger) • Imperial Chemicals Industries (ICI) created as counterweight to I.G. Farben (UK) • Formation of a European steel cartel by several European steel companies	• Foundation of Vickers Armstrong (UK)	• General Motors takes over Opel Werke (USA/Ger) • Farmers in the Soviet Union riot over collectivization • Soviet government offers industrial concessions to foreign enterprises	• Foundation of VEBA AG, a mining and electricity company (Ger) • Foundation of Unilever (UK) • General Motors buys a quarter of the shares in the German AEG electricity company (USA/Ger)
• H.R. Goddard invents the liquid fuel rocket (USA) • 15 Jul: First regular air route between Moscow and Gorkiy (USSR) • German company Benz produces trucks with diesel engines	• Mass production of Leica camera (Ger) • 12 Oct: First Zeppelin flight across the Atlantic Ocean from Friederichshafen to New York (Ger/USA)	• Hydrocarbon synthesis by F. Fischer and H. Tropsch leads to the development of synthetic gasoline	• 7 Jan: First demonstration of television by J.L. Baird (UK) • Wireless telephone service between London and New York set up	• First production of synthetic rubber (USA)	• 8 Feb: First international television transmission from London to New York by J.L. Baird (UK) • H. Geiger and W. Müller invent an instrument for measuring radioactive radiation	• P. Drinker invents the iron lung (USA) • Beginning of tractor production in Stalingrad (USSR)
• Hyperinflation after the occupation of the Ruhr by French and Belgian troops • Nov: Decree on the introduction of the Rentenmark and the establishment of the Rentenbank. Covering of this currency by goods instead of gold (Ger)	• Aug: Legislation on the introduction of the Reichsmark and a new set of regulations for the Reichsbank put into force (Ger) • Speculation in francs, but a sudden squeeze punishes the speculators (Fr) • Dawes loan issued to reschedule German reparations	• Apr: Restoration of the gold standard with the pound of the prewar parity (Ger) • Apr: Gold Standard Act (USA) • July: Law regarding the revaluation of loans and bonds, issued in Marks, fixing liabilities after inflation • Banking crisis and collapse of many banks (Sp)	• Inflation, followed by a de facto stabilization of the franc at devalued level (Fr) • Jul: New banking legislation, fixing the amount of government borrowing at 400 million Marks (Ger) • Banca d'Italia obtains a note-issuing monopoly (It) • Dec: Suspension of the Latin Currency Union as a result of French inflation	• 13 May: Collapse of the German stock market • Dec: New gold parity for the lira (It) • Dec: Decree by the Soviet government concerning a new organization of gold production (USSR)	• Jun: Devaluation of the franc. Introduction of a gold currency (Fr) • Sep: Currency and Banknotes Act. The figure of fiduciary money in circulation fixed at £260 million (UK) • Establishment of the Banco Exterior de España (Sp) • Central Bank of China, established in 1924 in Canton, becomes the state bank	• Issue of the Kreuger loan of $125 million for 50 years (Ger) • Sep: Collapse of the Allgemeine Österreichische Bodencreditanstalt, and its merger with the Österreichische Creditanstalt (Aut) • 22 Oct: Crash in the Wall Street stock market (Black Friday), and the beginning of the Great Depression
• Sep–Nov: Reorganization of the monetary system discussed, so that the covering of the currency is to be substituted by goods (Ger) • Nov: Dawes commission (USA) and McKenna commission (UK) established to decide on the regulation of reparations • Publication of A Tract on Monetary Reform by J.M. Keynes and Money, Credit and Commerce by A Marshall (UK)	• Apr: Restrictive credit policy adopted by the Reichsbank to defend the exchange rate of the Mark (Ger) • Jul: Beginning of the reparations conference in London. Discussion of the Dawes plan • Sep: Dawes plan put into force. No final regulation of the amount of German reparations. Annual rate of payment fixed • Nov: Strike of Austrian railwaymen	• Jul: British government grants miners special wages and established an arbitration committee to avoid a strike (Red Friday) • Aug: Legislation on protection tariffs for industry and agriculture put into force (Ger) • Aug: Strike of tram and bus employees in Paris (Fr) • Dec: Party congress of the Communist party of the Soviet Union (CPSU) agrees on a transformation of the Soviet Union from an agrarian to an industrial country	• 4–12 May: General strike organized by Trade Union Congress. Miners continue striking until December, when they exhaust their resources (UK)	• Italian Fascist party introduces new labor legislation, the Labor Card • German government warned by the agent for reparations to increase public expenditure • Dec: Party congress of the CPSU agrees on a measures for a socialist economy, the enforcement of industrialization and collectivization of agriculture	• Sep: Young Committee set up to regulate the German reparations • 1 Oct: First five-year plan in the Soviet Union. Concentration on heavy industry	• Jan/Feb: Conferences on the German reparations in The Hague and in Paris. Publication of the Young plan to regulate the reparation payments • Sep: French prime minister Briand proposes the establishment of a United Nations of Europe as a means of overcoming the difficult economic situation • Increase in the rate of unemployment in all European industrial countries
• Nov: Establishment of the Mission Interallié de Controle des Usines et des Mines (MICUM).	• Feb: Agreement between the UK and Germany reduces the reparation tax from 26% to 5% • Aug: Financial agreement between China and Germany • Oct: Germany signs agreements on trade with France and the UK	• Oct: Germany signs agreements on trade with Italy and the USSR	• Oct: First pan-European conference on the unification of Europe • Oct: Empire conference establishes the British Commonwealth (UK)	• Feb: Pilsudski's government approves freedom of movement between Poland and Danzig • May: First international economic conference in Geneva discusses the world economic situation • Aug: International congress of trade unions discusses the reduction of working hours	• Jun: Pan-American conference in Havana discusses the problems of trade between the American countries	• Jul: World congress of women's labor opened in Berlin
• Jan: French and Belgian troops occupy the Ruhr (Ger) • Nov: Revolt in Munich of the NSDAP under Hitler ends in failure (Ger)	• Italian Fascist party wins the elections with a majority of 65% • First Labour party minority government under J.R. MacDonald	• Massacre of demonstrating students in Shanghai by the British police initiates the National Revolution (China)	• May: Coup d'état by J. Pilsudski introduces a moderate military dictatorship in Poland	• Tanaka Memorandum reveals the new Japanese policy of expansion in Asia • UK severs diplomatic relations with the USSR	• Briand–Kellogg pact declaring war to be an unsuitable method of solving international problems is signed by 15 countries	• Austria becomes a presidential republic

49

Datafile

The 1920s was a decade of marked contrasts. Outwardly it was a prosperous time, seemingly confirmed by the growing consumption of new consumer durables and new leisure industries like the cinema. However, the decade was also characterized by economic instability, with marked fluctuations in the level of activity, for example the deep, sharp slump of the early 1920s. The growth of new technologically-based industries contrasted with the depressed state of major manufacturing sectors, established in the 19th century, like textiles and coal. Moreover, not all advanced economies shared equally in the industrial boom. This was most firmly based in the United States and France, but Britain, and Germany to some extent, experienced major structural problems, since the contraction of older manufacturing activity was not fully offset by the expansion of the new. Postwar recovery was uneven among the industrial and industrializing economies, and for most primary producing economies the 1920s was a period of depression, marked by falling prices.

▼ As well as being the world's leading producer of manufactures, the United States was also a major primary producer. American agriculture had a lean time during the 1920s, following the prosperity of the war years. The problems for American farmers stemmed from falling market prices, allied to relatively high production costs after 1920.

▶ Between 1921 and 1929 average real income per head in the United States increased by 37 percent, while industrial production rose by 90 percent. However, the pace of growth was not even, with falterings in 1924 and 1927 and there were major differences between sectors of the economy, and between different social and ethnic groups.

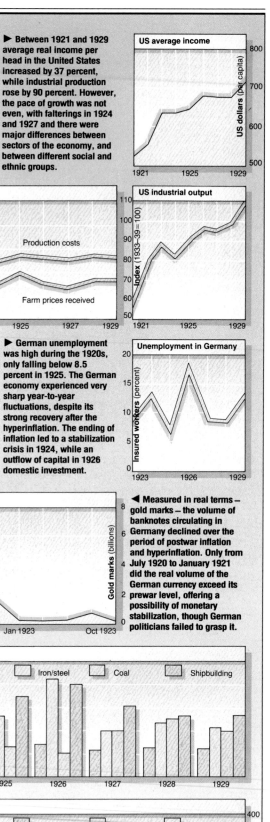

US average income

US agriculture

US industrial output

Japanese economy

◀ Japan had a balance of payments surplus during World War I, but in the 1920s imports exceeded exports in every year except 1926. Japan's international trading problems were exacerbated by the effects of the Great Kanto earthquake of 1923, which made it necessary to import reconstruction materials. The weak yen encouraged export growth.

▶ German unemployment was high during the 1920s, only falling below 8.5 percent in 1925. The German economy experienced very sharp year-to-year fluctuations, despite its strong recovery after the hyperinflation. The ending of inflation led to a stabilization crisis in 1924, while an outflow of capital in 1926 domestic investment.

Unemployment in Germany

International value of the franc

German banknote circulation

◀ Measured in real terms — gold marks — the volume of banknotes circulating in Germany declined over the period of postwar inflation and hyperinflation. Only from July 1920 to January 1921 did the real volume of the German currency exceed its prewar level, offering a possibility of monetary stabilization, though German politicians failed to grasp it.

▲ France experienced inflation throughout the first half of the 1920s as a result of unbalanced budgets caused by reconstruction expenditure in the devastated regions. There was a steady decline in the international value of the franc, as against the pound. The fall of the franc became a matter of public concern from mid-1923.

▶ After the postwar restocking boom broke in the summer of 1920, unemployment in Britain never fell below 10 percent. One of the major reasons why it remained so high was the difficulties experienced by the old "staple" export industries, especially shipbuilding. There were marked regional variations in unemployment levels.

Unemployment in UK

▶ After recovering sharply during the postwar boom, British exports, by value in current prices, remained stagnant throughout the decade. Britain's 19th-century export industries had lost their dynamism and this situation was aggravated both by sterling's return to its prewar parity in 1925 and by rising barriers to trade in the world economy.

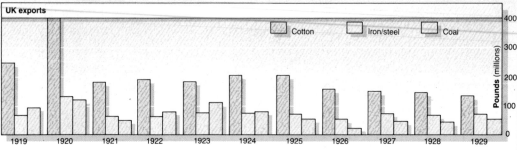

UK exports

THE POSTWAR YEARS

German reparations

A "return to normalcy"

French industrial modernization

Western aid for Eastern Europe

German hyperinflation

The transfer to new industries

Expansion in Japan

The new Soviet economy

At the end of World War I the common intention of political and industrial leaders among the liberal-capitalist economies of the West was a "return to normalcy" – putting the clock back to July 1914. In some economic realms this was possible, and the immediate postwar years were marked by rapid dismantling of the systems of state control erected during the war. But it was not possible to return to the world economy of 1914, as the delicate fabric of that entity had been torn apart by the war. Further, war-induced changes occurred at different rates among the economies of the world and consequently there were marked disparities between countries during the 1920s. This lack of homogeneity arose from a range of factors such as the prewar size of "new" industries within an economy and the pace of wartime and postwar inflation. Therefore the basic pattern – of a postwar boom, sharp and severe slump in the early 1920s, followed by recovery and even boom in the late 1920s – varied considerably from country to country.

After the war there was demand for everything, but above all for foodstuffs, industrial raw materials and producer goods. In particular, continental urban Europe east of the Rhine was experiencing famine in varying degrees, while the whole of Europe was short of energy. Consequently, the postwar restocking boom which carried through to the summer of 1920 was experienced most strongly by those industrial economies, such as Britain and the United States, which had intact productive capacity, and by the primary producing countries. The price bubble of this boom broke in mid-1920, by which time supply had got more into balance with demand, while the monetary authorities in Britain and the United States introduced measures to control the expansion of credit.

In Europe, with a few exceptions, inflation continued after 1920. A division can be made among European economies between those that experienced mild inflation until the mid-1920s, like France, and those – in particular Austria, Germany and Hungary – where inflation gathered such a pace that it became hyperinflation, destroying local currencies in 1922 and 1923. High rates of inflation were associated not only with expansion of the money supply, increased public borrowing and balance of payments deficits, but also with weak coalition governments.

▼ The 1920s were prosperous years in the United States, although the rich got richer at a faster rate than the poor became less poor. Further, the 1920s boom did not affect all regions equally. Abject poverty persisted amongst the blacks of the South and the whites in the southern Appalachians. City slums contrasted with the growth of a new suburbia characterized by imitation English Tudor houses.

▲ **World War I, which together with World War II has been called the European civil war, did not end in 1918. The Franco-German conflict continued as a dispute over reparations, leading in 1923 to the French occupation of the Ruhr. Berlin responded by directing passive resistance in this most important German industrial area. The occupying forces organized a separate civil and rail administration, seized banks and factories and isolated the Ruhr economically from the rest of Germany. Some French leaders even considered establishing a new independent Rhineland province.**

▼ **The Central Powers defeated Serbia in 1915. Part of the Serbian army retreated through Albania, and 150,000 people were finally taken to safety. The refugee problem was one that would escalate during the century, and fuel future conflicts.**

Japanese Overseas Expansion

Japanese colonial expansion began after the war with China in 1894–95, which led to Japan acquiring Formosa (Taiwan) and the Pescadores. Following the Russo–Japanese War (1904–5), Japan annexed Chosen (Korea) in 1910 and established spheres of economic influence in the Guangdong peninsula and South Manchuria. As a result of World War I, the Chinese treaty port of Jiao Xian was transferred from Germany to Japan, while some former German Pacific island colonies became Japanese mandates under the League of Nations.

Japan not only made territorial gains as a result of the war, but also enjoyed a balance of payments surplus, generated by the war-induced boom, totalling over 3,000 million yen for the period 1914 to 1919. This temporarily transformed Japan into a net international creditor. Some of this wartime windfall was used to make political loans to Chinese local and provincial governments. Japanese colonial trade, which had been insignificant before 1914 and still only accounted for 12 percent of total trade in 1918, rapidly expanded during the 1920s, comprising 20 percent of the total in 1929. Japan exported manufactures to her Asian colonies, taking in return raw materials and foodstuffs to feed the Japanese population, which grew by more than 25 percent between 1914 and 1930. The cultivation of Japanese-style rice was introduced into Korea and Formosa during the 1920s and by the end of the decade these two colonies had a rice output equivalent to an eighth of Japanese home production. However, the growth of cotton exports, particularly of yarn, to China slowed during the 1920s. Japanese development of its Asian colonies involved capital supplied by the state. One of the major enterprises was the South Manchuria Railway Company, which also controlled large-scale industrial undertakings.

German reparations

On 5 November 1918, German reparations following World War I were defined by the American Secretary of State, Robert Lansing, as the repair of all damages inflicted upon the civilian population of the Allies and their property by land, sea or air. Article 19 of the Armistice stipulated the restitution of the currency reserve of the Belgian National Bank, together with all documents, cash and securities removed from German occupied areas. This amounted in total to 8.5 billion francs, and Germany was also liable to pay several billions of gold marks through deliveries of materiel, together with 5,000 locomotives, 150,000 railway wagons, and 5,000 trucks. Such stipulations mounted in each monthly renewal of the armistice.

Not only was Germany required to pay reparations, but the territory of the Reich was reduced substantially, by 13 percent compared with 1914. As a result Germany lost 12 percent of its population, 16 percent of its coal production and 48 percent of its iron production. The division of territory in the east was the subject of plebiscites and these led to Allenstein, Marienwerder and western Upper Silesia deciding to remain with Germany. However, Danzig became a free city under League of Nations control. In the west the Saar was League-administered until 1935. In addition Germany had to surrender her overseas colonies and give up 80 percent of her prewar fleet. These changes dislocated the German economy and made reparation payments more difficult.

While the Reparations Commission was calculating the precise amount and schedule of payment, Germany had to pay 20 billion gold marks and deliver immediately 100 billion gold marks in bearer bonds carrying 5 percent interest from 1 May 1921. In addition, Germany had to defray the costs of the Allied army of occupation and Allied food relief. Further, before 1921 Germany had to hand over ships, animals, machinery, coal and chemicals, whose value would be offset against Germany's final liability.

The Reparations Commission only came into existence once the Versailles Treaty had been ratified by the Allies and had come into force, on 10 January 1920. However, its prime functions were largely bypassed through direct negotiations between the Entente and Berlin. Allied terms, after a meeting in January 1921 in Paris, laid down German initial payments of 2 billion gold marks, rising to 6 billion after 11 years and continuing for a further 31 years. In addition there were to be annual payments equivalent to 12 percent of the value of German exports for all 42 years, which meant that a part of the reparations settlement would apparently be matched to Germany's payments capacity. German counter-proposals were ignored and when Germany failed to accept the Allied terms, some cities in the Ruhr were occupied in early March 1921.

During the spring of 1921 the reparations question was in chaos. Finally an Entente summit drew up the "London Schedule of Payments", which in effect required Germany to make annual payments of 2 billion gold marks plus 26 percent

▲ French troops re-entered Strasbourg on 29 November 1918 after 47 years, but the economic reintegration of the provinces of Alsace and Lorraine took longer. It involved presidential decrees, as well as stipulations in the Treaty of Versailles that Germany granted duty-free entry to goods from the provinces for a five-year transition period. Nonetheless the economy of the provinces remained geared to exporting to Germany, a stance that could be undermined by the reimposition of a German protective customs barrier. Re-establishing French administration led to further cries for regional independence, especially in Alsace. Lorraine's dependence upon Germany was even greater as its steel and metal working industries were based upon Ruhr coking coal.

of the value of German exports, together with the supply of material and labor to make good war devastation and aid Allied economic development. Germany paid the first 1 billion gold marks, but by the autumn of 1921, with inflation mounting rapidly, it was difficult to see how the London Schedule could be maintained. Germany did make a payment in July 1922, but at the same time applied for a total moratorium for the rest of 1922, whilst maintaining the impossibility of making further payments over the following two years.

The critical factor was, of course, German inflation, but there was an increasing body of opinion within the Reparations Commission that held that the German government was responsible for the fall of the mark through its failure to balance the budget. The rift between France and Britain over the reparations question became open in August 1922, aggravated by rivalry in the Middle East. The British government stated that it would renounce all financial claims against its Allies and for reparations in return for a general settlement of inter-Allied debts. German inflation was now rampant: by November 1922 9,000 marks

were needed to obtain one dollar. But the French premier, Raymond Poincaré, would only accept a reparations settlement involving the cancellation of Allied war debts which also met the cost of the French reconstruction program in the devastated areas. At the Paris Conference of January 1923 the Reparations Commission declared that Germany was technically in default on payments and Poincaré, in conjunction with Belgium, dispatched a small contingent of engineers to the Ruhr. But this intervention was countered by a German campaign of passive resistance which turned the Ruhr occupation into a full-scale test of national wills.

The costs of German resistance were substantial and totally unhinged the state budget; it was abandoned in September 1923. The reparations problem was once again handed over to experts, but now with full and active American participation. The Americans had always made clear that their intention was to secure a moderate reparations settlement to pacify Europe and this is what the Dawes plan of 1924 involved. It laid down a schedule of payments for 64 years. The necessary resources were to be obtained half from German

► Ypres in Belgium was lost to the Germans, but then recaptured by British troops during October 1914. Thereafter the area experienced intense fighting, resulting in as many as a million deaths over the course of the war. The city's cathedral and Cloth Hall became physical symbols of the Entente's determination to resist German aggression. The result of trench warfare on the Western Front was a waste land. Ten *départements* of France had to be reconstructed. In 1923 it was estimated that 13 billion francs would be needed to complete the rebuilding of roads, railroads and canals, filling in trenches and shell holes, and the clearing of barbed wire and unexploded shells.

► The average Frenchman was averse to using checks, preferring cash both for transactions and for savings. Public confidence in the franc in 1920 was increased by the government's agreement to repay loans from the Bank of France.

▼ The Le Mans 24-hour motor race both proved the reliability of the automobile and attracted public attention. Between 1923 and 1938 the four main European car-producing countries manufactured ten million vehicles, with output growing faster than in the United States though from a lower base.

taxes and half from a mortgage on German industry and railways. The plan was to be initiated by a 0.8 billion gold marks external German loan.

Germany made reparations payments in the late 1920s as a result of American lending to Germany, while the reparations schedule was once more revised by the Young Plan of 1930. The Young Plan was made ineffective by the financial crisis of 1931, when inter-government debts were frozen for a year by President Hoover. In 1932, following the Lausanne Conference, Germany formally ceased paying reparations.

From September 1924 to the time of the Hoover moratorium, reparations totaled 10.8 billion marks, but over the same period German foreign indebtedness increased by 15.5 billion marks.

French modernization

The position of French agriculture was weak, but in sharp contrast France experienced an industrial boom during the 1920s, drawing its labor force from rural workers, who for the first time began to move in numbers to the towns and cities. Hydroelectricity, which had a prewar base, was used to power this boom, which led to technical developments in steelmaking and chemical manufacturing.

What best typifies the French industrial boom was the growth of the motor industry, from a prewar base. It was dominated by three firms – Renault, Citroën and Peugeot – which in 1928 accounted for 68 percent of sales of cars in France. Renault had been established in 1899, and by 1914 their works at Billancourt, Paris, occupied 150,000 square meters (1.6 million square feet). War demands expanded the size of the enterprise further and in the 1920s Billancourt became the largest automobile plant in Europe, fed by iron and steel from the former Thyssen works at Handange in Lorraine, one of the provinces now reclaimed from Germany. To Billancourt were added new plants in both the Paris region and the French provinces, while Renault also established assembly lines in six other countries, including Britain and Germany.

In many respects the French boom of the 1920s constituted the belated modernization of the economy, a process which had begun in the 1890s. It was aided by the reconstruction of the devastated northern provinces and by the fall in value of the franc during the first half of the 1920s, due to unbalanced state budgets arising from the financing of reconstruction, which gave French exporters a price advantage, especially as other

currencies were progressively stabilized from 1922. However, the financing of reconstruction also posed great problems for the French government. Government finances were heavily dependent on short – and medium-term loans, issued to supply resources for the reconstruction of the war-damaged areas in the expectation that they would ultimately be discharged by German reparation payments. But as the franc continued to fall, it became increasingly difficult to market reconstruction loans, and by late 1922 the French floating debt amounted to nearly eighty billion francs and was a potential source of inflationary pressure. Meanwhile, the vexed question of reparations dragged on. Cutting back government reconstruction expenditure was politically unthinkable, especially as priority had initially been given to industry and so there were still people in the war-torn regions who were living in terrible conditions. Poincaré's decision to occupy the Ruhr in 1923, in protest at what the French viewed as a deliberate German attempt to avoid the payment of reparations, stimulated bond sales for a short period, but eventually the government had to resort to the Bank of France for assistance. The franc continued to decline, but the main public concern was now with the rise in prices, which shot up by 15 percent, more in the case of foodstuffs. By January 1924 the situation had reached crisis proportions.

The mid-1920s in France were marked by continued inflation and the further decline of the international value of the franc. Between May 1924 and July 1926 there were 11 French governments, whose successive finance ministers attempted to deal with the joint problems of inflation and fiscal imbalance. Returning as prime minister in July 1926, Poincaré introduced measures which finally stabilized the franc at a level of one-fifth of its prewar value. This continued to give the French economy an export advantage for both visible and invisible trade until the total collapse of the gold exchange standard in 1931.

Eastern Europe

Apart from Czechoslovakia, the industrial boom of the second half of the 1920s made little impact on Central and Eastern Europe. This was an area of primary production – Europe's own prairies stretching eastward into Russia – and here, as in other areas of foodstuffs and raw material production, incomes were depressed by the fall in prices. The war had made Western Europe more self-sufficient, and all the primary producers suffered in consequence. The resulting economic and social problems were compounded in Central and Eastern Europe by ethnic antipathy, the new political geography set up by the Treaty of Versailles and economic self-sufficiency.

The region had been devastated by the war

▲ The number of motor vehicles in France increased from 125,000 in 1913 to 2.25 million by 1938. In 1938 Renault, Citroën and Peugeot supplied three-quarters of the French market. The technological leader was Citroën, which in 1919 produced France's first popular car, the A-1, and by 1927 was making 400 cars a day, using American methods.

The Italian Corporate State

After an unpopular war, the Italian economy was weak, with huge debts and low industrial production. The early postwar years were marked by inflation, strikes and social disturbances. Taking power in 1922, the Fascists revoked war taxes, liberalized foreign trade policy, and in 1926 passed legislation organizing unions and employers into corporations. The right to strike was abolished. In 1925 trade protection measures were reintroduced in conjunction with the development of the corporate system. Henceforth the Italian economy was to operate under a system of "semi-private and planned capitalism". The larger part of the population was eventually grouped according to occupation into corporations, and a Ministry of Corporations established in 1926, giving the Fascists control over the economy. Postwar state assistance to industry was continued, and the Istituto Mobiliare Italiano was founded in 1931 to provide long-term industrial loans. The Fascists undertook a large program of public works, which were much publicized but which did not significantly reduce unemployment.

▲ The Italian Fascists took power in October 1922, following their virtually unopposed March on Rome. Initially Mussolini organized a broadly based cabinet with representatives from four democratic parties. The Chamber gave Mussolini a grant of "full powers" for a year. The Fascists then subverted and reduced all rival party groupings by methods including violence, and developed a corporatist state which had links with the older managerial and political elite but which destroyed any interest groups attempting either to oppose or to contest with them as a rival. The Fascists utilized the wave of Italian modernism and fully appreciated the propaganda advantages of film. Mussolini laid the foundation stone of the Istituto di Luce, a state-funded film production organization.

◄ A leitmotif of Fascist propaganda was the past glory of Roman civilization, deliberately used to support the building of a modern state. This common strand ran through many Fascist developments, from reestablishing a colonial empire in North and East Africa to reinterpreting classical architecture and social institutions, such as the Forum. Many public works were undertaken under Fascist rule: new bridges, roads and canals were intended to provide work for the unemployed.

and received substantial Allied, mainly American, relief assistance in 1919 and 1920. This had been given as much for political reasons as humanitarian, since not only had food aid been regarded as the best defense against Bolshevism, but its provision also permitted the orderly rundown of American wartime strategic food stocks, so stabilizing price movements. The new national frontiers blocked trade, which was additionally hindered by high protective tariffs. Through these the agrarian states in Eastern Europe attempted to develop industrial sectors, while industrial economies such as that of Czechoslovakia sustained local agricultural production. General antipathy toward Austria prevented Vienna from fully reassuming its role as the financial and commercial hub of Eastern Europe. The problems of trade in the early 1920s were compounded by hyperinflation in Austria and Hungary.

Limited international cooperation

The needs of eastern Europe did prompt mutual cooperative programs undertaken by Western governments in the early 1920s. The Brussels economic conference of 1920, held under the auspices of the League of Nations, produced the Ter Meulen relief scheme and the International Relief Credits Program of 1920. A further economic conference was held in Genoa in 1922, but this had no major practical results. The only advance made in Brussels and Genoa that had lasting impact was the growth of the cooperation between central bankers, led by Montagu Norman of the Bank of England and Benjamin Strong of the Federal Reserve Bank of New York.

Norman had been made deputy governor of the Bank of England in 1918, and governor in 1920. He was therefore heavily involved in plans for postwar financial reconstruction, a three-stage process beginning with the stabilization of hyperinflation in Austria, Hungary and Germany, followed by Britain's return to the gold standard in 1925 and completed by the formation of the Bank for International Settlements during 1929 and 1930. Norman was a committed Atlanticist, and he developed a firm personal friendship with Strong. Both men were in agreement that international bankers had more chance than politicians of guiding the public in the acceptance and execution of policies requiring time and patience for their implementation. However, Norman was unable to call a conference of central bankers in the early 1920s, with the result that this "bankers' diplomacy" was never concerted and consisted of piecemeal initiatives for various programs.

It was however, bankers' diplomacy which gave financial substance to the stabilization programs of the Financial Committee of the League of Nations first for Austria and then Hungary. The bankers were generally believers in liberal capitalism and stressed the importance of "sound money", but this attitude did not take into account the structural problems which had been caused by the fragmentation of the Habsburg imperial economy. The new national boundaries made little economic sense. They separated coal from iron, and spinning mills from weaving sheds; railroad tracks were separated from their junction points and repair sheds, and industrialists from their bankers. Among the vanquished, local industry was opened to the full force of Western competition as a result of the economic clauses of the peace treaties.

◄ The Fiat car plant was a superb example of modernism in Italian architecture, carrying the idea of the mass assembly line throughout the building, so that the whole of the activity within the complex was in the form of a continuous flow. Fascism did not especially accelerate the technological transformation of Italian industry, but it encouraged centralization and thereby assisted the growth of big business. The Fiat works was actually modeled, in terms of the production process, on Ford factories in Detroit. In June 1927 the Fascist government provided tax advantages for mergers. The growth of modern Italian big business, with 266 mergers in 1928 and 313 in 1929, was coupled with a crude interpretation of scientific management, extending the working day from eight to nine hours and imposing wage cuts.

Inflation aggravated the already dire food situation within German cities and towns. The war had ended with the black market being the main source of food. Some relief was provided by American supplies in 1919 and Western private charity thereafter, especially the work undertaken by Quakers. German agriculture did slowly recover, but farmers and peasants were antagonistic toward the postwar continuation of the state-controlled economy. As a result soup kitchens and other forms of assistance became a common feature of urban life, while in the countryside, in what was called the "paradise of inflation", peasants were paying off their mortgages, rebuilding their farms, and restoring their herds to prewar levels.

German hyperinflation

Germany's own unique monetary experience began in 1921. During the initial years of peace the mark fell on the foreign exchanges, but internal prices rose more slowly, not immediately reflecting the external decline of the currency. This inflation had many roots: postwar shortages and dislocation, a balance of payments deficit, an unbalanced state budget and political instability.

The expansion of the German money supply was fed by the Reichsbank, which gave credits to the government to cover the shortfall of tax revenue as against expenditure, and to industry, initially at very low rates of interest – five percent in July 1922. From the end of 1922, as the mark fell daily on the foreign exchanges, domestic prices were immediately adjusted, with shops closing at noon to alter price tickets. So much money was needed for even simple transactions that it had to be moved in suitcases and perambulators, and its very production caused increasing problems. By August 1923, as many as 30 paper mills were supplying the Reichsbank with paper, to be turned into banknotes by 150 printing firms running 2000 presses night and day.

◀ As German inflation accelerated, prices became astronomic. Price labels had to become larger, just to accommodate the required number of zeros, with four eggs costing 40,000 marks. Carrying sufficient banknotes became an increasing problem: a whole basket of notes was needed in order to complete a very normal, everyday transaction. The shortage of food was an added and particular factor of the inflation, but the losses suffered by city dwellers because of high food prices were gains for those in the countryside.

The summer of 1923 in Germany was one of hopelessness. The mark had largely gone out of circulation to be replaced by dollars, if they were obtainable, or anything which retained its value. Otherwise transactions were made by barter. Many suffered great hardship. Those on fixed incomes, such as war pensions, were quite without financial resources, whereas those who had borrowed during the period of inflation were practically debt-free, because of the depreciation of the currency. On 15 November a new currency, the Rentenmark, secured against the fixed assets of all German industry and agriculture, was introduced. Its stability depended ultimately upon political stability, and the reparations problem was handed over to international committees of nonpolitical experts, which produced the Dawes Plan in April 1924. This was accepted by the Entente Powers in August 1924, and the Reichsmark was introduced on 30 August 1924.

The settling of the two German problems laid the groundwork for general monetary stabilization. Britain returned to the gold standard in April 1925, at the prewar parity of sterling to the dollar. By 1926, exchange rates were stable in 39 countries, and the financial resurrection of the world economy had been largely completed by 1928. Thereafter the only major countries which continued to have floating exchange rates were Japan, Portugal, Romania and Spain.

German recovery

Rebuilding the financial edifice was one thing, installing a mechanism to generate longterm stable growth was another. Initially the machine did not seem to work as liquidity and investment had to be provided by the United States through loans of various maturities to the constituents of the world economy. One of the major recipients was Germany.

Using American funds, often in the form of shortterm loans, German cities were rebuilt and German industry remodeled itself on the American pattern. One feature of the new order was electrification, even of the "older" industrial sectors of the economy such iron and steel and chemicals. This was coupled with advances in fuel economy to increase energy efficiency. Nonetheless, hyperinflation, stabilization, and subsequently rationalization, had a high cost in unemployment. German unemployment during the second half of the 1920s never fell below seven percent of the employed population; it was as high as 18 percent in 1926, and in 1929 – to all appearances the peak year of the decade – it was still 12 percent, some two million individuals.

British structural problems

From 1919 British industry gained in the short run from pent-up frustrated wartime demand. It was in a position to meet these orders before European competitors and provided better quality goods than wartime American or Japanese substitutes. Further, British prices were initially lower than American, an advantage which became greater from March 1919 when the sterling/dollar exchange rate was unpegged and sterling was allowed to float from $4.765 in March

▶ Berlin became famous, if not notorious, for its café society during the 1920s. Hugo Stinnes, the industrialist, was a prime example of those who did well out of the inflation. The contrast between such high living in Berlin's nightspots and the plight of the urban poor became the subject of stark caricatures by artists such as George Grosz, whose "5 o'clock in the Morning" contrasted all-night revelers with those struggling to work in the early hours.

1919 to $3.40 by February 1920. However, the immediate postwar export boom reinforced inflationary pressures within the British economy and gave industrialists a false perspective of what the future held, as it largely provided orders for the old "staple" industries like textiles and coal.

Domestic activity declined first, and the fall in primary product prices from mid-1920 resulted in declining overseas demand too. The effect in Britain was a sharp and severe slump until mid-1922. There then followed the "doldrums", the main casualties being the becalmed, over-capitalized industries of cotton textiles, coal and shipbuilding. The stagnation of these industries resulted in persistent high regional unemployment; total unemployment did not fall below one million throughout the decade. Politicians mistakenly diagnosed the cause as lying in the failure of world trade to recover fully in the 1920s, instead of recognizing that large sections of British industry were manufacturing products that were generally no longer wanted in quantity in the world market place.

The price of Britain's return to the gold standard was also high. The pound was overvalued, which reduced exports and increased imports, and interest rates were high, resulting in deflation. Further, the continuing dominance within the economy of the outmoded staple industries contributed to industrial difficulties. It could be argued that a high pound and high interest rates from 1925 actually accelerated much-needed structural change, but at considerable social cost. Substantial unemployment and industrial discord mounted, to culminate in the General Strike of 1926.

The American economy in the 1920s

The American economy also experienced a sharp depression in 1921, caused by a rapid decline of exports, which was felt first by producers of luxuries such as silk and motor cars. Yet from 1923 the American economy recovered and enjoyed a long boom to 1929, with only minor interruptions in 1924 and 1927. However, it was largely an industrial boom in "new" products – such as automobiles and electrical appliances like radios, irons and refrigerators. "Older" sectors – coal, cotton manufacturing, shipbuilding, shoe and leather manufacturing – either stagnated or declined, as in many European countries, leading to pockets of unemployment.

Like other primary producers, American agriculture experienced severe depression during the 1920s. It had prospered especially during the war, but by 1921 the increase in European agricultural output had made Western Europe more self-sufficient and less dependent on sources of sup-

▲ Modern mass demonstrations against unemployment had begun in Britain during the slump of the mid-1880s. At that time they were a reaction to cyclical unemployment, but society as a whole was unprepared for the deep structural unemployment of the interwar years, which mounted rapidly in the autumn of 1920 after six years of almost full employment during the war and postwar boom. The sudden rise in the number of jobless was put down to political and economic chaos in Europe.

Britain's Return to the Gold Standard

In 1924 the Conservative party won the general election in Britain, and Winston Churchill – who had been secretary of state for war and air between 1919 and 1921 – was appointed chancellor of the Exchequer. One of his tasks was to decide whether Britain should return to the gold standard, since the immediate postwar legislation placing a temporary embargo on the export of gold was about to lapse.

Churchill had little knowledge of economics, and therefore relied heavily on his advisers. The opinion of the Treasury officials and of Montagu Norman, governor of the Bank of England, was that a return would be advisable. This appeared to be backed up by a substantial majority of informed business, financial and political opinion. However, it was opposed by the economist J. M. Keynes on the grounds that a return at the prewar parity of $4.86 to the pound would overvalue the pound by some ten percent; this would reduce exports, increase imports, and lead to continuing high unemployment.

Churchill made up his mind to "return to gold", and gave his announcement as part of his budget speech of 28 April 1925. What his

advisers had not foreseen, however, was the German recovery of the late 1920s and the "cheap" exchange rates that were to be adopted by France and Belgium from 1926. As unemployment and industrial unrest grew, Churchill was to come to regret his acquiescence in Britain's return to gold.

▼ Winston Churchill, chancellor of the Exchequer, in 1925.

▲ Skyscrapers were a symbol of American progress and prosperity in the 1920s. Their construction was made possible by the availability of structural steel sections, and in Manhattan, New York, the lack of land on the island which constituted the city's central business district made them an attractive solution. The first such buildings had been put up in the mid-19th century. By 1910 there were 90 buildings in Chicago and New York which had more than ten stories and by 1920 there were 450. They proved to be even more potent as a symbol than as an architect's solution to a particular problem, especially the Empire State Building shown here under construction.

plies outside Europe. American farmers were confronted with a glutted market in which prices fell below the costs of production. In addition, they faced high freight and handling costs. This had particularly harsh consequences since many American farmers had borrowed heavily since 1915, both to purchase land and to buy equipment. Their financial difficulties in turn affected the rural American banks from which they had obtained their mortgages. In reaction to the rise in mortgage debts and the decline in land values, there was an exodus from the rural areas; the farm population fell by an average of over half a million a year during the 1920s. The area of land under production fell by over five million hectares between 1919 and 1924. The American government did intervene, initially with an emergency tariff in 1921 and with the Fordney-Maclumber Tariff in 1922, as well as through the revival of the War Finance Corporation in 1921, an Agricultural Credit Act in 1923, and an Agricultural Marketing Act in 1929; but it could not overcome the underlying problem of world overproduction and consequent agricultural depression. However, the low prices of foodstuffs helped the industrial boom, which also benefited

from the decline in the cost of raw materials.

The full development of manufacturing techniques introduced before the war led to increased efficiency, and labor productivity in the United States almost doubled over the decade. It was a model of technical prowess admired universally, even by Soviet Russia. But by the late 1920s the rate of growth of American consumption of the "new" products was beginning to tail off, and this was to have substantial effects upon industries where investment in production capacity had had to anticipate the growth of demand.

While American farmers went into default with their bankers, other primary producing countries sustained their positions during the mid-1920s by borrowing, on either the New York or London markets, since although holding increased stocks of produce was one answer to falling prices, it had to be financed, as did long-term debts already incurred. As in America, industrial consumers of primary products gained from the fall in their prices – the terms of trade moved in favor of the advanced industrial economies – but the diminished incomes of the primary producers meant diminished export markets for industrial producers. The underlying fragile framework

▶ The Great Kanto earthquake of 1 September 1923 devastated the entire region around Tokyo and Yokohama. Nearly seven hundred thousand households were damaged either by the earthquake itself or by the resulting fires, and the dead or missing totalled 105,000. The government embarked upon a major reconstruction program, earmarking 573 million yen to be spent over six years, while local public bodies contributed a further 230 million yen. Earthquake spending pulled Japan out of the sharp depression of the early 1920s but led to further inflation in the mid-1920s because the import of materials and equipment adversely affected Japan's already weak balance of payments position.

▲ Connections did develop between Bolshevik Russia and the West which led, for instance, to some American relief measures during the famine of 1920–21. During the mid-1920s the New Economic Policy allowed relative autonomy in many areas of the Soviet economy, enabling the further rebuilding of contacts with the Western economies, including the use of foreign engineers and experts and imported capital. When the first five-year plan was proposed, appeals were made to the West for economic assistance, as in this cartoon directly targeted on Western capitalists.

began to collapse at the end of 1927; the countries which were to compose the post-1931 sterling area experienced continuous international payments deficits from 1928 and by April 1930 nine countries, including Canada, Australia and New Zealand, had effectively devalued their currencies and abandoned the gold standard.

Japanese policies

While reconstruction and recovery in Central and Eastern Europe were affected and shaped by inflation and hyperinflation, the Japanese economy suffered an immense blow as a result of the Great Kanto earthquake of 1 September 1923. This caused substantial damage in Tokyo and Yokohama through the fires that followed, resulting in losses worth five and a half billion yen.

The economy underwent an inflationary reconstruction boom in the mid-1920s and the consequent depreciation of the yen on foreign exchange markets stimulated Japanese exports from 1924, while import growth slowed in 1925 and imports actually fell in 1926. The Japanese economy grew in real terms by 50 percent during the 1920s, the most marked trends being the quadrupling of electrical generating capacity between 1919 and 1930 and the expansion of steel production from 584,000 tonnes in 1919 to over two million tonnes by 1929. With these developments heavy industry began to overshadow textiles, but a more important development was the growing dominance within industries of a few firms, usually affiliated to the Zaibatsu. In 1928 these consisted of four industrial–financial conglomerates, of which the most important was Mitsui, which controlled 97 firms with a total capital of 1.6 billion yen.

In 1928 the yen fluctuated wildly on the foreign exchange market. In July 1929 Finance Minister Inouye announced a policy of monetary orthodoxy, involving balanced budgets and a return to the gold standard. The latter was accomplished on 11 January 1930, against a background of buoyant Japanese trade and low interest rates.

The Soviet Union

Soviet Russia was generally isolated from trends in the world economy during the 1920s. Initially the Bolshevik government passed land to local peasant committees which, in turn, largely redistributed it to individuals. The revolutionary land settlement was coupled with the nationalization of the banks, while manufacturing industry came generally under workers' control. However, until 1921 the country was engulfed in civil war and subject to foreign intervention which resulted in dramatic inflation, comparable to the German hyperinflation. Whatever direction took place during these years of "war communism" came through the Bolshevik party apparatus, local soviets and the Red Army. By 1921 agricultural output had fallen to about two-thirds, and industrial output to less than a third, of 1913 levels.

The reconstruction of the economy during the 1920s took place through the New Economic Policy (NEP), which brought to an end rationing and compulsory deliveries by turning distributions over to the market. The hallmark of the NEP in industry was cooperation with bourgeois technicians. It led to a remarkable recovery from the low base reached after the civil war but nonetheless gave rise to problems. As far as agriculture was concerned, individual initiative was encouraged, and a system of market prices was begun to spur the peasants to provide food for the urban population in return for industrial goods. Agriculture came to consist of peasant plots, mainly of medium size, which produced largely for local consumption. Industry suffered from a shortage of investment, which arose from low productivity and high wage costs.

In 1928 Stalin introduced the first five-year plan, which had ambitious growth targets and involved the collectivization of agriculture. This program was designed to operate through the now much stronger Bolshevik party apparatus, using the controls which had been developed by Gosplan, the main economic planning committee of the Soviet Union, in the years since 1921.

The New Economic Policy

By 1921 enforced nationalization and continued food shortages had drastically weakened the Soviet economy. In March 1921 Lenin introduced the New Economic Policy (NEP), which was characterized by relative economic freedom. Economic liberalization led to the emergence of small enterpreneurs – "the Nepmen" – paralleled in the countryside by the well-off peasants, the kulaks. The economy operated through a free market, but this change from "war communism" revealed substantial industrial unemployment and rural underemployment. Although re-establishing market forces, distribution remained a problem and there was an imbalance between high industrial and low agricultural prices. Further liberalization reversed the balance, producing relatively high agricultural prices from 1924. Small-scale private industry was encouraged to provide peasants with consumer goods. Opposition to the NEP within the Party grew from the fear that it would produce a wealthy peasant class with interests opposed to socialism.

▲ From 1920 there had been encouragement for the establishment of collective farms, but in the mid-1920s Russian agriculture flourished under the New Economic Policy with high prices and good harvests. This led within the Party to growing criticism of what appeared to be a pro-kulak policy. From the inception of the first five-year plan, the official attitude of the party changed. The kulaks — rich peasants who hired labor — were no longer regarded as a tolerated necessity, but as a hostile class which had to be destroyed. The campaign for collectivization began in May 1928. It generally required the use of the military, rather than being a democratic viillage decision, as suggested in this propaganda photograph.

◄ By 1927 Russian railroads were carrying as much freight as they had in 1917. The first five-year plan assumed that the existing rail network would cope, but winter transport crises in the early 1930s. Some existing lines were relaid and re-equipped. Two new routes were constructed, the Turkestan–Siberia railroad, shown here (actually the completion of a line begun under the czarist regime), and a second north–south line, the Karaganda railroad.

THE BLACK ECONOMY

In 1919 the United States Congress passed what became known as the Volstead Act, outlawing the manufacture, distribution and sale of alcohol. Throughout the 1920s and until 1933, the law – more popular in some states that others – made criminals out of millions of citizens who liked their drink. Prohibition also turned the gangster into a respectable criminal, being regarded by many as an honest bootlegger, trying to make a living like any other American.

Gangs had developed over the course of the 19th century, with the growth in the number of saloons, gambling houses and brothels. Gangsters turned to new avenues of criminality in the 1890s, capitalizing on the bitter conflicts between capital and labor. They supplied blacklegs and strikebreakers to the bosses and drew close to organized labor through victimizing those who defied union rules.

The car, the machine-gun and the telephone transformed the organization of gangs through enabling them to spread their influence to embrace whole cities and even states. The income required to equip gangs in this manner was provided by illegal traffic in alcohol. The further growth of gangsterism, and in particular the rise of gang bosses during the 1920s, was seen by many young Italian and Slav immigrants as the American dream being made reality.

During the early years of Prohibition – until 1923 – small gangs were hired by businessmen to protect their breweries and distilleries and to escort deliveries, while businessmen used political influence to gain immunity from the law. After 1923 big city gangs developed to control the illegal trade, either buying fake denaturing plants in order to secure the feedstock of raw alcohol or taking over breweries that produced "near beer", the legal product. Further, they controlled the production in the slum tenements of private illicit alcohol based on corn sugar. Some 3000 private distilleries, worth $50,000, were seized in 1929.

The criminal production and distribution of alcohol, coupled with smuggling from Canada, was tolerated in the urban northeast of America until the late 1920s. Revulsion developed with the move of organized crime into blackmail, "the racket", and the excesses of gang warfare. The economics of bootlegging was undermined by the Depression, the number of speak-easies in New York falling from 32,000 in 1919 to 9000 in 1933, and the private home production of beer and wine. During the Prohibition period, American consumption of wine, largely home produced, increased by 66 percent.

◀ ▶ Society's ambivalent attitude towards illicit production and distribution of drugs is now frequently the base for organized crime. Drug enforcement agencies of the 1980s – here displaying a haul of smuggled cocaine – are better organized and paid than the Prohibition Bureau.

▶ Modern society has attempted to discriminate between "soft" and "hard" drugs, with marijuana frequently being placed in the former category. Trade in it is barely disguised, and can provide entrepreneurial opportunities for members of outcast social groups.

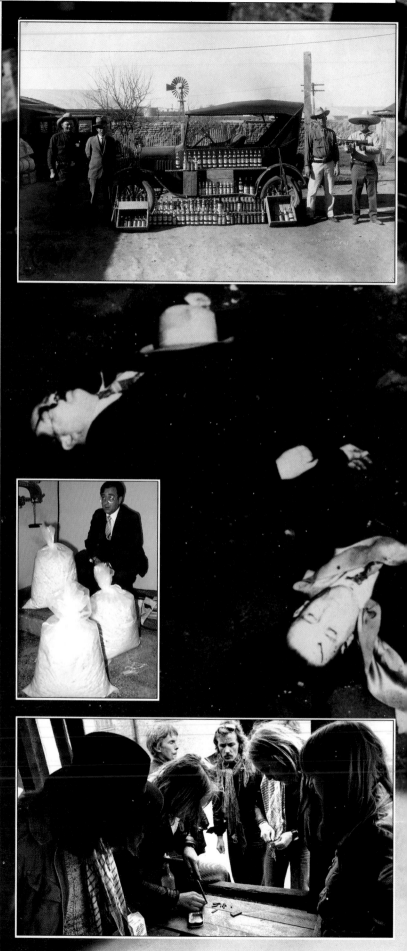

◀◀ Canada was one source of smuggled liquor for Prohibition America, Mexico another. Properly distilled spirits were prized, as one consequence of illegal production was death resulting from the use of wood alcohol. The Prohibition period was ushered in with 100 deaths in New York during the New Year celebrations of 1920, arising from the consumption of adulterated whiskey made from wood alcohol.

◀ The attempts to reform American morals by the law has also included the regulation of gambling; this, in turn, came under the sway of organized crime. Las Vegas turned the process on its head by offering state-controlled gambling through licenced casinos. This has led to close connections between gambling, the hotel business and entertainment industry.

▼ State economic controls in unpopular areas frequently lead to the development of fairly public black markets. Here a Chinese merchant examines a pair of jeans; such products command a high value in the East.

◀ Organized crime's control of the bootlegging trade led to overt gang warfare. On 14 February 1929 six gangsters were gunned down in Chicago. Gangleader George Bugs Moran had an uneasy truce with Al Capone through whom he was receiving smuggled Canadian Old Log Cabin whiskey. During early 1929 consignments of Old Log Cabin were hijacked and Capone presumed that Moran was responsible. An ambush was set up, and a police car bearing five men discharged over 100 machine-gun bullets at Moran's men.

65

Datafile

Advances in pure science in the 1920s were characterized by an expansion of our world view in many directions. In the new field of quantum physics, de Broglie and Schrödinger showed that matter exists fundamentally as both wave and particle at once. Heisenberg's Uncertainty Principle brought the fact of unpredictability into scientific practice, hitherto anchored on supposed predictability. And in 1929, Hubble established that the universe was constantly expanding.

Technology, too, was expanding, its expansion speeded by the incorporation of quantum theory and Heisenberg's discovery; and this led to the era of mass media communication and mass mobility which marked the 20th century. Other industries prospered on the back of communications and transportation, especially petroleum production – oil was dubbed "liquid gold". This industrial and technological proliferation also spanned the massive pollution problems of the later 20th century.

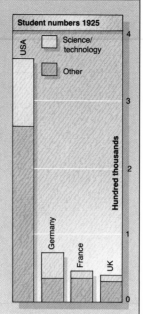

▲ Although the number of arts students was similar in the UK, France and Germany, postwar reconstruction of German industry coupled with generally high levels of unemployment encouraged many more students to study for a science or engineering qualification in the universities and technical schools.

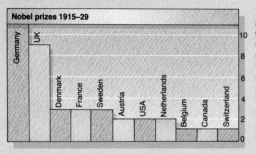

▲ The Nobel prizes awarded in science in this period were predominately given to scientists from Germany and the UK. Six scientists from Scandinavia were also honored. From Denmark Niels Bohr won the prize in physics in 1922 for his pioneering work on atomic structure. In 1920 S.A.S. Krogh had won in physiology. Working under Bohr's father Christian, Krogh had studied respiration and capillary blood vessels. Sweden won prizes in chemistry for Theodor Svedberg's work on colloids which showed visual evidence for the existence of molecules, and for studies of fermentation by Hans von Euler-Chelpin. A physics prize went to K.M.G. Siegbahn for work on X-ray spectroscopy.

► In the late 1920s European chemicals companies perceived that they could only compete with the giant Du Pont company in the USA if they formed larger units and sponsored large-scale research. In the UK four companies merged to form ICI in 1926. Its Dyestuffs division prospered in the 1930s.

◄ Based on highly creative work in organic chemistry, the synthetic materials industry in Germany grew rapidly to dominate world production at the outbreak of World War I. After defeat, however, the crucial German patents were siezed by the victorious powers and similar products were soon being manufactured elsewhere.

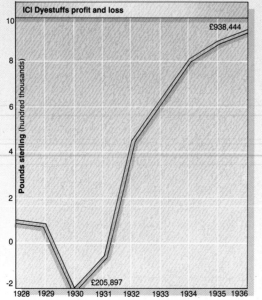

In the history of science and technology World War I (1914–18) proved to be very much a turning point, for it very soon changed the course of events in these fields. With the failure of either side to obtain a quick victory in 1914, the major powers involved prepared themselves for a long struggle. The potential importance of science and technology to the war effort was recognized, but the emphasis was placed on those sectors which either serviced the armed forces directly or assisted in maintaining the domestic economy. The general effect was that progress was made, but only on a relatively narrow front: research regarded as non-essential withered both through lack of funds and because so many scientists and technologists joined the services. Later, many specialists were recalled when it was discovered that they were needed for more essential work at home. The shadow fell also over peripheral countries, such as Switzerland and Sweden, who were not directly involved. Across the Atlantic, the USA stood aloof, having formally declared neutrality, which it was to preserve until 1917.

Science and technology in the 1920s

If we are to look for the greatest impact of science and technology on society in general we shall surely find it in the world of entertainment. The 1920s saw the burgeoning of public broadcasting on both sides of the Atlantic and the rapid commercialization of radio receivers: the amateur no longer had to build his own set but could buy one ready made, increasingly sophisticated, complete with loudspeaker in place of headphones. Cinematography, too, made immense strides, with the advent of both talkies and color.

Until after World War II radio and the cinema dominated the popular entertainment world, but a rival which was to outrival both was being conceived in the 1920s. In 1926 the British inventor John Logie Baird, amidst much publicity, gave demonstrations of television in London, using a photomechanical system. Baird's innovation was brought to its commercially viable, electronic form by others. Television was to become the Western world's staple medium of entertainment; whether it bestowed the gift of "far sight", as its name suggests, in any but the geographical sense is questionable. It certainly brought a revolution in the "turnaround time" of apparently hard information, and of artistic creation.

The automobile, too, may be regarded as in part a form of entertainment, for as well as being an increasingly popular mode of transport, much pleasure motoring was done. In Britain Herbert Austin launched his tiny but immensely popular Austin 7, the antithesis of the big automobiles of the trans-Atlantic world. The measure of progress is that in 1927 the USA alone produced 3.5 million automobiles.

TECHNOLOGY IN THE TWENTIES

The rapid growth of the automobile industry had far-reaching repercussions. The steel industry developed continuous strip-mills to produce the vast amount of sheets necessary for bodywork and the petroleum industry expanded to keep pace with the demand for fuel. The search for petroleum became wider and, literally, deeper: in 1927 a well in the USA reached a then record depth of 2,438m (8,000ft). In 1921 tetraethyl lead, a valuable antiknock agent, was hailed as a valuable means of economizing on gasoline. Half a century later, though, it was to be condemned on the grounds of atmospheric pollution.

By contrast, civil aviation made rather slow progress, mainly due to the lack of suitable aircraft; surplus military aeroplanes did not adapt well and it took time to design and build more suitable ones. But some events gave a glimpse of things to come. In 1919 John Alcock and Arthur Whitten Brown made the first trans-Atlantic flight

▼ An American 14in gun in use during the drive on the Argonne sector, France, October 1918. Mounted on a railroad wagon, it could be moved forward to keep pace with the advance.

and in the same year the brothers Ross and Keith Smith flew from London to Australia – though the journey took 135 hours. In 1924 a US Air Force team circled the globe: a year earlier repeated mid-air refueling had kept an aeroplane aloft for 37.5 hours. In 1923, in Spain, Juan de la Cierva was developing the principles of the autogyro, short-lived but the forerunner of the helicopter.

In the main, in the 1920s the great powers were licking their wounds and trying to restore their shattered economies. But even then there were rumbles of possible future conflict. In 1928 the French began to construct the Maginot line, a supposedly impregnable line of fortifications along the Franco-German border, which the Germans were to turn so easily in 1940. In Czechoslovakia, the weapon of the infantry man was being redesigned, with the development of the Z726 light machine gun, forerunner of the famous Bren gun used in World War II and later.

The origins and growth of photography

By 1900 the basic principles of still photography had been established, and the appearance of the first Kodak mass-produced camera in 1888 had made photography a popular amateur pastime. In 1900 one person in ten in the United States and in Britain owned a camera, though the hobby grew more slowly on the European mainland. But if the principles were established, major changes in both camera and filmstock lay ahead. Even up to World War II professionals used large cameras made with wood and brass. This was by then no longer technically necessary but a reflection of short-sightedness on the part of publishers. Up to 1940 *Life*, for example, refused to accept anything but 10x8in (25x20cm) contact prints. By then the far more convenient miniature camera, of which the 1925 Leica was the prototype, could produce equally good results on 35mm (about 1.4in) film. Most amateur photographers had by then turned almost entirely to roll-film, though in shorter lengths and larger sizes than 35mm.

A major problem in photography is to ensure that the image focused on the film corresponds with the picture desired. For this some form of viewfinder is necessary. This may be no more than two frames, arranged like the sights of a rifle, or a simple external optical series which reflects an image on to a small ground glass screen. These introduce problems of parallax – the fact that the axis of the camera's optical system is not indentical with that of the viewfinder. The twin-lens reflex was introduced by Rollei in 1929. This was essentially a double camera, the upper one of which reflected on to a viewing screen exactly the same picture as the lower focused on the film. The more compact single-lens reflex, in which the visible image was reflected by a mirror which dropped out of the way at the moment of exposure, appeared in the early 1930s.

The performance of lenses was also much increased. As early as 1902 the Tessar lens had an aperture of f4.5, but Leica had reduced this to f3.5 by 1925 and in the early 1930s apertures as large as f1.8 had been achieved. Corresponding improvements were made in shutter speeds. The popular Compur camera, made by the Deckel Company of Munich, had a fastest speed of 1/250th second when introduced in 1912 but this had been increased to 1/500th by 1935.

The advent of the talkies

The beginning of the cinema can be precisely dated: on 28 December 1895 the brothers Auguste and Louis Lumière displayed a moving picture on a screen to a paying audience at the Grand Café in Paris. At the time the event attracted little notice but it marked the start of a vast new industry which grew with remarkable speed. Initially its main centers were in France and Britain, but by 1915 the United States, and Hollywood in particular, had taken a decisive lead: at the outbreak of World War I American investment was in excess of 2.5 billion US dollars. The appeal was to a mass audience (though serious full-length dramas such as The *Battleship Potemkin* directed by the Russian Sergei Eisenstein, appeared as early as 1925) and the repertoire was broad, ranging from news features, identified particularly with those produced by the French businessman Charles Pathé, to slapstick comedies such as those of Mack Sennett's Keystone Company in Los Angeles, which made Charles Chaplin's first film.

From the beginning it was appreciated that an audience did not readily take to sitting in silence watching a flickering picture with the action explained only in short written captions on the screen. From the earliest days it was, therefore, customary for cinema managers to employ a pianist who played an impromptu accompaniment, endeavoring to match the mood of the music to the action on the screen. The ultimate goal, however, was to make the characters speak for themselves as the film was shown. An obvious solution, and one quickly tried, was to record the speech on a gramophone record and to play this in step with the film. Unfortunately, the results tended to be bizarre, as it was then technically impossible to synchronize the sound and the actions: characters said one thing and did another.

◀ Many stars found it difficult to make the transition: an exception was Greta Garbo, here seen with G. Brown in *Anna Christie* (1930)

▶ Two types of sound track were developed: the variable-area and the variable-density (shown here).

◀▲ By the early 1930s talkies had almost wholly superseded silent films. A problem with early equipment was how to muffle the sound of the camera so that it was not recorded on the sound track of the film being shot. Cameras were first placed in soundproof booths as here.

One solution was to record the sound as the film was made on a special sound track along its edge. Two systems were developed. In one the sound was recorded in terms of the varying opacity of the track; in the other a serrated track was formed, the pattern of the serration corresponding to the sound. In either case, the sound was regenerated by means of a tube- (valve-) amplifier system such as was used for radio transmissions. Not surprisingly, one of the pioneers of sound films was the American Lee De Forest, who had introduced the triode tube into wireless circuits in 1907. His phonofilm system of 1926 was unsuccessful, however, until improved as Movietone. The advent of this had dramatic success. In 1930 the number of American cinemas wired for sound increased from 8,700 to 13,500, and only 5 percent of films made were silent. The talkies eclipsed the silent film almost overnight.

▲ Although Thomas Edison's own inventions in the field of cinematography were of minor importance, he did become heavily involved in the organization of the film industry and particularly in the standardization of film and equipment. This picture shows film being shot in his studio in the Bronx, New York.

The advent of talkies had far-reaching effects on film production. On the one hand, a new kind of actor was required and many of the celebrities of the silent days found the new medium beyond their powers. There were also technical problems. Silent films could be produced in a hubbub of noise but talkies demanded a silent studio. Even the sound of the cameras was obtrusive: at first they were housed in soundproof cabins but later noiseless cameras were developed.

Although the American inventor Thomas Edison contributed little to cinema hardware, he did have a considerable influence on the organization of the rapidly growing new industry. In particular, he sensed the importance of standardizing film size and speed so that films could be shown without adaptation at cinemas anywhere in the world. At the beginning of the century he introduced a standard of 35mm (about 1.4in) width for film, with four perforations per inch (2.5cm), and 16 frames per foot (30cm). This was adopted internationally in 1909 and remained in use for 20 years. Projection speeds were not so closely monitored, however, and cinema managers anxious to give customers value for money could speed films up considerably. To cope with the new problems of sound reproduction a standard of 24 frames a second was adopted.

The World Power Conference

The worldwide concern of the late 20th century for adequate sources of power for industry and domestic uses is nothing new, but in the early years of the century the main concern was not the possible exhaustion of fuel supplies but how to keep power generation in step with demand. Anxiety about the management of electricity supplies led to the establishment of an International Electrotechnical Commission in 1906, with representatives from 19 countries.

A much more effective and influential organziation emerged after World War I as a result of the widespread desire to create effective international organizations and promote the regular exchange of information in a wide variety of fields. This was the World Power Conference, which first met in London in 1924 in connection with the British Empire Exhibition at Wembley.

It was organized by Britain and supported by all the Great Powers. The 40 countries represented included Germany and the Soviet Union. In all there were almost 2,000 delegates who considered "the power resources of each participating country and the extent to which they had been utilized" . and how "to provide adequate opportunities for the cooperation of all nations in the development of power resources".
Information presented at the Conference was afterward published in five volumes of Transactions.

It was perhaps ahead of its time, in that many countries had not even established national standards for electricity generation and transmission by 1924. But it continued to meet at intervals and after World War II was reconstituted as the World Energy Conference and then as the World Energy Council.

Instant visual communications: television

In the 1920s the public accepted as a matter of course sophisticated methods of communication that had within living memory been regarded as marvels of applied science. The telegraph and telephone systems had worldwide networks based on tens of thousands of kilometers of conducting wire and the possibility of transmitting sound without any wires at all had become reality: public radio broadcasting was in its infancy but growing rapidly. The cinema was entertaining millions by recording scenes on film and reproducing them on the screen later. One gap remained to be filled, however, in this complex pattern of communication: that of seeing events as they occurred, just as radio made it possible to hear speech as it was uttered.

As with so many technical advances, it is impossible to attribute the invention of television to one individual, but there is no doubt that the person occupying the center of the stage in the 1920s was John Logie Baird. He devised a photomechanical system in which the picture was scanned by a fast-rotating disk containing a series of holes arranged spirally: in this way, the whole picture would be scanned in the course of one revolution. The light signal from each hole was then turned into an electric signal via a photocell and a corresponding radio pulse was generated. The receiver consisted of a similar disk system: as the varying light signals passed in succession through the holes a picture corresponding to the original was built up on a screen. There was no great originality in this, for such a rotating-disk system had been patented by Paul Nipkow in Germany as early as 1884 – though at that time, of course, with the thought in mind of a cable connecting transmitter and receiver. Nipkow did not pursue his idea, but it was taken up by a Russian, Boris Rosing, in 1906, taking advantage of the cathode ray oscillograph invented by the German physicist F. Braun ten years earlier. This made it possible to eliminate the second disk and to modulate instead the spot of light which moved at great speed along parallel lines in the tube, thus giving – through the phenomenon of persistence

▲ Baird's original television equipment was very primitive, based on scanning an object with a fast-rotating disk, with a series of holes punched spirally on it: the whole picture was thus scanned in one revolution. The light transmitted by each hole was then turned into an electric signal by a photocell. At the receiver the process was reversed. In the event, however, this photomechanical system was not on the main line of evolution: the future lay with all-electronic television.

... so distinct was the scene shown on the large screen that the watchers forgot the race in face of the miracle that brought it before their eyes. Many of us can remember the thrill of these first "moving pictures". They flickered and spluttered, but out of the haze we saw men move about ...

"DAILY HERALD"
REPORT ON TELEVISING OF
THE 1932 DERBY

I am afraid if this invention becomes too perfect it will cause most people to spend their evenings at home instead of visiting the theatre.

R.C. SHERRIFF, 1930

of vision – the illusion of a continuous picture. However, signal amplifiers were then insufficiently developed for clear pictures to be produced. Meanwhile, in Britain, A.C. Swinton proposed, but did not develop, yet another system, in which both transmitter and receiver were based on the cathode ray oscillograph.

Baird persevered, and on 27 January 1926 gave the first demonstration of true television before an audience in the Royal Institution, London. In September 1929 the British Broadcasting Corporation began television broadcasting with the Baird system and so, too, in the same year, did the German Post Office. Baird was a good publicist and among his more spectacular achievements were a trans-Atlantic broadcast in 1928 and the showing, in a London cinema, of the finish of the 1931 Derby horse race. Nevertheless, his success was short-lived, for his photomechanical system was not on the true line of evolution. Others had reverted to Rosing's all-electronic system. Among them was one of Rosing's students at St Petersburg (now Leningrad), Vladimir Zworykin. After the revolution in 1917 he fled to America and joined RCA, becoming director of research in 1929. In this capacity he contributed much to the development of an all-electronic transmission/reception system as visualized by Swinton.

◀ Although the best-known, Baird was by no means the only inventor working on television in the 1920s. In the United States F.E. Ives – primarily interested in color photography and photoengraving – explored other possibilities for long-distance picture transmission. This cover of *Le Petit Inventeur* ("The little Inventor") (1928) gives an optimistic vision of a videophone system in which the picture was displayed with the aid of neon tubes. It did not prove to be a practicable proposition.

◀ The work of J.L. Baird in Britain on a photomechanical system of television was complemented in the USA in the early 1920s by that of C.F. Jenkins and P.T. Farnsworth. Both used a perforated scanning disk similar to that of Baird. The success of cinematography encouraged the belief, not to be fulfilled, that photomechanical equipment could be equally effective in television. The National Broadcasting Company became interested and made some experimental transmissions. Here Felix the Cat pirouettes in front of a television camera (1928). As the inset shows, the resulting picture was recognizable but of very poor quality. Not until the advent of all-electronic equipment in the 1930s was the future of television assured.

Datafile

Medical advances ensured that epidemic diseases were generally kept under control during World War I. Although the influenza epidemic of 1918 showed the limitations of scientific medicine, the postwar period saw renewed activity in clinical medical research. Numerous breakthroughs were achieved in surgery, with the production of new drugs, and in preventive medicine as for tuberculosis. There was also a vogue for psychoanalysis.

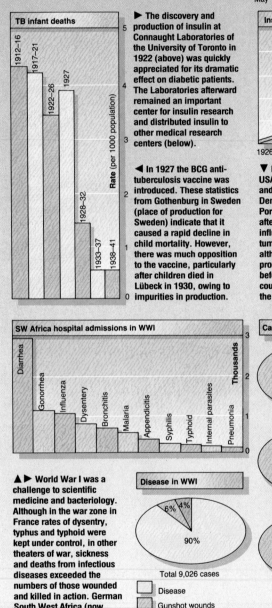

Insulin production 1922

► The discovery and production of insulin at Connaught Laboratories of the University of Toronto in 1922 (above) was quickly appreciated for its dramatic effect on diabetic patients. The Laboratories afterward remained an important center for insulin research and distributed insulin to other medical research centers (below).

◄ In 1927 the BCG anti-tuberculosis vaccine was introduced. These statistics from Gothenburg in Sweden (place of production for Sweden) indicate that it caused a rapid decline in child mortality. However, there was much opposition to the vaccine, particularly after children died in Lübeck in 1930, owing to impurities in production.

▼ Mortality rates for the USA in 1920, for England and Wales in 1921, for Denmark in 1921 and Portugal in 1920 show the after-effects of the postwar influenza epidemic. Cancer tumors are a new feature, although these were probably under-diagnosed before as well as in certain countries as suggested by the statistics for Portugal.

▲► World War I was a challenge to scientific medicine and bacteriology. Although in the war zone in France rates of dysentry, typhus and typhoid were kept under control, in other theaters of war, sickness and deaths from infectious diseases exceeded the numbers of those wounded and killed in action. German South West Africa (now Namibia) exemplifies the problems of campaigns in the less favorable non-Western European areas. Hastily organized military forces from the Union of South Africa attacked German territory during 1914 and 1915, but suffered more from infectious diseases (above), heat, lack of water and sandstorms than from gunshot wounds (right).

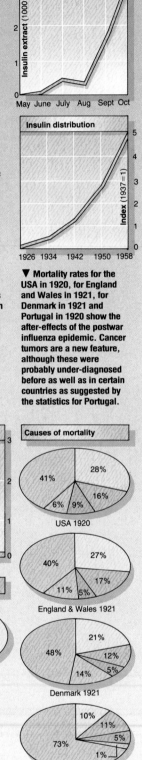

Insulin distribution

Causes of mortality

USA 1920 — 41%, 28%, 16%, 9%, 6%

England & Wales 1921 — 40%, 27%, 17%, 5%, 11%

Denmark 1921 — 48%, 21%, 12%, 5%, 14%

Portugal 1920 — 73%, 10%, 11%, 5%, 1%

□ Heart disease
▨ Influenza/pneumonia etc
▨ Tuberculosis
□ Cancer
▨ Other

Disease in WWI

90%, 6%, 4%

Total 9,026 cases

□ Disease
▨ Gunshot wounds
▨ Heat

For most of the world, World War I was not a time conducive to original work in the biological sciences and medicine: many research workers were diverted to work of immediate military importance. Even in the USA, not directly involved until 1917, a slowing down was apparent. Alexis Carrel, for example, who had left France in 1906 to continue his research on organ transplantation and tissue culture at the Rockefeller Institute in New York, became involved in the treatment of deep wounds by continuous irrigation with sodium hypochlorite. In Britain, F.W. Twort was called away for army service and could not exploit his exciting discovery (1915) of bacteriophages – viruses which can infect bacteria.

However, the war years were by no means wholly unproductive. In 1915 K. Yamagiwa and K. Ichikawa reported the carcinogenic (cancer-producing) effect of coal tar, starting a new line of cancer research which remained useful for the rest of the century. In social medicine there were some curious developments. In 1916 Margaret Sanger opened the first birth-control clinic in the USA. In 1920 France made abortion illegal, while the newly founded Soviet Union legalized it. In Britain, Marie Stopes pioneered work on eugenics and birth control (her then controversial *Married Love* appeared in 1918). Three years later she founded the first birth-control clinic in Britain.

The 1920s saw a marked change of emphasis in the approach to medical problems. Before the war research was largely in the hands of professionally qualified physicians and surgeons who guarded their position jealously. Afterward, there was an increasing contribution from workers trained previously in physical and biological sciences. Hans Berger, for example, who introduced electroencephalography (EEG – electrical monitoring of brain activity) in 1929, began life as a physicist before turning to psychiatry. EEG was soon used not only to investigate mental disorders but also to diagnose physical diseases of the brain.

This trend was particularly well illustrated in the field of vitamins and hormones. Although very different in origin – vitamins are ingested with food and hormones are secreted by the endocrine glands – they have one important feature in common: though needed only in minute quantities, both are essential for maintaining the body's metabolism in proper balance. The existence of both had been recognized by the early years of the century but their identification as specific chemical substances was possible only by using a multiplicity of physicochemical techniques. Major achievements were the isolation of insulin by F. Banting (1922) and of vitamin C by A. Szent-Györgyi (1928).

TOWARD MODERN MEDICINE

The impact of World
War I on medicine

Pioneering work in
surgery

Calmette, Guérin and
the conquest of
tuberculosis

The discovery of insulin

The origins and spread
of psychoanalysis

The rediscovery at the turn of the century of Mendel's classic work on inheritance, by H. de Vries and others, had initiated an increasingly intense international program of research on the mechanism of inheritance at the cellular level. In this field important landmarks were the American geneticist T.H. Morgan's *Physical Basis of Heredity* (1919) and his *Theory of the Gene* (1921). Important contributions were also made in the USA by H.J. Muller, who made meticulously careful studies of the conditions under which wholly new characteristics appear in living organisms, a phenomenon known as mutation. In 1927 he showed that by exposure to X-rays the natural mutation rate in fruit flies might be increased as much as 150 times.

Surgery and transplants

In the 19th century two major developments in surgery had much improved both the patient's comfort and his chance of survival. On the one hand, anesthesia had made it possible for surgeons to perform much longer and more com-

plex operations than were feasible when the patient was conscious. On the other, the use of aseptic techniques, and close attention to hygiene generally, much reduced the risk of postoperative infection, which was all too often fatal. In the early 20th century techniques were still primitive and great advances lay ahead, but two important principles had been established. Nevertheless, there were still areas where surgical intervention was hazardous.

The biggest problems lay with organs whose activity had to be sustained without interruption to maintain life. An important example was surgery of the chest, where opening the thoracic or chest cavity containing the lungs led to their collapse. Here an important development was one effected by Ferdinand Sauerbruch, who was appointed professor of surgery in Zuricn in 1910. He designed a special operating chamber, outside of which was the patient's head and the anesthetist. His body, and the surgeon, were inside the chamber which was maintained at a reduced pressure to prevent lung collapse. Zurich

▼ On all fronts, World War I cost 6 million dead and 12 million wounded. Medical services in the field worked under primitive and difficult conditions. Here a doctor treats a casualty at a captured German ammunition dump at Oosttaverne, Belgium (1917).

▲ Many of those who survived their injuries were left badly disfigured. Plastic surgery was still primitive, so many ex-servicemen, such as this Frenchman, could only hide their injuries with masks.

▼ Sadly, the making and fitting of artificial limbs became a considerable postwar industry. Some specialist firms were founded, others diversified into limb manufacture. The big demand encouraged improvements in design, especially in articulation.

abounded in sufferers from diseases of the lung who had come to seek relief in sanatoria in the mountains, and his technique soon became widely adopted. In 1908 F. Trendelenburg attempted surgical removal of a pulmonary embolism (blockage of tissue in the lungs) but this technique was not mastered until 1924. For patients whose respiratory muscles had been severely affected – as after poliomyelitis (a form of muscular paralysis) – the "iron lung" developed by P. Drinker in 1929 was a major advance.

For the sufferer from heart disease, however, the surgeon could still do little. The medical literature contained occasional references to successful surgery after stab wounds and similar mishaps but for chronic conditions the prospects were poor. The introduction of sympathectomy (cutting off a part of the sympathetic nervous system) for the relief of angina by the Romanian surgeon Thoma Ionescu in 1916 was a small but significant development.

Although intracranial surgery had long been practised – some skulls from prehistoric sites reveal successful trepanation, perhaps for the relief of depressed fractures of the bone – even in the 19th century the mortality rate was very high. In the main, this was because the methods of general surgery were used. Progress began to be made only when more specialized techniques were developed, notably by Harvey Cushing in the USA. The secret of his success was exceptionally comprehensive diagnosis beforehand, using specialized methods, and meticulously careful surgery, often lasting many hours. He was particularly successful with brain tumors and tumors of the acoustic and optic nerves. He also made a special study of the pituitary gland located at the base of the brain. It is perhaps the most important of all the endocrine (or hormone-secreting) glands, having an influence on all the others. His reputation attracted disciples from all over the world, who returned to their own countries to set up clinics using his methods.

While neurosurgical techniques were being developed to deal with pathological disorders of the brain and nervous system, others were seek-

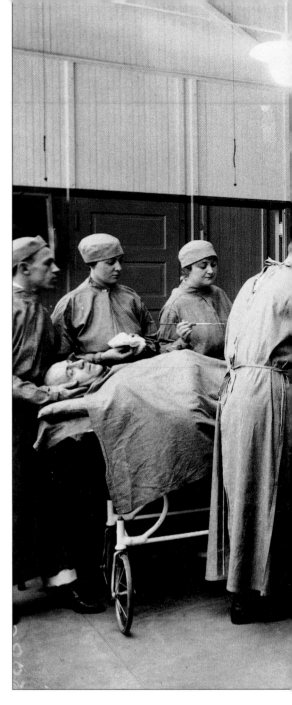

ing subtler methods to diagnose and treat disorders of the mind. In Paris J.M. Charcot (1825–93) had turned his attention from diseases of the nervous system to problems of human behavior, especially hysteria. Among his students in the latter part of the 19th century was the Austrian Sigmund Freud, pioneer of psychoanalysis. Initially derided, his concept of psychoanalysis – developed with C.G. Jung, A. Adler, and others – eventually became accepted and the International Association for Psychoanalysis was founded in 1910. Freud was elected a Foreign Member of the Royal Society in England in 1936. He continued his research and teaching for many years, until obliged to leave Vienna in 1938 as a consequence of the Nazi occupation of his country. In this field conventional experimental approaches had little validity and new ones had to be found. Among them was the famous ink-blot test for intelligence, personality and emotion devised by the Swiss psychiatrist Hermann Rorschach in 1921.

Try to recall the patient's face in every instance and a general picture of the case.

(Re patient with gastric ulcer) Hard-working, law-abiding, porridge-eating, God-fearing Scot ... Good fellow and we want to help him. Fifty percent of diagnosis in G-1 disease lies in the history so get a good one.

HARVEY CUSHING

During the 20th century organ transplant operations became a normal, albeit highly specialized, feature of medical practice. Important contributions were made in the early years of this century. Among the pioneers was Alexis Carrel, working at the Rockefeller Institute in New York. There he developed a considerable interest in organ transplantation where, among other problems, earlier workers had found difficulty in reestablishing a satisfactory blood supply to the organ transplanted: the usual outcome was thrombosis (blood clot) or stenosis (narrowing of a blood vessel). Carrel overcame this by developing new techniques of suturing (joining) blood vessels and succeeded in removing entire organs from animals and replacing them in their original position. By working with single animals he was able to avoid the rejection symptoms which remained a major problem in organ transplants in human patients.

Carrel also did original work in the field of tissue culture. He succeeded in maintaining cells alive in nutrient solution long after the animal from which they had been derived had died. Much later, in 1935, he devised a mechanical heart to maintain circulation during cardiac surgery.

In the treatment of infectious diseases the climate of medical opinion at this time favored the use of vaccines, where there had already been a long series of successes and new ones were being recorded. A major advance was the introduction of BCG vaccine in 1927 for protection against tuberculosis. By contrast, the track record for chemical agents had been disappointing. Salvarsan and neosalvarsan had proved valuable against syphilis, but side-reactions could be severe and even fatal. In 1924 German chemists produced plasmoquine, a synthetic alternative to the long-established antimalarial drug quinine.

This was an unimpressive record but with the benefit of hindsight it is possible to see that the tide was beginning to turn. In 1927 G. Domagk, director of research in experimental pathology and bacteriology with the great German chemical company I.G. Farben, was sufficiently optimistic to embark on a systematic search for chemical agents which might control some of mankind's most serious diseases such as meningitis, tuberculosis and pneumonia – the latter, in particular, dreaded as "the captain of the men of death". Progress was slow but faith and patience were rewarded in 1932 with the discovery of the first of the sulfonamide drugs, a truly revolutionary advance. In 1928 another discovery was made which passed virtually unnoticed at the time but was destined to prove even more revolutionary. In that year a British bacteriologist, Alexander Fleming discovered penicillin.

Research into microorganisms

When bacteria were first observed it seemed that they must be the smallest of all living organisms. Soon, however, just as the physicists were discovering that atoms were not after all the smallest units of matter, it became clear that there were forms of life smaller than bacteria. Around the turn of the century it was discovered that a number of major diseases – including poliomyelitis, foot-and-mouth disease and tobacco mosaic disease – were caused by infective organisms so small that they would pass through filters which would trap bacteria. Unlike bacteria, they could not be propagated in inanimate media but only in susceptible living cells, such as yolk of egg. In 1915 F.W. Twort, working in London, discovered that some viruses, which he called bacteriophages, can infect and destroy bacteria. War service made it impossible for him to continue his work at that time and it was left to Félix d'Hérelle in France to investigate the phenomenon more closely.

Until the advent of the sulfonamides and antibiotics the main weapon against infectious diseases was immunization, a system of prevention rather than cure. In the 1920s the most deadly of the endemic infections was still tuberculosis and the introduction of an effective vaccine in 1927 was a major step forward. Its inventors were two French biologists, L.C.A. Calmette and Camille Guérin and after them was named BCG (Bacille Calmette-Guérin) vaccine. It was derived from bovine tubercle bacilli whose virulence had been reduced by cultivation in ox bile.

Tuberculosis can attack many organs of the body, but especially the lungs. It has been considered as one of the great scourges of mankind since the earliest recorded history, but until the advent of vaccines and drugs such as isoniazid little could be done for sufferers. The merits of

▼ Until the development of BCG vaccine in 1927 by Albert Calmette (inset top) and Camille Guérin (below), of the Pasteur Institute in Paris, there was no effective protection against tuberculosis. The vaccine was of no value to those already infected, for whom the only recognized treatment was prolonged rest and plenty of fresh air and sunshine. The supposition was that this would stimulate the blood supply to the lungs and increase resistance to infection. A favored venue was Switzerland, but for the many who could not afford this there were many national sanatoria. Here children are treated for TB by exposure to ultraviolet lamps (London, 1930).

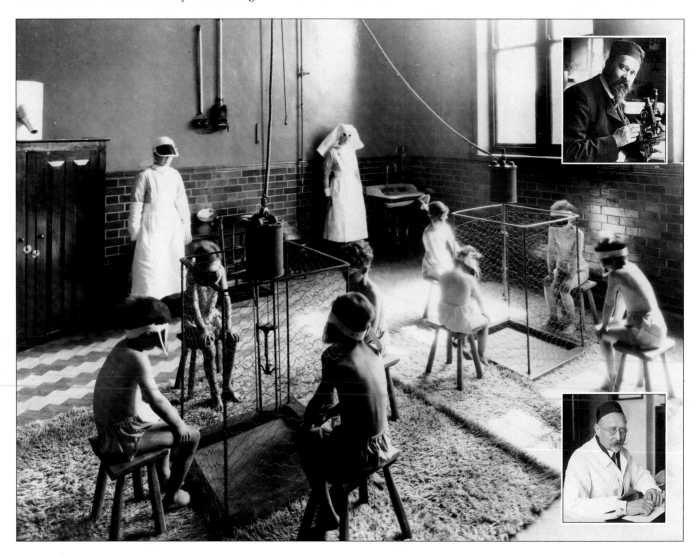

▲ In the conventional open-air treatment of tuberculosis, much importance was attached to plenty of sunshine. In the pursuit of this no expense was spared for those who could afford it. This sanatorium at Aix-les-Bains in southeast France had a rotating upper storey so that patients faced the sun all day. There was also – especially on the Continent – faith that spa treatment also could be helpful, and doubtless the site of this sanatorium was chosen so that patients could receive both treatments.

▶ Thanks to the development of vaccines and tuberculo-static drugs, the incidence of tuberculosis has been much reduced. Even so, in the late 20th century mortality worldwide was still around three million annually, three-quarters in developing countries. This poster, issued by the American Red Cross in 1913, is a grim reminder that TB was once one of the great killers worldwide – the white plague.

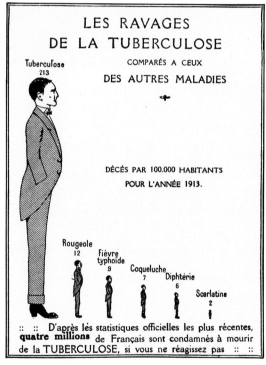

LES RAVAGES
DE LA TUBERCULOSE
COMPARÉS A CEUX
DES AUTRES MALADIES

Tuberculose
213

DÉCÉS PAR 100.000 HABITANTS
POUR L'ANNÉE 1913.

Rougeole
12
Fièvre
typhoïde
9
Coqueluche
7
Diphtérie
6
Scarlatine
2

:: :: D'après les statistiques officielles les plus récentes, **quatre millions** de Français sont condamnés à mourir de la TUBERCULOSE, si vous ne réagissez pas :: ::

We learn from an experience of thousands of cases all over the world that BCG nearly always yields sufficient protection

ALBERT CALMETTE, 1933

fresh air and sunshine were preached, but sanatoria were palliatives rather than cures.

Vitamins and hormones

Diabetes is an age-old scourge. In many cases the symptoms may be slight, or even pass undetected, but in severe ones increased susceptibility to infection, loss of weight and impairment of bodily functions generally cause serious illness or death. The discovery of an effective treatment for this widespread disease was one of the major medical triumphs of the 1920s.

The nature of the disease was by then well understood through research in various countries. The root cause was that groups of cells in the pancreas, the Islands of Langerhans, fail to secrete a substance which regulates the metabolism of sugars. In 1920 F.G. Banting, a young

orthopedic surgeon, established himself in practice in Toronto, Canada, and also obtained a post as demonstrator in physiology in the University of Eastern Ontario, working in the laboratory of J.J.R. Macleod. There he became interested in diabetes and invited the cooperation of a young medical student, C.H. Best. Reviewing earlier work he came to the conclusion that if he tied the ducts of the pancreas the gland would atrophy except for the Islands of Langerhans, and that from this residue he might be able to extract the active substance, insulin. This approach proved effective and the first successful clinical trial was carried out with the crude extract in January 1922. Thereafter, there remained two major problems: first, to prepare insulin in sufficient quantities; second, to devise means of administering controlled doses to patients.

The question of supply was partially answered by an extraction process developed by enlisting the help of a young biochemist, J.B. Collip, who used as his source pancreas glands (sweetbread) obtained from a local abattoir. By 1926 insulin was available in pure crystalline form, which made precise dosage much easier, and the new drug became generally available for all who needed it.

In 1923 the Nobel Prize for Physiology or Medicine was awarded jointly to Banting and Macleod, an honor all the greater because it is rare for the award to be given so soon after the discovery it marks.

The discovery of insulin is important in itself because it made possible the effective control – though sadly not the cure – of a major disease. But it was important, too, as one facet of a growing understanding of human physiology and thus of the treatment of other similar diseases.

Many of the glands of the body secrete products through clearly defined ducts and have a fairly local action. But not all glands have such ducts. The so-called endocrine glands secrete physiologically active substances into the bloodstream and thus affect the body generally. Collectively, the active substances created by endocrine glands are known as hormones, a term first used in 1905. Hormones are essentially chemical messengers which serve to keep the whole complex metabolism of the body in balance. Over- or underactivity of an endocrine gland can give rise to a variety of very specific symptoms. Thus an overactive thyroid, producing thyroxine, causes exophthalmic goiter: underactivity results in myxoedema, a condition distinguished by mental slowness, sluggish metabolism and loss of hair. Such effects were beginning to be understood around the turn of the century and led to the development of a new branch of medicine, which the Italian physician Nicole Pende named endocrinology in 1909.

Development followed two major lines. First, there was increasing knowledge of the role of individual endocrine glands and the hormones they secrete. Second, and no less important, it was recognition that these glands do not act individually but in concert: unraveling their complex interaction was, and still is, a task of great difficulty.

One of the pioneers was the Argentinean physiologist Bernardo Houssay, who followed up Banting's research and discovered that the hormone of the pituitary gland, a tiny organ at the base of the skull, is closely linked with that of insulin. The sex hormones, produced in the testes and ovaries, profoundly affect sexual activity and fertility and determine secondary sexual characteristics such as facial hair.

Hormones are specific chemical substances but have widely differing structures. they are all remarkable for their extremely high physiological potency: very minute amounts produce profound effects. Thus insulin is a complex protein. Thyroxine, however, is relatively simple and is remarkable for its high content of iodine; the small thyroid gland may hold as much as one-third of the iodine in the whole body. It was synthesized in 1927.

Yet another hormone-related disease began to yield to treatment at the end of the 1920s. This was Addison's disease, an age-old scourge but one not clearly identified until 1849 by the British physician Thomas Addison. He could do no more than describe the syndrome, but it is in fact due to atrophy of the adrenocortical glands. The most obvious symptoms are weakness, loss of weight and brown pigmentation of the skin. In the absence of treatment the outcome is usually fatal. In 1929 W.W. Swingte and J.J. Pfiffuer, in the USA, prepared active extracts of the gland and a year later they found it effective in the treatment of Addison's disease. In 1934 E.C. Kendall isolated the hormone itself. Now the condition can be successfully controlled by regular treatment with corticosteroids.

Hormones are created within the body but another class of essential natural products, the vitamins, are ingested as part of the diet. Like hormones, vitamins are remarkable for their extremely high physiological activity. Although a very little goes a very long way, deficiency can have very serious, even fatal, consequences. As with hormones, the effects of vitamin imbalance were familiar long before their causes were understood. Scurvy, for example, had been well known as a scourge of seamen, more particularly on long voyages without fresh provisions. In the 18th century James Lind (1716–94) recommended the use of lemon juice for its prevention and cure. The results were dramatic, and when his recommendations were accepted – albeit very tardily – scurvy virtually disappeared from the British Royal Navy. A similar connection between diet and disease was demonstrated by Christiaan Eijkman in 1890. In 1909 the German biochemist W.U. Stepp demonstrated that chemically pure fats lack an essential food factor, which was later identified as vitamin A (1913).

By the beginning of World War I it was clear that there was a relationship between diet and certain kinds of disease – some of them very prevalent and serious – but this was very far from identifying the basis of the relationship. For health, a proper balance of the main nutritional elements – protein, carbohydrate and fat – was necessary, but it was evident that other factors were essential, through only in very small

◀ Although diabetes was clearly recognized as early as the 2nd century AD, it was not effectively brought under control until the discovery of insulin by Banting and Best in 1922. This tragic photograph shows a child of three weighing only 7kg (15lb) – afflicted with the disease in that same year.

▼ Diabetes is caused by failure of the pancreas to produce sufficient insulin. The basis of treatment is to administer the hormone regularly to balance the deficiency. The original source was animal pancreases obtained from abattoirs. This picture shows the first stage of the extraction process (grinding the animal material) at the Indianapolis plant of the American pharmaceuticals company Eli Lilly in 1923.

The Origins and Spread of Psychoanalysis

Psychoanalysis is a method of treatment of the neuroses (minor mental disorders) which developed into a general psychology. Its originator was Sigmund Freud (1856–1939). Freud began his professional career as a research worker in the physiological institute of Ernst von Brücke in Vienna, but financial pressures forced him to embark upon private medical practice (from 1886). Dissatisfaction with current methods of treatment of the neuroses impelled Freud to abandon hypnosis and other methods of suggestion in favor of "free association". By encouraging patients to reveal whatever thoughts were passing through their minds, Freud hoped to uncover the origins of their neurotic illnesses which, he was convinced, were caused by traumatic events in early childhood. The first psychoanalytic book, *Studies on Hysteria*, which Freud wrote jointly with Josef Breuer, was published in 1895.

As Freud's ideas developed, a small group of interested physicians began to meet at his apartment and, in 1907, the first psychoanalytic society was formed. An International Association for Psychoanalysis followed in 1910, and by the outbreak of World War I psychoanalytic societies existed in Zurich, Munich, Berlin, Budapest, England and America. Interest in psychoanalytic theories was fostered by the high incidence of various types of neurotic breakdown ("shell shock") during the war amongst serving members of the armed forces.

By the 1920s psychoanalysis had become influential in intellectual circles throughout Europe and America. Freud's insistence on the central importance of the individual's sexual development opened the door to freer discussion of sex. Freud's concept of the unconscious, and his rediscovery of the importance of dreams, encouraged painters, sculptors and writers to experiment with the fortuitous and the irrational. Movements like Dadaism and Surrealism owe a great deal to psychoanalysis. Although many Freudian theories have not stood the test of time, Freud has had an inescapably powerful influence upon man's view of his own nature.

▶ Magritte's *Reckless Sleeper* (1927) with Freudian symbols.

amounts. In 1912 the Polish biochemist Casimir Funk suggested the name vitamine for such necessary food factors, in the belief that they all belonged to a class of chemicals known as amines. However, this assumption proved wrong and in 1920 the modern spelling vitamin was introduced to avoid confusion. One of the pioneers in the study of vitamins was Frederick Gowland Hopkins of Cambridge, who shared a Nobel prize with Eijkman in 1929. But although there were clear ideas abut their role, vitamins remained anonymous until 1926, when vitamin B1 – deficiency of which causes beriberi – was isolated in pure crystalline form. Two years later vitamin C – the antiscurvy vitamin – was similarly isolated and in 1933 it was made synthetically. In 1929 vitamin K was isolated, followed by vitamin D in 1931.

This emergence of the vitamins from the shadows was one of the greatest medical events of the 1920s and today a multitude of vitamins find their place in the world's pharmacopoeias. More than this, however, it became general practice in the food industry to fortify certain foods – such as margarine and dried milk – with vitamins to ensure that the population at large had a sufficiency of them – a very important public health measure.

Vitamins differ enormously in their chemical constitution and there is thus no single technique for their isolation, which is further complicated by the fact that they occur in very low concentrations – sometimes a few parts per million – in admixture with scores of other different, and irrelevant, substances. Two considerations are paramount, however. The first is identification of a relatively rich source: for vitamin C. Szent-Györgyi used Hungarian red pepper (paprika). The second is to find a suitable test organism – usually a small laboratory animal – which can be used to follow the vitamin through successive stages of purification.

THE GLAMOR OF TRAVEL

In the early 20th century, especially after World War I, comfortable travel for the well-to-do became big business. Luxury liners crossed the Atlantic, vying for business by advertising their speed, comfort and style; aircraft and airships allowed the rich to move ever more quickly around the globe; and the rail service, in Europe at least, was in its heyday, both for comfort and the comprehensiveness of the network. In the most renowned towns and cities of the world stood luxury hotels, trading on their cosmopolitanism and the quality of their service, which harked back to the more settled world of the 19th century. The rich had a network of glamor, through which they could tour the world without disturbing their illusions or their sense of their inalienable rights of privilege.

The network was an extension of the Grand Tour, itself a tradition whereby young aristocrats completed their education by a leisurely tour around the cultural highspots of Europe. With the establishment of travel agencies such as Thomas Cook's and the publishing of guides to the sights of Europe (such as Baedeker's guides, published from the 1840s), the tour became accessible to a much broader spectrum of people. Cook's first European tour had been organized in 1851, and from 1867 they began to offer hotel coupons. Twelve years later they entered the banking and foreign exchange business, and thus offered their clients a complete travel service.

Luxury rail carriages, the Pullmans, were introduced into Europe from the United States in the 1880s. But the years after 1918 saw a proliferation of Grand Expresses – the Orient Express, which plied between Paris and Istanbul, and similar services such as the Golden Arrow, the Rheingold and the Blue Train. Luxury liners flourished in the years before 1914, and then again after World War I. With the trend towards air travel by people more concerned to arrive quickly than to travel in style, the liners sought new trade by offering leisurely cruises around the cultural highspots of the world. They thus enjoyed a golden summer in the 1930s. For travelers on these ships and trains, traveling could be better than arriving.

The airship attempted to compete in providing a service that combined speed with comfort, and the largest airships could carry more than 100 passengers across the Atlantic in less than three days. Unlike travel by rail or sea, air travel remained almost entirely a luxury activity until World War II and the advent in the early 1950s of the first jet airliners. Prices began to fall in the mid-1950s, and by the mid-1970s only some 20 percent of transatlantic passengers were paying the full fare. As packaged holidays brought the exclusive resorts within the reach of most people in the industrialized countries, the old exclusive hotels were swallowed up in a mass of uniformity and high-rise concrete. Those seeking the glamor of travel had to seek ever more original ways of making a journey an event of thrill and challenge.

▲ Switzerland had become an important tourist resort in the 1860s. Winter sports were developed by Sir Henry Lunn, who, on a visit in 1883, recognized the possibilities arising from introducing skiing from Norway. This 1900s tour is being escorted up the Mont Blanc glacier at Chamonix.

▲ Flying was a glamorous pursuit from the mid-1920s until the early 1950s, with adventurous and dangerous flights in the 1930s by well-off couples receiving substantial press publicity. In the 1930s aircraft were specifically developed, such as the D.H. Moth series, for private touring and many flying licenses were held by society ladies.

► International aircraft flights, particularly flying-boat routes involving overnight hotel stays at exotic locations, creamed off the wealthy from the custom of the luxury liners in the 1930s. The ships built for transport were increasingly redeployed for cruising.

DEUTSCHE AFRIKA-LINIE
Schnelldienst nach
Südafrika

► Growing passenger numbers in the 1960s took the edge off the glamor of air travel, particularly through congested terminals. Airports were redeveloped, but often lagged behind traffic growth. Airport designed was revolutionized by the new approach taken at Schipol, Amsterdam.

► The rising incomes of the advanced industrial economies during the 1960s resulted in a growing màrket for travel. The more ambitious young Westerners developed a new "Grand Tour", to the Orient. For many American students this was but an extension of backpacking around Europe.

▲ The availability of international travel has also led to it being used as a vehicle for fund raising for charity. Sponsoring was developed as a way of financing scientific expeditions, as well as more imaginative sports, such as mountain-cycling. This has now been taken a stage further, with commercial and private sponsoring to raise money for a charitable cause.

THE
UTOPIAN
VISION

"Victorious troops…march through London, day by day, with bands playing and colors flying, to be reviewed by the King. What with brilliant sunshine and the consciousness of being a victorious race, the crowds in the streets have lost the looks of strain and anxiety and have become smiling and buoyant."

BEATRICE WEBB, 1919

"I have today given two minutes to praying for our dead and two hours regretting I am not one of them. They 'live' in a world where bread is not needed; I am condemned to 'exist' in a land which threatens to starve me."

EX-SOLDIER'S LETTER to *The Times*, 11 Nov 1919

"What sad sights there were for the observant in the streets and cafés of the once gay city of Vienna. The postman…was dressed in rags….Uniformed officers sold roses in the cafés. Delicate women in faded finery begged with their children at street corners. Grass was growing in the principal streets. The shops were empty of customers. There was no roar and rush of traffic…Frequently [horses] dropped dead in the streets of hunger…tens of thousands of child lives and old lives have been ended by famine and the diseases of famine; whilst over a long period the number of suicides from hunger and despair amounted to scores in every week."

MRS. P. SNOWDEN, 1921

"The impotence of God is infinite."

ANATOLE FRANCE, 1925

"The nationalism of Indian thought is a composite product possessing unity from this point of view alone, that it is aimed at the system of authority which the British have established in India…The conflict of civilizations in India, so far as it exists, instead of being the cause of the political discontent is in reality its effect."

N.C. CHAUDHURI, 1926

"We want to liberate the sex impulse – which is part of the heritage of humanity – from the impression that it is always to be surrounded by negative warnings and restraints, and to place it in its rightful place among the great and formative things of every healthy and joyous boy and girl."

THE ARCHBISHOP OF CANTERBURY, 1928

	1919	1920	1921	1922
Rural life	• Fiat begins manufacturing tractors (It) • Poor harvest and lack of manpower lead to famine in eastern Europe. Increased demand for US wheat pushes prices to $3.50 per bushel	• American Farm Bureau is established to mobilize US farmers' political efforts • Massive drought begins in Russia • A mere 20% of virgin forests in USA remain uncut	• Aug: Russia suffers devastating famine with up to 18 million starving • E.M. East and G.M. Shull perfect a hybrid corn (maize) strain that will greatly improve crop yields	• 14 Oct: Agrarian law in Finland distributes land among the peasantry • Lenin allows for the existence of small private farms to boost production (USSR)
Industry and labor	• Jan: Miners' strike in favor of nationalization and a six-hour day (UK) • May: Establishment of the International Labor Organization (Swi) • 2 Mar: Foundation of the communist Third International • Steelworkers strike in the USA until 1920	• 1 Mar: US returns railroads to private ownership • 1 Apr: German Workers Party becomes the National Socialist German Workers Party • 16 Oct: Coal miners strike begins (UK) • Unemployment insurance introduced in Austria and Britain	• 13 Jan: General Confederation of Labor (CGT), the heart of the syndicalist movement in France, dissolved by court order • Feb: UK unemployment surpasses one million • 31 Mar–1 Jul: Coal strike due to the rejection of nationalization proposals (UK)	• Feb: Strike of German railroadmen • 6 Mar: General strike breaks out in Johannesburg (SA) • 1 Apr–4 Sep: UMW leads a massive coal miners' strike (USA) • Montecatini chemical company is founded and grows to become Italy's second largest industry
Government and people	• Dec: UK Sex Disqualification Removal Act opens professions to women • Eight-hour day introduced in France, Netherlands and Spain • Women enfranchised in Czechoslovakia, Belgium, Germany, Netherlands and Sweden	• 28 Aug: Ratification of 19th Amendment enfranchises women in federal elections (USA) • 10 Sep: Indian National Congress votes in favor of Gandhi's program of noncooperation with the Indian government • Abortion is legalized in Soviet Russia but outlawed in France	• 8 May: Sweden abolishes capital punishment • 19 May: New immigration legislation strictly limits entry in proportion to the nationalities already present (USA)	• 13 Feb: Campaign of civil disobedience suspended by Indian National Congress due to violence • 22 Sep: Women granted the same citizenship and naturalization rights as men (USA) • Empire Settlement Act Britain pledges to promote emigration to Australia
Religion	• 28 May: Romanian Jews are emancipated and given rights of full citizenship • 18 Jul: Reichstag votes against the separation of Church and State (Ger) • Benedict XV revokes a decree forbidding Catholics from participating in politics	• 12 Jan: Reports suggest the massacre of up to 12,000 Jews in the Ukraine • 11 Aug: First ecumenical conference brings together Eastern, European and US churches in Geneva	• 1–6 May: Anti-Jewish riots by Arabs in Palestine, in protest at the increased influx of Jewish immigrants	• Jan: Death of Pope Benedict XV, succeeded by Pius XI • 27 May: Vatican objects to Britain's proposed mandate in Palestine, because of the privileged position it gives to Jewish concerns • 1 Nov: Mustapha Kemal abolishes the sultanate in Turkey
Events and trends	• 6 Mar: UK Board of Trade Report reveals that women in paid employment has risen 1.2 million since 1914 • 28 Oct: National Prohibition Act passed in the USA, severely restricting sale and manufacture of alcohol (taking effect 16 Jan 1920) • 28 Nov: Nancy Astor is the first woman MP in the UK parliament	• Feb: Hitler and the National Socialist German Workers Party publish their program for a Third Reich • 13 Jun: International Feminist Conference opens in Geneva (Swi) • Social reformers found the American Civil Liberties Union	• 13–22 Jan: Italian Socialist Party splits into moderates and radicals at a congress in Livorno • 17 Mar: London's first birth control clinic opens to bitter opposition (UK) • Height of Gandhi's civil disobedience movement in India; though the movement is nonviolent, terrorist violence occurs frequently	• 10 Mar: Gandhi is arrested and sentenced to six years imprisonment (Ind) • 31 Dec: US figures reveal a total of 57 lynchings for the year • Country Club Plaza, the world's first shopping center, opens in Kansas City (USA) • Radio is used as an advertising medium for the first time (USA)
Politics	• 23 Mar: Mussolini forms the Fascio di Combattimento (It) • 28 Jun: Treaty of Versailles creates several new European states	• 10 Jan: League of Nations is founded in Geneva (Swi) • Mar: UK parliament passes the Home Rule Bill dividing Ireland into North and South	• 17 Mar: Lenin announces his New Economic Policy (NEP), introducing partial capitalism • 10 Apr: Sun Yixian elected president of China	• 28 Oct: Fascists march on Rome, and Mussolini becomes prime minister of Italy on 25 Nov • 6 Dec: Establishment of the Irish Free State

1923	1924	1925	1926	1927	1928	1929
• 6 Mar: 15,000 Norfolk farmhands go on strike for higher wages (UK) • Dec: 73,500 animals have been slaughtered during a foot and mouth epidemic (UK) • Continued export of corn after the recent famine in USSR	• Oct: Up to seven million people reportedly starving after failure of the harvest (USSR) • Introduction of the first effective chemical pesticides	• 16 Sep: Liberian land is opened to rubber cultivation by Harvey Firestone • 28 Dec: Land law in Poland passed to provide for the distribution of 500,000 acres of land to the peasantry annually for ten years	• Trofim Lysenko first gains notice in the USSR by putting ideology ahead of science in farm policy	• Perfection of the mechanical cotton picker in Texas reduces the need for field workers, thereby spurring black migration to the urban north (USA)	• Jan: International Famine Relief Commission reports that Chinese peasants are selling children to obtain food • Oct: Stalin launches land collectivization with the first Five-Year Plan. Millions of kulaks (farm landlords) are murdered or exiled to Siberia (USSR)	• 15 Jun: Congress passes the Agricultural Marketing Act encouraging farmers' cooperatives • Africa's Serengeti National Park formed after complaints about hunters using Model T Fords in the bush
• Jul–Aug: Seven-week dock strike in London (UK) • United States Steel Corp reduces the working day from twelve to eight hours • Wilhelm Messerschmidt establishes his aircraft manufacturing firm (Ger)	• 29 Jan: End of an eight-day rail strike (UK) • 16 Feb: Dock strike closes every port in the UK • Nov: Railroadmen strike in Austria • International Business Machines (IBM) Corp is organized in New York (USA)	• Jul: British government grants miners special wages and establishes an arbitration committee to avoid a strike • Aug: Tram and bus employees strike in Paris (Fr) • 12 Aug: Reports of numerous deaths during riots by striking cotton workers in Tientsin (China) • Miners' strike for 170 days in the USA	• 12 Mar: Italian senate passes an industrial relations law abolishing strikes • 3-12 May: General strike cripples Britain, after sympathy strikes by those supporting the refusal of coal miners to accept wage cuts • 2 Nov: Formation of Imperial Chemical Industries (ICI) is announced (UK)	• 18 Feb: 65,000 Shanghai workers strike to protest against the presence of foreign soldiers (China) • 23 Jun: UK Trade Disputes Act outlaws sympathetic strikes and compulsory political levies • 10 Nov: Dividend of $62 million is announced by General Motors, the largest in US history • Pan-American Airways is founded (USA)	• 1 Aug: Morris Motors begins a new model, the Morris Minor (UK) • Merger creates the Colgate-Palmolive-Peet Co (USA) • General Motors (USA) takes over Opel Werke (Ger) • Wave of strikes by textile workers, railway workers and others in Bombay, indicating the influence of the communists (Ind)	• 1 Dec: Ferrari founded at Modena (It) • Lufthansa is organized as the German national airline • British unemployment tops 12%; in Germany, 3.2 million are unemployed • Grumman Aircraft Engineering Corp organized (USA) • World Congress of Women's Labor opens in Berlin
• Apr: National Birthrate Commission reports recommends the teaching of sex education in schools and homes (UK) • 8 Jun: Bill approved by Mussolini gives women municipal voting rights (It) • First forced labor camp established by Lenin in the Solovetsky Islands; slave labor will be used extensively in construction projects (USSR)	• 12 Apr: Congress approves the Johnson-Reed Immigration Act restricting Japanese immigration (USA) • 13 Nov: Mussolini introduces a bill granting women the vote in national elections (It) • Mongolian women enfranchised on equal terms	• Apr: Britain and Australia begin funding the migration of British families to Australia • 8 May: Bill passed making Afrikaans the official language of the Union of South Africa • Jun: MPs pass a bill excluding blacks, coloreds and Indians from skilled or semiskilled positions (SA)	• 5 Jan: First widows pensions paid out at British post offices • 2 May: India allows women to stand for election to public office • 25 Nov: Mussolini restores the death penalty (It)	• 17 Oct: Norway elects its first Labor government • Italian Fascists introduce the labor card • German government warned by the agent for reparations to increase public expenditure	• 29 Mar: House of Commons passes the Equal Franchise Bill giving the vote to all women over 21 years (UK) • 12 May: Italy reduces its electorate to three million by abolishing female suffrage and limiting male suffrage to those paying over 100 lira in rates • Soviet Union introduces compulsory military service	• 11 Jun: Soviet working day reduced to seven hours • 10 Mar: Egyptian government grants women limited rights of divorce • 6 Dec: Turkish women enfranchised • Romanian women granted equal voting rights
• 7 Jun: Pope Pius XI condemns Franco-Belgian military occupation of the Ruhr • Jul: Treaty of Lausanne begins a huge transfer of population including the movement of 388,000 Muslims from Greece to Turkey	• 3 Mar: Abolition of the Caliphate (Islam's spiritual leadership) by Mustapha Kemal (Turk) • 28 Sep: Gandhi starts a 21-day fast in response to Hindu-Muslim rioting (Ind)	• 30 Jan: Turkish government expels Constantine II (Greek Orthodox Patriarch of Constantinople) from Istanbul • 1 Apr: Hebrew University in Jerusalem opened by Lord Balfour (Pal) • 6 Oct: Archbishop of Canterbury blames low church attendance on poor teaching and outdated clergy (UK)	• 11 Feb: Calles government nationalizes all Church property (Mex) • 31 Jul: Mexican priests begin a strike after enforcement of anticlerical clauses in the 1917 constitution (until 1912) • 2 Apr: Martial law is declared in Calcutta after the outbreak of Hindu-Muslim rioting. Similar disturbances occur in Rawalpindi in June (Ind)	• 3 May: Sikhs and Muslims clash during riots in Lahore (Ind) • 19 Aug: Orthodox Church recognizes the Soviet government (USSR) • 15 Dec: House of Commons rejects the new Book of Common Prayer (UK)	• 9 Apr: Turkey abolishes Islam as state religion • Papal Secretary requests that Catholics not associate with Fascists (It)	• 11 Feb: Lateran Treaty establishes The Vatican as a sovereign city state • 4 Aug: 250 killed in Arab-Jewish clashes over Jewish demands to exclusive use of the Wailing Wall • 11 Aug: Chaim Weizmann forms the Jewish Agency in Zurich (Swi)
• Jun: Ku Klux Klan claims to have one million members (USA) • Nov: Germany crippled by inflation, with a loaf of bread costing 200 billion marks (US$1 = 4 trillion marks) • Mothers' Day first celebrated in Europe • Gregorian calendar introduced in the USSR, replacing the Julian calendar	• Aug: Severe floods in China kill 50,000, leaving two million homeless • 4 Nov: Texas elects Miriam Ferguson, the first woman state governor (USA) • Foundation of Imperial Airways (UK)	• Mar: State of Tennessee bans teaching of the theory of evolution. A violation of this law brings the highly-publicised "Scopes Monkey Trial" (USA) • Apr: Founding of the SS (Schütz Staffel) in Germany • 8 Aug: First National Congress of the Ku Klux Klan (USA) • American Medical Association endorses birth control	• 21 Jan: Makwar Dam opens on the Nile in Egypt, due to fears that irrigation in Sudan might deprive Egypt of enough water for its crops • 28 May: 1,200 reported killed by a cyclone and tidal wave in Burma • 31 Aug: 15,000 people reported heading for the new diamond field in the Transvaal (SA)	• 12 Aug: 80,000 Bolivian Indians revolt against the government • First World Population Conference is organized by Margaret Sanger • UK petrol prices drop to 1902 levels • Borden Co introduces homogenized milk (USA)	• 15 Feb: Oxford English Dictionary, the world's biggest etymological dictionary, published in twelve volumes • 5 Aug: International Socialist Congress opens in Brussels • 3 Nov: Latin alphabet introduced in Turkey – all Turks under 40 years are obliged to learn it • More than 1,500 Americans die from drinking bad liquor	• Jan: King Amanullah restores the veil for women and abandons European clothing (Afg) • May: 3,000 die in Persian earthquake • 22 Sep: Confrontations between armed groups of communists and Nazis in Berlin (Ger)
• 1 Jan-26 Sep: French troops occupy the Ruhr, and a policy of passive resistance is instigated by the German government	• 22 Jan: Ramsay MacDonald forms the first (minority) Labour government (UK) • 6 Apr: Fascists win sweeping victory in Italian general election	• 12 Mar: Death of Sun Yixian (China)	• May: Marshal Jozef Pilsudski becomes dictator of Poland • 25 Dec: Death of Japanese emperor Yoshihito, succeeded by Hirohito (until 1989)	• 31 Jan: Control over Germany turned over from the Allies to the League of Nations	• 8 Jun: Beijing surrenders to Jiang Jieshi, and the capital is moved to Nanking (China) • 27 Aug: Kellogg-Briand Pact renouncing war is signed by 63 nations (Fr)	• 22 Oct: $30 billion in capital disappears as Wall Street collapses on Black Friday. Beginning of the Great Depression

Datafile

Before World War I it looked as though Western capitalist industrialization was destined to conquer the world. But the Russian Revolution ushered in a new social and economic order planned and imposed by a doctrinaire one-party state. Despite the first communist regime's initial failures and the human cost of forced social change, the Soviet "model" would eventually reshape the destinies of one-third of mankind.

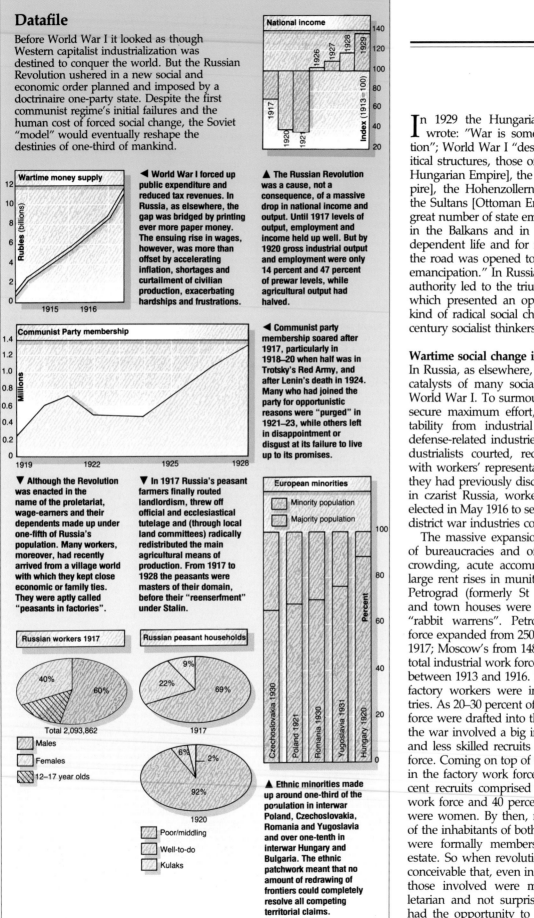

National income

◄ **World War I forced up public expenditure and reduced tax revenues. In Russia, as elsewhere, the gap was bridged by printing ever more paper money. The ensuing rise in wages, however, was more than offset by accelerating inflation, shortages and curtailment of civilian production, exacerbating hardships and frustrations.**

▲ **The Russian Revolution was a cause, not a consequence, of a massive drop in national income and output. Until 1917 levels of output, employment and income held up well. But by 1920 gross industrial output and employment were only 14 percent and 47 percent of prewar levels, while agricultural output had halved.**

◄ **Communist party membership soared after 1917, particularly in 1918–20 when half was in Trotsky's Red Army, and after Lenin's death in 1924. Many who had joined the party for opportunistic reasons were "purged" in 1921–23, while others left in disappointment or disgust at its failure to live up to its promises.**

▼ **Although the Revolution was enacted in the name of the proletariat, wage-earners and their dependents made up under one-fifth of Russia's population. Many workers, moreover, had recently arrived from a village world with which they kept close economic or family ties. They were aptly called "peasants in factories".**

▼ **In 1917 Russia's peasant farmers finally routed landlordism, threw off official and ecclesiastical tutelage and (through local land committees) radically redistributed the main agricultural means of production. From 1917 to 1928 the peasants were masters of their domain, before their "reenserfment" under Stalin.**

▲ **Ethnic minorities made up around one-third of the population in interwar Poland, Czechoslovakia, Romania and Yugoslavia and over one-tenth in interwar Hungary and Bulgaria. The ethnic patchwork meant that no amount of redrawing of frontiers could completely resolve all competing territorial claims.**

In 1929 the Hungarian historian Oscar Jászi wrote: "War is sometimes a kind of revolution"; World War I "destroyed four petrified political structures, those of the Habsburgs [Austro-Hungarian Empire], the Romanoffs [Russian Empire], the Hohenzollerns [German Empire] and the Sultans [Ottoman Empire]. In consequence a great number of state embryos in Central Europe, in the Balkans and in the Baltic grew into independent life and for many millions of people the road was opened toward national and social emancipation." In Russia the collapse of imperial authority led to the triumph of a socialist party, which presented an opportunity to impose the kind of radical social change envisaged by 19th-century socialist thinkers.

Wartime social change in Russia

In Russia, as elsewhere, labor problems were the catalysts of many social changes ensuing from World War I. To surmount labor bottlenecks and secure maximum effort, cooperation and adaptability from industrial workers (especially in defense-related industries), governments and industrialists courted, recognized and bargained with workers' representatives and leaders whom they had previously disdained or despised. Even in czarist Russia, workers' representatives were elected in May 1916 to serve on 20 regional and 98 district war industries committees.

The massive expansion of war industries and of bureaucracies and office work caused overcrowding, acute accommodation shortages and large rent rises in munitions towns, above all in Petrograd (formerly St Petersburg). Tenements and town houses were converted into workers' "rabbit warrens". Petrograd's industrial work force expanded from 250,000 in 1913 to 417,000 in 1917; Moscow's from 148,000 to 206,000. Russia's total industrial work force increased by 13 percent between 1913 and 1916. By 1917 65–75 percent of factory workers were in defense-related industries. As 20–30 percent of the 1914 industrial work force were drafted into the armed forces by 1917, the war involved a big influx of less experienced and less skilled recruits into the industrial work force. Coming on top of the 30 percent expansion in the factory work force in 1909–13, by 1917 recent recruits comprised over half the industrial work force and 40 percent of all factory workers were women. By then, moreover, three-quarters of the inhabitants of both Petrograd and Moscow were formally members of the peasant social estate. So when revolution occurred in 1917 it is conceivable that, even in Petrograd and Moscow, those involved were more peasant than proletarian and not surprising that when workers had the opportunity to take over industry they had little readiness to do so.

THE BOLSHEVIK EXPERIMENT

From war to revolution

In 1915–16 social unrest and morale were not palpably worse in Russia than in other belligerent states. Indeed, the Russian war effort, production and employment held up well. There were military successes against Austria-Hungary. There was little loss of ethnically Russian territory. Italy and Austria-Hungary seemed to be in greater trouble than Russia. Yet in March 1917 (old style, February) revolution broke out in Russia. It involved bread riots in Petrograd, strikes, the mutiny of city garrisons, the abdication of the czar, the reemergence of workers' soviets (councils) and the emergence of a self-appointed Provisional Government. Why did this occur?

It has been argued that revolutions do not just "happen", that they must have instigators and that any talk of "spontaneity" masks a failure or unwillingness to identify the culprits. But, despite allegations of wartime "subversion" from various quarters, and much political agitation and propaganda, the March revolution was a spontaneous outburst and caught politicians off guard.

The March revolution was mainly a product of wartime dislocation of transport and urban provisioning; a six-fold increase in prices since 1913; the discreditable conduct of government (including the antics of the court mystic Rasputin); and local difficulties caused by Germany's naval blockade of Petrograd. However, the spontaneous activities of self-appointed war industries committees, Red Cross committees, the union of local government bodies, cooperatives and village communes in support of Russia's war effort meant that "Without realizing it, the Russians were beginning to govern themselves. The revolution had not yet been thought out, but it existed in fact" (M. Ferro).

The unstable outcome of the March revolution was that the workers, soldiers and peasants who had toppled czarism became the main powers in the land, yet they expected the relatively impotent

▼ Putting on brave faces, Moscow workers celebrate May Day 1918. The Bolshevik "workers' state" had already started down the road of brutal repression of other socialist and revolutionary groups and dissident workers.

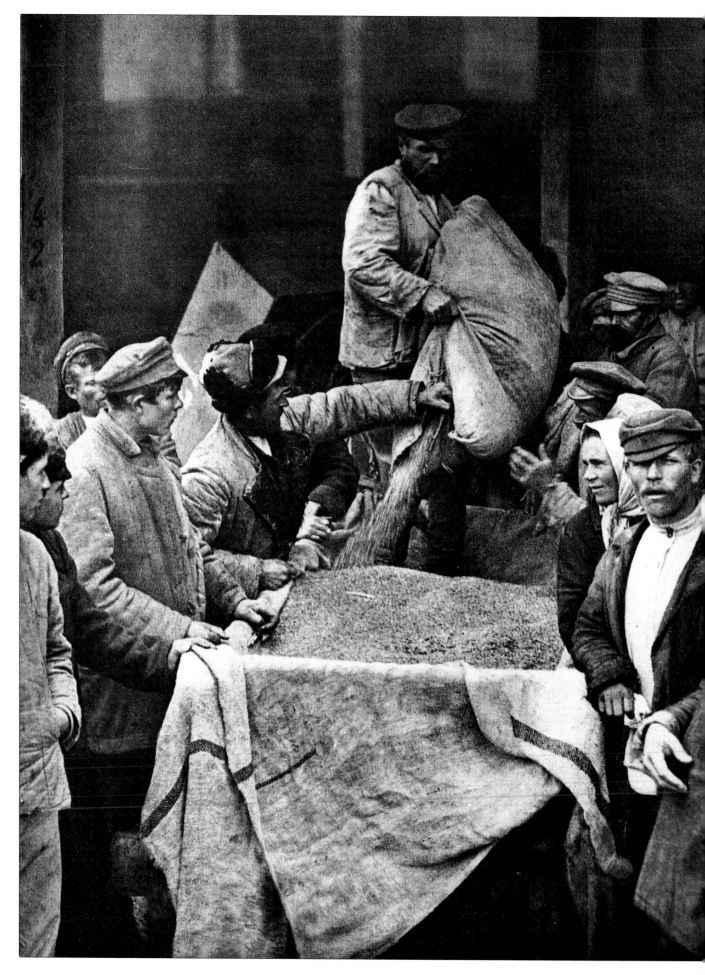

properted classes to keep the responsibility of governing. The instability of "dual power" ended with the Bolshevik socialists' seizure of power from the Provisional Government in November 1917 (old style, October). Lenin – the Bolsheviks' leader – claimed to be taking power for the soviets and on behalf of the proletariat – the mass of laboring men and women.

Social consequences of the Bolshevik coup

Lenin launched the Bolshevik bid for power with schemes for social reconstruction in mind. The basis was to be the nationalization of land, industry and the controlling financial apparatus. As Lenin wrote in 1918, "Capitalist culture has created large-scale production, factories, railways, the postal service, telephones etc., and *on this basis* the great majority of the functions of the old state power have become... reduced to such exceedingly simple operations of registration, filing and checking that they can be performed by every literate person." Thus "We, the workers, shall organize large-scale production on the basis of what capitalism has already created, relying on our experience as workers."

The Bolshevik seizure of power through and for the soviets and factory committees momentarily reflected the interests and wishes of many industrial workers. In November 1917–January 1918 (new calendar) there was a honeymoon period, during which workers and factory committees enthusiastically used up remaining stocks of materials, fuel and capital. But workers' support for the Bolsheviks, soviets and factory committees rapidly dwindled, as it proved impossible to deliver on the promises made and expectations raised. Employment, food supplies and real wages not only did not increase, but from January 1918 began to fall catastrophically. The truce between the new Bolshevik government and the Central Powers (signed on 3 December 1917), the ensuing peace negotiations and cessation of Russia's war effort caused a 70–80 percent reduction in employment in defense-related industries. Unplanned spontaneous demobilization of the 7-million strong armed forces further swelled unemployment and threw transport and distribution into deeper chaos in the winter of 1917–18. Since mounting hardships could no longer be blamed on capitalism, millions of starving, unemployed and disillusioned workers blamed incompetent Bolsheviks, soviets and factory committees for their desperate plight and for having cheated them with promises and panaceas. Peace, workers' control and the Bolshevik policy of "All power to the soviets" had solved nothing and had rendered the crisis even more insoluble.

During 1918 the Bolsheviks increasingly resorted to repression of workers' protest, forcible dissolution of hundreds of workers' soviets and imprisonment, exile or execution of opposition socialist leaders. This struggle played a critical role in the emergence of a one-party police state. The party and the security police decided who was a "counterrevolutionary", a power that was freely abused. Already by May 1918 Lenin was publicly demanding "unquestioning obedience... to the one-man decisions of Soviet directors, of

◄▲ **Sickening contrasts between official Soviet propaganda pictures of well-stocked shops and granaries (left and opposite) and the grim realities of widespread malnutrition, destitution and disease (above) added insult to injury. They reinforced a growing popular revulsion against the consequences of revolution and civil war: regimentation, requisitioning and repression. In 1920-21 grain output was only half the prewar level, and in 1921-22 Russia was ravaged by famines and epidemics centered on the Volga basin. They caused around 5 million deaths. Women and children suffered terribly. Gangs of abandoned children roamed towns and villages, begging, scavenging and stealing.**

the dictators elected or appointed by Soviet institutions, vested with dictatorial powers". As Lenin told the 1919 congress of the Communist party (as the Bolsheviks had renamed themselves in 1918) "the Soviets, which by virtue of their program are organs of government by the working people, are in fact organs of government for the working people by the advanced section of the proletariat", meaning the Communist party. Dictatorship of the proletariat became dictatorship over the proletariat and, if proletarians resisted, against the proletariat.

The Bolshevik police state

The Bolshevik coup led by Lenin resulted in the execution of some 200,000 opponents in his six years in power (compared with 14,000 executions under the last czar) and to the creation of a one-party police state. (The political police expanded from 15,000 under the last czar to 250,000 in 1921.) Worst of all, Lenin plunged Russia into a wholly avoidable civil war in 1918–21, by forcibly suppressing in January 1918 a new constitutent assembly (his party had won only 25 percent of the 42 million votes in the November 1917 elections).

It is painful for me...to see how the peasants are ordered around in the localities.... You have to explain and prove things to peasants, not simply use rigorous and iron discipline against them, not beat them into submission; you have to have the patience to talk to the peasants. It's no good just terrorizing the peasants. Is that not right, comrades?

RED ARMY COMMANDER
JULY 1919

Soviet society and the New Economic Policy

By 1921 Russia's civil war (which had raged since 1918), the Russo-Polish War of 1920 and the reabsorption of the Ukraine, Transcaucasia and Central Asia had reduced Russia to a state of economic collapse, epidemics and famine. The industrial work force had been more than halved in size. The Revolution had devoured its children.

To provide a breathing space to enable Russia to recover, Lenin launched his New Economic Policy (NEP) in March 1921. Its essence was the restoration of a market-based, mixed economy, in which only the "commanding heights" of finance, transport, large-scale industry and foreign trade remained in state control. Simultaneously, however, Lenin set out to consolidate one-party rule. Party appointees replaced elected officials, and there were prohibitions on "factions" within the ruling party and on independent trade unions, professional associations, schools and publications and on opposition parties. But, having monopolized political power in the hands of the party leadership and especially in those of the general secretary (a post which Joseph Stalin's astute exercise of patronage quickly elevated to the status in effect of party boss soon after he obtained it in 1922), the party felt a growing need to try to convince the public that this was still their revolution rather than exclusive "party property".

To promote broader identification with and support for this Soviet regime, the party promoted (within officially prescribed parameters) an unprecedented eruption of experimentation, iconoclasm, creativity, festivity, revolutionary cinema and mass organizations. It made particular efforts to increase peasant, female, ethnic minority and intelligentsia support for and commitment to the party and the Soviet regime.

The Indian summer of the commune system

Under NEP the Russian peasantry enjoyed a large measure of autonomy. Some 90 percent of all peasants used the opportunity to hold their lands and to administer their villages on a communal

Lenin also unleashed an uncontrollable "Red Terror" against rival socialists and against massive peasant and proletarian opposition in 1918 (ostensibly against the relatively insignificant and peripheral "counterrevolutionaries" and "foreign intervention"). This civil war and the ensuing famine and economic collapse were to cost over 12 million lives in 1918-21, about four times the 3.2 million lives lost by Russia in 1914-17 and over twice the 5.5 million lives lost in 1926-39 (in Stalin's Purges, rural collectivization, epidemics, and the 1932-34 famine), according to the sober calculations of F. Lorimer, B. Kerblay and S. Wheatcroft. As the radical historian Yuri Afanafiev told the Supreme Soviet in February 1990, the Soviet state was founded on violence and terror, which its founder elevated into principles of government.

One of the principal reasons for the enormous human and economic costs of the early years of Soviet rule was that the Bolsheviks seized power with no agreed or worked-out blueprint for the "socialist" society they hoped to build. Marxist orthodoxy had never envisaged that the first and only "proletarian dictatorship" could arise in a peasant society. The Bolshevik leadership seized the opportunity to take power in November 1917 because it might never have arisen again. However the vast number of Marxist writings offered no thought-out or unambiguous guidance on policies that should be pursued by a "dictatorship of the proletariat" in an industrialized society, let alone in a predominantly peasant society. Marxists had embraced the idea of "planning" as a panacea for the "anarchy" and "waste" of commodity production. But until 1924 they remained blissfully ignorant of *how* to plan, of the various possible *forms* of planning, and of the various possible relationships and contradictions between central and local planning and workers' control and the market, or even of where to start. Until the 1930s planning was just one of many socialist slogans, devoid of real substance; planners were just groping in the dark.

Soviets and Social Organization

The Bolshevik party seized power in November 1917 behind Lenin's slogan "All power to the soviets." But what were the soviets? The word *soviet* simply means "council." Soviets or councils of workers' deputies first arose in the 1905 Revolution, when factories in St Petersburg and Moscow elected delegates to coordinate strike movements. The soviets became embryonic organs of popular power, establishing workers' militias and printing presses.

Suppressed after 1905, soviets reappeared in 1917 after the March Revolution, but this time peasants and soldiers imitated the workers and formed soviets. As various soviets coordinated opposition to the Provisional Government an improvised national network and hierarchy of soviets emerged with an All-Russian Congress of

Soviets at the top which elected a 300-member All-Russian central Executive Committee.

"All power to the soviets" was never understood to mean "All power to the Bolshevik party." Soviets were originally seen as organs of dispersed, decentralized power and direct democracy, in which Bolsheviks could coexist with other parties. But the Bolsheviks quickly monopolized and centralized power in the Soviet system. Local budgets and appointments came under central control, rival parties were terrorized and suppressed, lower soviets became passive executors of the policies of higher tiers; key policy-making decisions and debate shifted to the ruling Party. The soviets became the official structure for the Bolshevik state, yet it has never been imitated by other communist states.

▲ A village soviet in the Volga region, c.1930. A nationwide network of village soviets (*selosoveti*) was established in 1918-20, in a political endeavor to wean the Russian peasantry from their peasant-administered village commune system. The village communes or "land societies" (as they became under Soviet law) were seen by the Bolsheviks as irritating obstacles to party penetration and control. However, village soviets failed to attract much peasant support.

basis in accordance with peasant custom. They farmed their fields on an independent family basis and carried out widespread "land reorganization" involving division and resettlement of communes and villages scattered over excessively large areas, and the consolidation of scattered and excessively narrow strips (reorganizing 27 percent of cropland by 1927). From 1913 to 1929 the sown area rose by 13 percent and production of cash crops and potatoes rose two and a half times. The average size of peasant farm allotment in the Russian federation rose from 14ha (35 acres) in 1913 to 18ha (44 acres) in 1927, and in

1925–29 average Soviet grain yields per hectare were 12 percent higher than the 1909–13 level.

It might have been expected that this agricultural policy would have led to the reemergence of the so-called *kulaks* or rural "bigmen". But the cumulative concentration of agrarian capital, land and production in the hands of a rural wealthy class was inhibited by the prohibition of the private purchase and sale of land, legal restrictions on private employment of hired labor, and by the strength of communal landholding. Even official Soviet accounts generally concede that the so-called kulaks comprised only 2–5 percent of the

The Bolshevik Revolution and Women's Emancipation

The Bolshevik Revolution was a milestone in the struggle for women's emancipation. It was the first occasion on which complete economic, political and social equality of males and females became an officially proclaimed goal of a state.

World War I had greatly expanded the roles, public recognition and self-confidence of women in Russia, as elsewhere. Thousands of Russian women had distinguished themselves as army nurses, auxiliaries and doctors. In industry, women took over jobs vacated by male conscripts. Malnourished women nevertheless staged serious food riots in April and June 1915, and food riots and strikes by working-class women were the catalysts of the Revolution of March 1917. During 1917 leading feminist organizations redoubled their support for Russia's war effort. In return, the Provisional Government enfranchised all adults over the age of 20 in July 1917. Russia was thus the first *large* country to confer equal political rights. In mid 1917 Russia's women also won rights to serve as lawyers and jurors and to equality of opportunity, pay, benefits and titles in public employment *before* the Bolshevik takeover.

The successes of liberal feminism in 1917 galvanized Russia's ailing socialist women's movement. In 1917 leading Bolshevik women established a Bureau of Women Workers, resurrected the Bolshevik women's newspaper and founded new publications. The same women organized the First All-Russian Congress of Working Women in November 1918. There Lenin declared that "A primary task of the Soviet Republic is to abolish all restrictions on women's rights", as "the success of a revolution depends on the degree to which women take part in it". Out of this congress arose the energetic *Zhenotdel* (women's department) of the Communist Party (1919–30).

In late 1917 and early 1918 Bolshevik family reforms established a basic juridical framework around which equality of the sexes could gradually be built or attained, primarily within marriage. The reforms conferred legal recognition only on marriages recorded in civil registry offices; completed the equalization of male and female rights to hold and inherit property, be household heads, take employment, conduct business and reside where each chose, begun in 1912–14; equalized the rights of legitimate and illegitimate children; established liberal, equal, quick civil divorce (at the request of either spouse and subject to alimony for unemployed exspouses); and proclaimed equal male and female rights and obligations to work. The revised Family Code of 1926 further liberalized divorce procedures, permitting "postcard divorce" (postal notification of divorce in uncontested cases).

However, heated public debate during the revision of the Family Code in 1925–26 revealed significant peasant hostility to the liberal divorce laws, not so much on religious as on practical grounds. Divorce might be relatively straightforward in towns and cities where divorcees could often move to new accommodation and jobs. But for multigenerational peasant households which were also production units, divorce could be economically disastrous for the divorcees and their dependent relatives, splitting up peasant family farms. The same debate revealed a widespread tendency to blame Soviet family

reform for alarming crises in family life in 1918–26: soaring divorce rates and juvenile delinquency; resurgent prostitution; endemic sexual promiscuity and venereal disease; and millions of homeless waifs and orphans and abandoned, destitute wives. Such phenomena were mainly consequences of World War I, the Civil War, economic collapse, famine and epidemics, but many people blamed the Communists' attacks on the family and religion, and their "free-living" and "free-loving" moralities.

Marxism and Leninism were committed to encouraging high birth rates and to the idea of motherhood as a social duty. Abortion was legalized in 1920, not to increase women's freedom to choose whether or not to have

children (although women had the final say in practice), but as a "lesser evil", to reduce the health and mortality risks attendant upon illegal "backstreet" abortions. (Unqualified abortionists were made liable to criminal prosecution.)

In Russia, unlike the West, the struggle for women's emancipation was joined to a quest for total reconstruction of society. The ascendant intelligentsia increasingly saw women's emancipation not as a discrete goal in its own right but as one element in a wider transformation of society. This gave women's emancipation greater initial prominence in post-revolutionary Russia than in the West, but it also contributed to the subsequent subordination of women's emancipation to economic, political and military goals.

◀ **Alexandra Kollontai, author of *The Social Bases of the Woman Question* (1909) and Russia's foremost Marxist proponent of sexual liberation. Rebutting liberal feminists, she insisted that emancipation involved much more than obtaining equal political, legal and educational rights and professional opportunities. Fundamental redistribution of economic power was requisite for sexual equality.**

▶ **A civil marriage, 1922. The civil wedding procedures adopted by civil registry offices (popularly known as ZAGS) lasted about 20 minutes and emphasized simplicity and privacy. They could be supplemented by church wedding ceremonies, but these no longer had any legal standing. Moscow's civil registry office reported that only 12 percent of marriages were supplemented by religious ceremonies in 1928, whereas 58 percent of births and 66 percent of burials were still marked by religious ceremonies. Religious ceremonies were most persistent in rural areas.**

◀ **An election poster exhorts all working women to support industrialization, large-scale socialized agriculture, cultural revolution, "proletarian self-criticism" and the defense of the Soviet Union, under the Leninist party. In 1920 Lenin had declared that "In order to achieve complete emancipation of women and to make them really equal with men, we must have a social economy and the participation of women in general productive work. Then women will occupy the same position as men."**

ОВЛАДЕВАЯ ТЕХНИКОЙ, БУДЬ В ПЕРВЫХ РЯДАХ СТРОИТЕЛЕЙ СОЦИАЛИЗМА

▶ **Women were urged to master technology and be in the front ranks of the builders of socialism. "In the course of two years of Soviet power", Lenin claimed, "more has been done to emancipate woman, to make her the equal of 'the strong sex', than has been done in the past 130 years by all the advanced, enlightened 'democratic' republics of the world put together".**

agrarian population in 1928–29, as against 15 percent in 1914, and that they produced 20 percent of peasant grain in 1926–27, compared with about half before 1914; Western estimates are much lower. Either way, it is difficult to take seriously the Bolshevik alleged notion of a kulak threat to the Soviet regime.

On the reverse side of the same coin, there was almost no rural proletariat or "semi-proletariat" and the soviets could hope to attract much class-based rural support. Many peasants were put off or perplexed by the party's obsessive class-rhetoric, and also by its "militant atheism", its closure and desecration of thousands of churches and mosques, its persecution of Christian and Muslim clergy and its formal (albeit skin-deep) commitment to women's emancipation.

NEP as "New Exploitation of the Proletariat"

Relative to other groups, the main loser under NEP was the much-diminished working class. Many workers felt betrayed, denied the deference they deserved in the dictatorship of the proletariat, and exploited and manipulated by a self-serving bureaucracy. Some saw the restoration of a market system as an unpalatable restoration of capitalism, a sell-out and a defeat, rather than as a welcome escape from the rigors and privations of a siege economy. Many resented the growing powers and privileges of the bureaucracy, the continuing decline of "workers' control" in industry and of democratic accountability in public administration, the rampant corruption and nepotism, and the regime's concessions to the peasantry, to "Nepmen" (traders and industrialists), to the intelligentsia and to ethnic minorities, allegedly at the workers' expense. Real wages remained well below the paltry 1913 levels until as late as 1926.

In 1928 the statutory working year was lengthened from the 267 days of 1913 to 300 days. Workers felt threatened by serious urban unemployment. The number of unemployed hovered around 1.2 million in 1924–28, jumping to 1.7 million in April 1929. In mid 1929 45 percent of the unemployed were women, 17 percent were youths and many were peasants who had recently left their land in search of new opportunities. Even in 1928 the number of wage and salary earners was only just above prewar levels at 11.6 million (versus 11.2 million in 1913). The number of industrial wage earners was 2.8 million (versus 2.5 million in 1913) and women comprised 28.5 percent of factory workers (versus 31 percent in 1913 and 40 percent in 1917).

As elsewhere, it seems that 1920s unemployment bore most heavily on female workers, seriously undoing their wartime occupational advancement. Only in teaching, nursing, medicine, office work and as students in secondary and higher education did the 1920s see Russian women making further major advances. Peasant and working-class women were still confined to drudgery and looking after Soviet males.

Workers also felt exploited by Leninist enthusiasm for piecework and F.W. Taylor's "scientific management". A Central Labor Institute was formed in 1920, especially to promote "scientific

▲ An Uzbek woman removes the veil. In the predominantly Muslim and Turkic Republics of Soviet Central Asia the near-complete absence of industrial workers encouraged the Bolsheviks to seek alternative sources of support. Most notably, they mobilized Muslim-Turkic women. Sweeping social reforms, however, met fierce resistance or caused widespread social problems.

organization of labor" based on time and motion studies, the definition of output quotas or work norms for each job, and remuneration of workers in accordance with the degree to which they "fulfilled" or "overfulfilled" their norms. Work norms based on time-and-motion studies were introduced from 1924 and by 1928 62 percent of all industrial workers were on piecerates. These favored the fittest workers at the expense of the unfit, the old, the inexperienced, etc. Most unpopular were the differential or "progressive" piecerates, rewarding above-quota work at progressively higher rates, which became widespread under Stalin. Workers were not enamored of NEP, but there was far worse to come.

The springtime of nations

After the Bolshevik Revolution the Russian Empire in effect broke up. Separate states emerged from once imperial territories in Eastern Europe (Poland), along the Baltic (Lithuania, Latvia, Estonia and Finland) and in the Ukraine, Transcaucasia, Central and East Asia. Between 1920 and 1921 the Communists reestablished control over all these states except those in Europe and the Baltic and in July 1923 adopted an all-union constitution. The initial plans for a federation and the subsequent Communist nationalities policy were directed by Joseph Stalin.

The forcibly reincorporated Ukrainian, Transcaucasian and Central Asian nations were first of all thoroughly subjugated and then permitted significant areas of cultural autonomy. Each of the major ethnic minorities (except Jews) was in due course granted its own separate Soviet Socialist Republic. Especially under NEP, these Republics vigorously promoted vernacular education, literature, art, architecture and music. The 1920s saw a remarkable flowering of national cultures which, while a surrogate for true independence, occurred on a scale that would have been unthinkable under czarism. With hindsight, one can see that this period sowed the seeds of the long-term survival and growth of nationalism and separatism in the Soviet Union by fostering the "emblems" of nationhood.

In 1924, as people's commissar for nationalities, Stalin set forth guiding precepts for the "eastern" Soviet Socialist Republics. These included the aims to "develop national culture [but also] training Soviet, party, technical and business cadres from the local population". These were to

► In 1926 the Soviet Union was a multinational federation comprising 147 million people, 47 percent of whom were non-Russians. The 31 million Ukrainians were the largest European nation to have been denied full sovereignity and independence since the 1920s. The Soviet Union contained 17 million Turkic peoples and about 19 million Muslims (13 percent of the total population). Except for the 4 million Turkic, Muslim and largely nomadic-pastoral Kazakhs and 2.7 million widely dispersed Jews, each major nation within the Union had its own "Union Republic" or "Soviet Socialist Republic" (SSR) with its own "Republican" government and formal rights of self-determination and secession. But the bundle was tightly bound together by the Communist party's monopoly of power and decision-making.

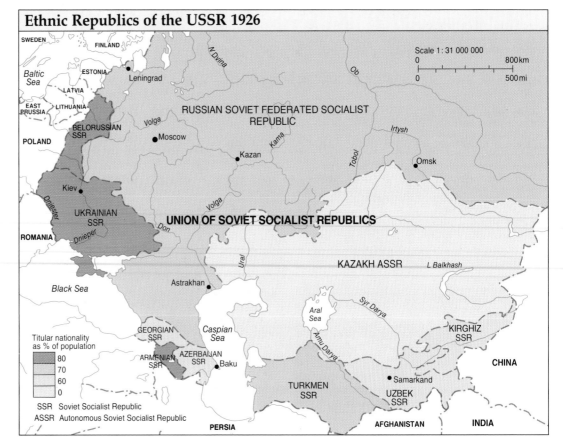

Ethnic Republics of the USSR 1926

Scale 1 : 31 000 000

0 — 800 km
0 — 500 mi

SWEDEN
FINLAND
Baltic Sea
ESTONIA
Leningrad
LATVIA
EAST PRUSSIA
LITHUANIA
N. Dvina
Ob
RUSSIAN SOVIET FEDERATED SOCIALIST REPUBLIC
BELORUSSIAN SSR
Volga
Moscow
Kama
Irtysh
POLAND
Kazan
Tobol
Omsk
Kiev
Dnieper
Volga
UKRAINIAN SSR
UNION OF SOVIET SOCIALIST REPUBLICS
ROMANIA
Dniester
Don
Ural
KAZAKH ASSR
L Balkhash
Black Sea
Astrakhan
Aral Sea
Syr Darya
KIRGHIZ SSR
GEORGIAN SSR
Caspian Sea
CHINA
ARMENIAN SSR
AZERBAIJAN SSR
Baku
Amu Darya
Samarkand
TURKMEN SSR
UZBEK SSR

Titular nationality as % of population
80
70
60
0

SSR Soviet Socialist Republic
ASSR Autonomous Soviet Socialist Republic

PERSIA
AFGHANISTAN
INDIA

become, in effect, foot troops of the Soviet regime. "Proletarian in content, national in form – that is the universal culture towards which socialism proceeds... Proletarian culture does not abolish national culture, it adds content" – the national cultures of the new Soviet national republics were to be inbred with the Soviet as well as national foundation myths, emblems and values. Moreover, Stalin maintained that socialist revolution, "by stirring up the lowest sections of humanity and pushing them into the political arena", was responsible for a national awakening of hitherto submerged nationalities. Finally, Stalin warned against mechanical attempts "to transplant models of economic construction comprehensible and applicable in the center of the Soviet Union, but totally unsuited to conditions in the so-called border regions". those "guilty of this deviation fail to understand... that, if work is not adapted to local conditions, nothing of value can be built" and "they degenerate into Left phrasemongers", divorced from the masses. The opposite "deviation" lay in "exaggerating local features...hushing up socialist tasks, adapting to the tasks of narrow nationalism" (*Pravda*, 22 May 1924). Stalin thus left himself plenty of scope for accusing local Soviet elites of either excessive or insufficient nationalism and served notice that either "deviation" could land them in political hot water. Stalin was laying a minefield which would claim many victims during his long reign.

The "Green Rising" in peasant Europe

The working classes were not the only people "on the move" in post-1917 Europe. There was also a groundswell of peasant-based movements right across Europe, from Ireland and Scandinavia through Germany and the Slav world. This "Green Rising" was accelerated by the emergence of self-consciously peasant nation states in Ireland, the Baltic littoral, Eastern Europe and the Ukraine, by the largely peasant revolution in Russia in 1917, by the growing politicization of peasantries during and after World War I, by electoral competition between rival mass movements, and by the international ideological appeal of "blood and soil" nationalism and Russian agrarian socialism (the latter mainly among Slavs and Romanians). Moreover, the widespread adoption of universal suffrage and elementary schooling in Europe after 1917 benefited peasants more than any other class, as did the continuing spread of cooperative networks.

In Eastern Europe peasants achieved new social prominence thanks to radical land redistribution. In all countries except Poland and Hungary large estates were eliminated. Both native and foreign estate-owners were expropriated. Their lands were transferred to peasants in the form of small freeholdings. As the British writer G.K. Chesterton wrote in 1923 "what has happened in Europe since the war has been a vast victory for the peasants".

▲ Young and old reading a local newspaper in Yakutsk, Siberia, 1929. While failing to precipitate "international proletarian revolution" in the West (which Lenin had hoped would come to the aid of Soviet Russia), the Soviet regime more successfully championed "national liberation" in the East, starting with the creation of SSRs and ASSRs (Autonomous Soviet Socialist Republics) in Soviet Asia and the People's Republic of Mongolia in the 1920s. By instigating "national liberation" in the East, Lenin set out to tip the balance of world power against Western imperialism.

DEVIANTS

Deviants are societies' scapegoats. Every community has its "nuts, sluts and perverts" although life-styles and motives which are ridiculed or discriminated against in one epoch might become conventional or at least acceptable in the next. Having a child outside marriage once caused a woman to be utterly rejected; it is now common in many societies.

Some deviance has always been tolerated; for example the "court fool" or the "village idiot" of the rural past and, more recently, teenage rebellion. Defining deviance is a power struggle between contending groups over where the line should be drawn between acceptable and unacceptable behavior. If deviants lose, at best they face ostracism, at worst legal sanction – both intended to punish the offender and to act as a deterrent to others. Over time this has meant death, arrest, prosecution, imprisonment or compulsory treatment. If deviants win, the boundaries of tolerance shift.

Deviance takes many forms. Moral deviance often becomes political opposition. Suffragettes chaining themselves to fences in the early 20th century were seen as scandalous. Today in most countries the vote for women is beyond contention. In the 1980s the stand taken by British women against the siting of cruise missiles at the US air base at Greenham Common in England was initially ridiculed, but the missiles were eventually removed. The concern for environmental issues is no longer just the hobbyhorse of an eccentric few but a matter of international concern.

All societies have their economic deviants. Over half a century of centralized planning did not purge entrepreneurs and black marketeers from socialist countries. In capitalist societies some have eschewed competition by adopting alternative life-styles while others have survived by operating in the underground economy, avoiding regulation and as pedlars of contraband or sexual services.

Social deviants offend because they subvert prevailing and reassuring certainties about normality. Alcoholics, psychiatric patients, drug abusers, homosexuals or prostituted women are regarded by the moral majority as not just outrageous but prone to trouble and crime. They are thought to prey on innocent and unwary victims and some forms of deviance do have serious social consequences, dragging families into poverty, transmitting venereal disease, thieving to sustain drug habits and the spread of the AIDS virus through needle sharing by heroin addicts. But deviants not only offend, they also suffer, from discrimination in jobs, social services and the courts. The stronger amongst them have challenged their victimization. Prostituted women in the developing world have formed organizations to fight toward decriminalization and for protection, homosexuals in the West have challenged pejorative labeling and stereotyping. The weak, however, are still ultimately dependant upon the slow shift of social perception.

▶▶ Inside a mental hospital. Many such institutions are located far from city centers, removing from society the sense of embarrassment felt at the plight of the mentally ill. Isolated locations provide tranquility for patients but also add to feelings of alienation.

▶ A member of the Salvation Army visits old people. Dedicated members of voluntary organizations have shown some of the greatest concern for marginal members of society.

▼ The "old man of the road" – attractive at a distance, an outcast if he approaches.

▼ *Three Prostitutes on the Street* by Otto Dix, 1925. In the 1920s antiestablishment culture in Germany celebrated outcasts such as prostitutes and homosexuals. It was repressed by the Nazis.

▲ At the state level, pressures to conform have been strongest in the 20th century in totalitarian societies. For example, Soviet governments have removed and imprisoned millions of supposed enemies of communism, such as these prisoners engaged in forced labor near Tiflis in Georgia.

▼ Members of a gang of "Hell's Angels" who use appearance, behavior and contrary values to shock the rest of society. Their self-confidence, however, is based on the creation of conformity within their own groups.

ERROR, DECEPTION AND FRAUD

Science is a set of rules that keeps the scientists from lying to each other. Breaking these rules is unbecoming to scientists. Society wants science to be good, true and beautiful. In real life, performance does not always conform to the ideal. Over the years there have been many examples of scientific misdemeanor, ranging from innocuous error, due to faulty observation or negligence, to intentional "massaging" of data or downright fraud.

The outmoded Lamarckian view of heredity, which assumed that physical characteristics acquired during life could be inherited by subsequent generations, received support in the first three decades of this century by experiments conducted by Paul Kammerer of Vienna on salamanders and frogs. One experiment which was considered critical involved the midwife toad *Alytes obstetricans*. This toad mates on land and does not have horny pigmented pads on its thumbs (nuptial pads), like other toads which mate in water. Kammerer kept his *Alytes* toads in water for several generations, forcing them to mate there. After several generations some of the male toads developed the nuptial pads; Kammerer claimed that this new character became hereditary. There ensued a long controversy between Kammerer and the Mendelian geneticists. In 1926 the American herpetologist G.K. Noble visited Kammerer's laboratory and found that the coloration on the thumbs of Kammerer's specimen of *Alytes*, suggesting nuptial pads, was due to indian ink injected under the skin. Kammerer, though claiming innocence, was discredited, and committed suicide. Nevertheless his experiment served to bolster Lamarckian ideology in the Soviet Union during the period of Lysenko.

Trofim D. Lysenko, a soviet agronomist active during the period 1929–1960, won Communist Party support for his version of Lamarckian philosophy. His activities led to the annihilation of the science of genetics in the Soviet Union. Lysenko first gained recognition for his rediscovery of "vernalization" (when plant seedlings and seeds are kept wet and chilled during the winter, they sprout and mature earlier in summer). He denounced Mendelian genetics, and denied the existence of chromosomes as the bearers of heredity. He fanatically insisted on the correctness of his pseudoscientific ideas and completely ignored the evidence to the contrary from Western science. He succeeded in forcing collective farmers to attempt his impractical ideas on hybridization in plants, cross-fertilization in rye, transformation of one species of plants to another. Many of Lysenko's experiments were bolstered with manipulated data. By 1948 Lysenko became so powerful in Soviet agricultural science, that many of his opponents, the classical geneticists, lost their jobs and were exiled to concentration camps, only because they dared to contradict Lysenko. Lysenko was not discredited until 1965, after the fall of Stalin and Khrushchev, his main supporters. His teachings and theories then quickly became obsolete.

◀▼ In 1912 the scientific establishment was hoaxed into accepting that fossils excavated in Sussex, southern England, provided evidence for a primitive stage in human evolution. It was not until 1953 that part of the skull was shown to be an animal bone.

▼▼ The fossilized *Archaeopteryx* found in the 19th century, was hailed as evidence for the link between flying reptiles and birds. In 1985 a group of scientists claimed the fossil was a fraud. The controversy has not been finally settled.

▲ Trofim Lysenko (right) showing the results of his hybridization experiments to Soviet farmers in the 1930s.

▶ In 1989 two scientists claimed in a press conference to have achieved nuclear fusion at room temperature. Subsequent testing of their work revealed that the reactions they had observed were chemical ones.

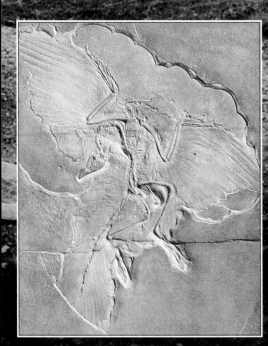

Datafile

Throughout Western Europe the war of 1914–18 brought devastation but also hastened the passing of social welfare legislation, of which there was a wave in the early 1920s. The period saw greater personal freedom as social conventions were relaxed, and also saw real advances in the conditions of labor in both Europe and America. There was more time and scope for home life, modest prosperity, and the concept of "leisure" began to have meaning even for workers. Yet at the same time it was a period of reaction in which, after initial reverses, ruling classes reasserted themselves and, in America especially, sought to impose a moral conformity quite at odds with the carefree image of "the roaring twenties".

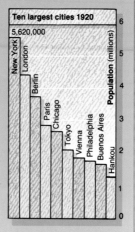
Ten largest cities 1920

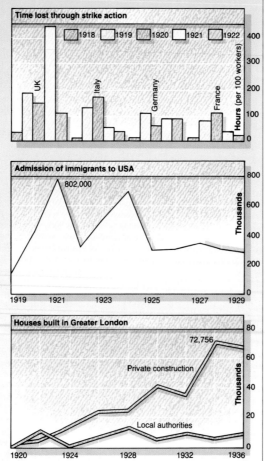
Births and deaths 1925

◀▲ By 1920 American prosperity was reflected in the fact that New York had become the largest city in the world (above). Some cities outside the West were also growing fast. In Europe the 7 cities of more than 1 million inhabitants of 1910 were to be 16 by 1940. Birth and death rates continued to fall (left) but the pattern of much higher rates in the east and south than in the north and west of Europe became even more pronounced. The proportion of children in the Western European population was disproportionately low.

▶ The period immediately after World War I witnessed unprecedented labor unrest with British workers leading the way. The British government used troops against strikers. In Italy industrial unrest culminated in some large-scale factory occupations. However, militancy there and in other countries was generally short-lived.

▶ Disillusionment with Europeans after the war heightened American fears of being swamped by poor immigrants from Europe. The National Origins Act of 1924, designed to stabilize the ethnic composition of the population, reduced immigration but represented the repudiation of America's tradition as a haven refuge.

▶ Lloyd George's scheme of building "homes fit for heroes" after the war was a turning point for the public provision of housing in Britain, even though it was soon dwarfed by the boom in private house-building. Houses were relatively cheap, costing on average about twice the annual salary of a lower professional man.

Time lost through strike action

Admission of immigrants to USA

Houses built in Greater London

For those in the West who lived through the war years of 1914–18, the war they called the "Great War" was a catastrophe. Yet now it seems that contemporary perceptions exaggerated the extent of change caused by the war. There certainly were major changes, perhaps especially the end of European ascendancy in the world economy. In the 1920s the United States emerged as the dominant economic power, offering unparalleled prosperity to its people and a style and way of life to the world. But the lines of social change are more difficult to discern.

In Europe it is most helpful to think of the war as having etched out and emphasized particular changes that were already underway. In general it enhanced the power and improved the position of organized labor. It threw further into doubt the future of the middling classes. It encouraged unprecedented intervention by governments and thereby hastened change in state–society relationships, while at the same time helping to ensure the continuity of social power in Western Europe.

In the United States the war encouraged a mood of disillusionment and reaction and introduced an era of political conservatism and social conformity. This was all in spite of the popular image of a new, freer way of life.

Population movements and family policies

Precisely how many lives were lost during the war is debated – a common estimate is that 9 million combatants were killed. The losses of war fell particularly heavily on France, the population of which had been growing more slowly than that of other powers. By the late 1930s it no longer really counted as a major power because of its loss of manpower. The postwar period saw a major influx of immigrants, accounting for three-quarters of the increase in the population in France between 1920 and 1930 – mainly Poles, Spaniards, Belgians and Italians. French governments pursued policies to encourage population growth.

Yet the war and the later economic depression accelerated the long-run trend toward smaller families in Western Europe and North America – also extending it to the working classes. They also encouraged the practice of contraception. Contraceptives had already been quite widely used amongst the middle classes but during World War I working-class soldiers were issued with them as a protection against venereal diseases. As a result there was a sudden diffusion of knowledge of contraception. Marie Stopes' *Married Love* was published in the UK in March 1918 and her *Wise Parenthood* in November of the same year – marking a greater openness about sexuality. The long-run differences between the richer north and west of Europe, with their smaller families and slowing rate of population growth,

LIBERTY AND REACTION

and the poorer south and east became much more marked.

The growth of large cities went on in Europe and North America. Suburbia expanded. The population of the French department of Seine-et-Oise, outside Paris, for example, increased by 50 percent between 1921 and 1931 as transport became easier. In Britain there was a significant drift of population to the southeast around London, and away from the areas of the older heavy industries. Meanwhile the great movement of Europeans to North America came to an end. There was now widespread feeling that the "Anglo-Saxon" stock of America was being swamped by the "new immigrants" from poorer parts of the Old World. The National Origins Act of 1924 reduced immigration to 165,000 a year and extended national quotas in a way which discriminated against the "new" immigrants.

▼ The entombing of the unknown soldier beneath the Arc de Triomphe symbolized for France the loss of one-tenth of its menfolk in the war.

The onward march of labor?

The urgency of wartime production demands strengthened the hand of organized workers generally. In Britain, at least, the living standards of the working class also rose, especially among those at the bottom end of the scale. As a result there was considerably less poverty after than before the war. Elsewhere in Europe, especially in Germany and Austria-Hungary, the war usually brought greater material suffering than in Britain but everywhere workers became more organized and more militant. Even in a country outside the conflict like Spain the war years were part of "a revolution of rising expectations" which also led to a rush among employers to form associations.

The war period itself and especially the period immediately afterward saw an enormous surge in union membership and quite unprecedented industrial conflict. Regimes feared the prospect of

imminent revolution following the Bolshevik example in Russia. Yet as early as 1922 the threat of the contagion of revolution had receded as the varying mix of repression and conciliating reform applied by governments took effect. A notable effective reform was the granting of the eight-hour working day, which became nearly universal. It seems likely that popular support for revolutionary social change was anyway much weaker than contemporaries believed. A study of workers in the Ruhr, for example, has shown that their demands at this time were essentially economic and that "theirs was much more a social protest movement than a wish to achieve major political and other structural changes". Critically, too, the left in Germany split between reformist/revisionist wings aiming to work within the existing system, and the revolutionaries. The German Communist party (KPD) broke away from the Independent Social Democrats (USPD) in December 1918 and continuously challenged the SPD-dominated government during a period of near-revolution. It was met with sometimes brutal force as the SPD, in its effort to secure stability and the independence of Germany, was driven to reliance on the army and conservative forces profoundly mistrustful of socialism. There was direct repression of worker militancy in Britain and France too. Police forces were used to break up demonstrations and strikes, and in Britain wartime legislation allowed the government to declare a state of emergency to deal with the rail strike in 1919 and again in 1920–21. The left split in Britain and France in 1920 and in Italy and Spain in 1921.

One reason for the divisions in working-class movements was that social reforms started in some countries before the war, and extended during and after it, increased the interest of organized labor in the existing economic system. Concessions made by ruling groups to a large extent worked. The early 1920s saw a wave of social legislation throughout most of Europe, extending social insurance for the elderly, widowed and orphaned, making provision for unemployment and for subsidizing housing. Reform went farthest in the country where organized labor was strongest – Britain. A ministry of health was established in 1919 and national health insurance became universal for the working class in 1920. The Housing Act of 1919 obliged local authorities to meet housing needs and so established the "council house" in the social landscape. The Unemployment Insurance Act of 1920 extended that of 1911. The years to 1939 saw more and more legislation which brought real benefits: by 1935 the working class received 91 million pounds more from the state than it paid in taxation.

Labor militancy in the 1920s

After the storms of 1919–20 workers were increasingly pushed onto the defensive politically, and were variously absorbed in economic reconstruction and modestly increasing living standards, or in confronting unemployment. The nine-day General Strike of 1926 in Britain, which has sometimes been seen as the high watermark of labor militancy, was essentially a defensive action. It developed as a response to attempts by mine owners to extend working hours and cut pay. Its defeat was followed by antiunion legislation and a great drop in militancy (fewer working days were lost because of strikes in the whole period between 1927 and 1939 than in 1919 alone).

In Germany many of the workers' gains had been lost by 1924. Unemployment increased and union membership declined. Business amalgamations created huge firms and units of production in iron and steel and chemicals. The increased strength of employers was shown in November 1928 when a quarter of a million iron and steel workers were locked out during a dispute. French unions were weaker anyway, and cheap immigrant labor kept down wage increases. But France also had the fastest growing European economy in these years and average incomes rose by nearly 40 percent (1913 to 1929). The establishment of Fascist power in Italy, meanwhile, saw the removal of the rights of opposition trade unions by 1925, and thereafter the incorporation of workers' organizations into the Fascist movement. In Spain the socialist leadership cooperated with the dictator Primo de Rivera (1923–30).

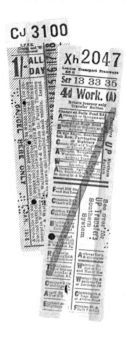

▲▼ Tickets for London trams (above); and the fight of suburban travelers to get home by tram during the national rail strike of 1919. In this one year 35 million days were lost to strikes in Britain and seemed near revolution.

European elites and middle classes

A leading historian of the 1920s, C.S. Maier, argues that "European social hierarchies have proved remarkably tenacious". It is widely accepted that after the upheavals of the war and its immediate aftermath the social order of western Europe emerged more or less intact. The war enhanced the position of workers, brought benefits to some members of the upper classes and assisted the upward mobility of others – notably those businessmen whose activities related to the war effort and who were drawn more directly into government. But the war also precipitated the decline of those aristocrats and gentry who had remained dependent upon title and landed wealth alone, and it had a particularly damaging impact upon the middle classes.

Together with the aristocracy, the middle classes lost relatively more men during the war than the working classes. Increased taxation in wartime affected them too and those who depended on rents or fixed incomes were especially hard hit. Wartime and postwar inflation eroded the savings of all the middle classes and the reduced spending power of others also hit the incomes of shopkeepers and craftsmen. Though middle-class incomes, relative to those of workers,

▲ Mounted police in action against strikers in London during the nine days of the General Strike in May 1926. Class divisions never stood out more strongly in Britain. Working-class communities showed immense solidarity in support of miners who were threatened by proposals for the reorganization of the coal industry. On the other hand middle-class volunteers helped the (well-prepared) government to maintain essential services. Yet both sides sought to avoid violence and it became clear that the labor leadership did not seek revolutionary change.

◄ The establishment of the 8-hour day, for which these workers from the Paris Metro demonstrated, was achieved at last in France in 1919. The limitation of the working day marked both new industrial time discipline and the clearer separation of work and leisure.

Life in English Suburbia

Suburban development around London began before the end of the 19th century, when a contributor to *The Architect* described the modern suburb as "a place which is neither one thing nor another; it has neither the advantage of the town nor the open freedom of the country, but manages to combine in nice equality of proportion the disadvantages of both". In spite of such disdain many common people preferred a semidetached house with a bit of garden to tenement flats in the city. The housing boom after World War I, and the extension of the Underground and Metropolitan railroad systems – beginning with the continuation of the Hampstead line out to Hendon beyond North London in 1923 – saw the development of huge new housing estates around the city, served by new multiple stores, banks and branches of the building societies. The local Woolworths "was increasingly the focus of popular life", and by bringing down retail prices Woolworths, together with the building societies and the "Never-Never" (the instalment system of payment for consumer goods such as sewing machines, vacuum cleaners and wireless sets) "made it financially possible for people of small means to take over new houses" (R. Graves and A. Hodge). Houses built mostly of red brick, costing around £1,000, belonged to people with incomes of £5-10s per week, and were given individuality or "personality" by their architects with pebble-dash, half-timbering and unexpected minor features. The poorer classes were given less fanciness in council estates and new tenements built in slum-clearance schemes. Though there was jerry-building, housing regulations brought better standards which resulted in improvements in health and "the elevation of slum-dwellers to lower middle-class rank by virtue of such amenities as gas, electricity, bathroom and water-closet". Yet still the new suburbs attracted scornful upper-class comment. The remark of the writer Osbert Lancaster is characteristic: "It is sad to reflect that so much ingenuity should have been wasted on streets and estates that will inevitably become the slums of the future". In practice social classes were increasingly separated by the layouts of the new estates, and the effects of the Town Planning Act of 1932 were to perpetuate this cleavage. Status divisions were almost literally built in to British society at this time.

The life of English suburbia has been supposed dull and restricting, and to have encouraged "a privacy of loneliness and tedium". Thus the British writer George Orwell wrote: "Do you know the road I live on? Even if you don't you know fifty others like it. You know how these streets fester all over the inner-outer suburbs. Always the same. Long, long rows of little semi-detacheds... The stucco front, the creosoted gate, the privet hedge and green front door". And yet, just as the country house on the green outskirts of the city met the aspirations of the wealthy, so a semidetached in the suburbs seemed the way to independence and social consideration for the lower middle-class and many workers. A larger proportion of the population emerged from World War I with these aspirations of home ownership, a quiet family life, leisure activity and domestic comforts. "The home" became for them the supreme object of attention, to be embellished with labor-saving devices like the Hoover vacuum cleaner. These

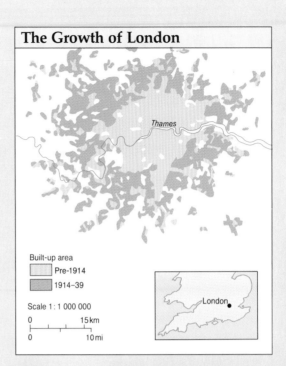

The Growth of London

Thames

Built-up area

Pre-1914

1914–39

Scale 1 : 1 000 000

0   15 km

0   10 mi

London

◀ About one-third of the increase in the English population between the wars was found in Greater London. Suburbs grew rapidly on all sides of the city in response to the demand for new housing which attracted much adverse comment, though it was evidently what people wanted.

▼ ▶ The new suburban houses were smallish, semi-detached, usually tiled and lighter and airier than Edwardian houses had been (below). They had larger gardens and space for sheds and garages. There were over one million privately owned cars by 1930, of which the favorite model was the "Baby" Austin (right).

had generally recovered by the mid-1920s, the undermining of their positions during the war led many members of the middle classes to support the "new European right" – "comprising distressed farmers, retired officers, intellectuals and university youth, clerical employees and hard-pressed small businessmen and traders [who had, even before the war] embraced a strident chauvinism, anti-semitism and anti-parliamentarism" (Maier). It was such people, or sometimes members of Catholic groups, who formed the ranks of the various volunteer corps which fought against socialists in Germany, France and Spain. They thus contributed to the defense of bourgeois Europe while posing a sinister threat to liberal institutions.

The way in which regimes achieved or maintained stability after the war represented an important change in the way in which power was exercised, marking a shift from the ideals of 19th-century liberalism. The urgency of wartime production had required harmonious industrial relations. The war thus both established the legitimacy of unions and their leaders and increased the significance of employers' associations. It had also caused states to intervene and acquire new powers to control prices, allocate materials and regulate labor. The autonomy of markets thus tended to be eroded, and decision making to shift from parliamentary assemblies to negotiation and bargaining between the state and major organized ("corporate") interest groups. In sum the war produced a trend toward "corporatism" in which key decisions are made by corporate groups, or these groups and the state jointly, and individuals have influence only through their membership of corporate bodies (such as trade unions, professional associations or business corporations). Corporatism is reflected in the Stinnes-Legien agreement between union leaders and employers' representatives in Germany, which was made on 15 November 1918 – only four days after the Armistice. In return for recognition of many trade union bargaining rights and the eight-hour day, manufacturers were assured of their leadership of industry. Similar sorts of agreements were at least considered in Britain at this time; and somewhat later in the 1920s corporatism became established as a principle of rule in fascist Italy. But the extent of the trend toward corporatism in the 1920s should not be exaggerated. In Germany, for example, the Ruhr lockout of 1928 showed how far power had swung back to employers and the old privileged groups which had in fact run things throughout.

Industry and workers in America
Across the Atlantic, in the United States, the war had encouraged an inward-looking, intolerant nationalism, known as "100 percent Americanism". In the name of the war effort, there was an assault on civil liberties and repression of dissent. The pro-business Harding administration after 1920 sided with employers. Union membership fell from 5 million in 1920 to 3.5 million in 1929.

At the same time, as industrial production almost doubled in the 1920s, industrial workers

aspirations were fostered by developments in retailing. The provision and advertising of branded goods simplified shopping, and fast-cooked foods (like "Quick Quaker Oats") arrived in the shops. Packaging changed too, and in the 1920s cellophane wrapping came into general use, banishing the flies from grocers' shops. There was, contemporaries wrote, "a new found pride" among young women "who wished everything to conform in cleanliness and respectability to their new domestic standards". The same young women now dressed in clothes made from the new fabric – artificial silk – called "rayon", which made both for a quicker turnover of fashions and for their adoption even by relatively poor people. "It was now at last possible to mistake working-class girls for titled ladies, if one judged by dress".

The suburban growth was fostered by the growth of productivity in the 1920s and 1930s, especially in new industries based on electricity and the automobile. But these developments took place mainly in the Midlands and Southeast, which accumulated wealth and population and power. A social gulf opened up between these areas and the older industrial regions which persisted through the century. The divide was remarked upon by the British novelist J.B. Priestley when, in 1933, he described three different Englands: the "old country of history"; the England of 19th-century industrialization; and then 20th-century England, "springing up unplanned and shapeless – an England of...thousands of semi-detached houses, with advertising hoardings everywhere". Here there is another hint of disdain. Yet, as the historian K.O. Morgan says, "The majority of the population found that life was acceptable and in many ways agreeable. If one explanation for the lack of social change amidst unemployment and depression lies in the lack of political power vested in the old industrial areas, another lies in the increased commitment to a pleasing form of suburban life by larger and larger sections of the population".

achieved new prosperity. Working conditions were improved as employers, in order to head off labor unrest, developed "welfare capitalism" – including profit-sharing, life insurance and pension plans, and company recreational facilities. The mix of repression and conciliation applied in America as it did in Europe. But as in Europe, some areas of old heavy industry lay outside the general prosperity. Agriculture was generally depressed and the countryside in America (as in Europe) lagged behind in the rise in living standards.

America's prosperity was based on the chemicals industry and the manufacture of new synthetic textiles (rayon) and plastics. The electrical industry was also important: in 1912 only 16 percent of the population lived in dwellings with electricity, but 63 percent in 1927. Electrical household appliances – cookers, irons, refrigerators, toasters – were mass-produced for the first time. Meanwhile the production of automobiles trebled in the 1920s.

Industrial growth in this period was based upon increased productivity resulting from technological innovation and the application of "scientific management". Its key idea – to take

control of production away from workers by making it independent of their knowledge and skill – had been elaborated by F. W. Taylor before the war, but actually implemented in only a very small number of plants. The approach required detailed study of industrial processes to break them down into simple operations. It began to come into its own in the 1920s – in both the United States and Europe – together with the principles of mass production pioneered by Henry Ford: flow (assembly line) production of highly standardized products, often involving special-purpose machinery.

Such mass production presupposes mass consumption, in which advertising plays a crucial role, and market management – of which a bold example was the purchase by General Motors, Standard Oil and Firestone Tires of urban electric trolley systems. They then dismantled the systems to ensure the dominance of motor transport. Mass production also involves intensely hierarchical, top-down management and authoritarian work relations. These features of "Fordism" – mass production and consumption, centralized organization with rigid job specifications, reliance on semiskilled workers and collective

▲ A gathering of the Ku Klux Klan in West Virginia, 1924. Open only to "native born, white American citizens" the Klan by then had more than 2 million members, mainly among disadvantaged blue-collar workers, clerks and small business people in fast-growing cities of the mid-West, Southwest and the Pacific Coast. Its hostility ways at first directed not so much against blacks as against Catholics, Jews and "foreigners" who "with drink, dancing and short skirts" were accused of undermining American values.

▼ A last drink before Prohibition made drinking illegal in America in 1920. Rural Protestant fundamentalists were strong supporters of what President Hoover described as "a great social and economic experiment", sought by the high-minded idealists of American Progressivism since the Civil War had boosted alcohol consumption. But it proved impossible to enforce because so many people, including the very rich and the immigrant working class, were strongly opposed to it.

bargaining, and commitment to standardized products (cultural products like films as much as chocolate bars) – together constituted the dominant economic culture of the middle part of the 20th century. It powerfully influenced experiments in the construction of socialism (usually obsessed with scale) – as well as market societies until later in the century when it was challenged by more flexible production methods.

Conformity and reaction

The defensiveness of American society was shown in the "Red Scare" of summer 1919 and was also reflected in the terrible outbreak of racial violence which followed the influx of blacks into northern factories during the war. In the postwar recession white workers felt that blacks threatened their jobs and homes.

From this time onward race became a crucial factor in urban labor markets, dividing workers against themselves. The colorful founder of the Universal Negro Improvement Association, Marcus M. Garvey, won a following for a time among the black urban masses when he sought to stimulate pride in black achievements. But his movement was undermined and had collapsed by 1923, leaving only "garveyism" as an inspiration for later black nationalists.

Defensiveness also manifested itself in an intolerant moralism rather at odds with the image of the age of jazz and the automobile and of greater social freedom and leisure. The attempt to enforce moral and intellectual conformity by law is epitomized by Prohibition and by anti-evolutionism, first established in law in Tennessee in March 1925. The legislation reflected the strength of religious fundamentalism and anxiety in the south about the basis of white racial supremacy. Ethnic and racial tensions also underlay the rise of the Ku Klux Klan, founded in Georgia in 1915, as a vehicle of militant patriotism.

Organized Crime

▲ The studied calm of Al Capone.

Alphonse Capone, born in New York in 1899, became the most famous gang boss of all in the 1920s, the violent but formative years of organized crime in America. Capone was reputed to have owned banks, real estate firms, hotels and other investments, bringing in more than 60 million dollars annually. His imprisonment in 1931 for tax evasion may, however, have been engineered by more progressive syndicate groups because he attracted too much publicity and attention from the law, which obstructed the development of organized crime.

Ethnic criminal groups like the Mafia, with their origins in the armed bands of Sicilian landowners, laid the foundations of 20th-century criminal syndicates. Prohibition then marked a turning point, for the supply of illicit liquor to a national market with deliveries to thousands of "speakeasies", meant that criminals had to become businessmen owning distilleries and breweries and distribution networks, albeit with protection rackets enforced by their private armies. Their operations taught the gangs the need for national cooperation. Johnny Torrio, a Neapolitan, was elected president of the Unione Siciliane, and brought together a convention of major crime groups in 1929 to formulate a national policy. Capone perhaps stood in the way of this rationalization of crime. Organized crime was in some ways an outgrowth of the corrupt economic practices of late-19th-century America, and there has been close liaison between the syndicates and the political and business establishments. But organized crime has also been encouraged, paradoxically, by America's Protestant tradition, for attempts to legislate morality, as with Prohibition, have always created criminal opportunities in their evasion. The crime syndicates, described by a presidential commission as "a society that seeks to operate outside the control of the American people...working within structures as complex as those of any large corporation" have extended their operations from the traditional lines of gambling, loan-sharking, labor and business racketeering, and narcotics, into new ones such as credit-card and real-estate fraud, as well as into legitimate business operations.

Women and the family

After the war the great social and cultural trends of prewar industrial society continued. Although differences were to persist between urban and rural settings, between rich and poor, with increasing urbanization notions of personal happiness and the desire for security began to change the goals and nature of marriage more widely.

For women, marriage was to become increasingly their "career". It denoted status and security, both of which were absent in most fields of employment open to them. The media began to promote motherhood and better housekeeping in advertising and women's magazines. Fashion journals and designers followed suit: "How to attract a man" and "How to please one's husband" were the kind of maxims which channeled women's interests, their expectations and aspirations. This renewed focus on women's reproductive roles after the war was accompanied by a retreat of feminism from the doctrine of individual equality toward an acceptance of sex-role divisions in society. The programs of the women's movements thereafter sought to protect the interests of mothers and housewives, abandoning earlier demands such as the right to abort or the right of married women with children to work outside the home.

Complex reasons underlie this shift. The increasing obsession with the birthrate after the war, for example, put feminists on the defensive. It was suggested that it was women's moral or even national duty to "cooperate in the preservation of the nation". In all the industrialized countries the low birthrate was widely attributed to the growing independence of women. In Germany feminists were accused of undermining the nation; in others they were stigmatized for wanting to destroy the family.

In nearly all countries feminists responded by mounting pro-family campaigns in an effort to halt the downward trend of birth rates. Other agencies helped along and the celebration of "Mother's Day" (in the United States from 1914, in Germany from 1922) became a great commercial success. In France mothers of numerous children were awarded the *medaille de la famille*. Already by 1920 employment figures for women had "normalized" and now varied little from those before the war. Except for some advances in the professions such as medicine and law, women's positions seemed not to have been changed by the war at all. In many countries women were granted the vote, but on the whole it brought them only symbolic equality.

Yet there were some important if limited changes resulting from the war. They mainly affected younger women who, during the war, had been "out in public" on their own as never before. This undoubtedly fostered new expectations of personal freedom and independence, especially as the whole notion of women in public (as distinct from the home) had become more respectable during the war. Supporting the national effort and working in new surroundings also raised women's consciousness and made them more confident. These less concrete yet threatening changes to the traditional image and

role of women were difficult to offset, especially as a whole new industry of recreation and fashion now began to "market" the modern trends. Thus motherhood, or rather the perceived lack of it, received new attention.

Married women were increasingly barred from the professions or dismissed upon marriage. In the postal services in Germany, for example, the total number of married women was reduced between 1922 and 1923 from 2,718 to 21. Among the workers, married women in the labor force were stigmatized and accused of taking men's jobs away. Would-be working women were channeled into so-called "caring" occupations in social welfare, child or health care – or at universities into the "female" professions. In secondary education, the curriculum for girls continued to incorporate an emphasis on housekeeping and childcare. "New opportunities" for women began to mean better conditions in the home, improved child and maternity welfare, and a better education for their children. While new welfare legislation and extended family benefits on the whole improved the quality of material life within the family, they also served to reinforce women's traditional roles.

In this decade of so-called moral decadence, and of a general erosion of acquiescence, the family was blamed, as it had been and was to be again and again, for all the social and moral ills of society. The family was held to be at risk: "it was weakening". Parents were seen to be losing control over their offspring as adolescence was emerging as a distinct phase in the life of individuals. It was the result of a delay of his or her entry into the sphere of productive work through longer education. Social concern that children should be brought up according to cultural and social ideals and the increasing attention paid to them created what the historians Mitterauer and Sieder called a "kind of hiatus", a period of initiation into society by external institutions (schools, job-training, clubs or youth organizations).

▲ Modern technology was soon to become indispensable for the wife and mother. This advertisement shows the leisurely pace of washday with an *Easy* machine.

▶ In spite of war, defeat and social democracy, German society in the 1920s still bore the stamp of its aristocratic traditions. Guests at the wedding of the grandson of Count Otto von Bismarck (German chancellor until 1890) to Anne Marie Tengbom are waving the newly married couple off to their honeymoon.

▼ Holidays abroad remained the privilege of the rich during the 1920s, but lower-middle-class and even some working-class families were beginning to have holidays in their own country, as did this German family seen at a seaside resort.

▲ Mass production of records transformed the leisure time even of the poor, as the introduction of gramophones to pubs and cafés brought to them the newest fashions in music and dance.

▼ In some American municipalities "indecent bathing" was banned in the 1920s; in others "petting" was made a crime. Anything authorities deemed obscene or immoral was liable to suppression or seizure, as for example these unfortunate women bathers.

By the end of World War I the young had begun to form an important social group through which nations hoped to transmit their "cultural heritage" of work ethics or moral values. The extent to which they could be influenced in order to ensure socio-cultural continuity became more pressing, once young people were beginning to be organized by political parties, or formed their own organizations. This seems to have happened on a wider scale in Germany than elsewhere, where a youth movement began to emerge before the war. In other countries the young grouped together after the war often out of protest against conformity and authoritarianism. In prosperous America such youthful rebellion has been described as a reaction against the prevailing social norms, sexual taboos and double standards of "Victorianism".

A significant feature of the 1920s was the spread of Freudian ideas throughout Europe and America. This also increased the number of apostles cí sexual freedom. Although profoundly anti-feminist, Freudian ideas eventually proved to have a generally liberating effect also on young women, pointing the way beyond feminism. The "advocates of women's rights" of that time gave short shrift to "radical" women such as Victoria Woodhull, Marie Stopes or Helene Stoecker who promoted sexual freedom. Instead they joined the ranks of those who expressed indignation over the new "immorality" of the twenties. They also supported the new moves to make the diffusion of knowledge of contraception illegal (in Sweden such a law had been passed already, in 1911). Yet the use of contraceptives increased despite statutory obstacles – to what extent among the unmarried is difficult to assess. The existing trend of rising nonmarital intercourse certainly continued, but the number of illegitimate births also continued to fall until World War II (as it had done, with variations from country to country, from the mid-19th century or so, though not in Sweden until the 1930s).

"Nothing and no one was in its place anymore, everything was possible", reflected the German philosopher Helmut Kuhn, in response to the changes in Europe after the war. Change was too fast. Although individual morality had already become a matter of public concern long before the war, bringing along new types of social reform through state intervention, the postwar period saw the convergence of more active forms of state control, as expediency, class or political interest began to replace the notion of "the rights of the individual". With regard to women, this can be clearly sized up by the way in which, even among the feminists, vocabulary such as "rights" or "justice" had begun to recede as a justification for female suffrage, and moral imperatives moved into the forefront of the struggle.

Feminist ideas of the 1920s

The granting of female suffrage in most Western countries soon after the war was celebrated by women as a main victory on the road to their liberation. At the same time, however, it was seen by politicians and suffragists alike as a means of controlling society in the interests of the "stable" part of the population, the middle classes. In the end women were given the vote either to stave off a proletarian revolution, or as Sir John Hall, the main advocate of votes for women in New Zealand, put it, because female suffrage would "increase the influence of the settler and family man, as against the loafing single man".

The feminists' promotion of motherhood as women's primary role after the war was illustrative of a more long-term reorientation of feminist ideology. Feminists had started off as liberal individualists, asserting that there were no innate differences in reason or ability between men and women, and had fought for "equal" opportunities on "equal" terms for women, only to retreat to a position where these innate differences became the basis for feminist demands. This was to be a crucial development in all industrializing nations, as it endorsed the concept of separate spheres of action for men and women. The feminists' new rationale built on that 18th- and 19th-century proposition that women's moral superiority was inborn and a consequence of their function as mothers. Thus suffrage had been widely demanded on the grounds, that once in government, women could help curb immorality and disorder.

This move toward the right with the feminists' retreat from liberalism was part of a general change in the nature of liberalism itself. At this time liberals came to endorse state interventionist and collectivist solutions to social problems in order to preserve social peace – often in order to preempt solutions suggested by the left. Liberalism became a "Janus-faced political ideology", as Richard Evans termed it, and feminism shared its characteristics: "The way in which problems of social control featured in the actual granting of female suffrage illustrates the extent to which the feminists owed what many of them saw as the crowning victory to these more conservative implications of the liberal creed".

▲ A much publicized aspect of women's revolt against the restrictions placed on their behavior and appearance was that they demanded and sometimes asserted the right to drink or smoke in public, as in this English restaurant.

▼ The images on these powder compacts convey a sense of the new freedom young women claimed in the 1920s. The use of cosmetics no longer implied a wearer's easy virtue. Advertising now reminded women of their duty to keep young and beautiful and face powder promised an "irresistible complexion".

The freedoms of the "roaring twenties"

A new trend of leisure and youth culture took its cue from the cinema as the new "movies" from Hollywood began to offer notions of "another life". America's jazz, played by New Orleans black musicians, grew increasingly more popular. It inspired new dance forms – the Charleston and "Black bottom" – all visually suggestive, which was proof for the period's moralists to believe that the collapse of all morality was imminent. Most parents felt lost in the face of such rapid change among the young; and most young people did think of themselves as wild and daring. There were probably fewer changes in sexual behavior than contemporaries believed, but there was experimentation, and new romanticization of love as the notion of sexual fulfillment in marriage was being discussed more openly.

The "modern" young woman, who no longer behaved as she used to do, filled a special niche in society's concern for stability, as she threw off the restrictions which traditions had placed on appearance and behavior. The "new" woman smoked in public, took part in entertainments outside the home, at cinemas, the dance halls; she wore boyish hairstyles, makeup and shorter dresses. She seemed to prefer carefree pleasure-seeking rather than preparing herself for her serious duties as future wife and mother. New employment opportunities in the expanding service sector, where young women worked as typists, telephonists, secretaries, or as clerks, had made this short period of carefree life between school and marriage possible. It was a period of idealized freedom and temporary independence and of equally idealized dreams of marriage – a form of escapism, reinforced by Hollywood cinema and the new novel.

PLAY AND GAMES

The idea that the world of the child is entirely separate from that of the adult is a relatively recent one. A hundred years ago, blind man's buff was a game for the whole family, and even today, in many parts of the world, adults and children play games together – charades, cards, ball and board games. It is usually through games that adults find it easiest to spend recreation time with their children, because "playing by the rules" imposes a structure and competition that resemble aspects of daily life. In this way, games teach children valuable life skills, not least of which is that when they lose, the world does not come to an end.

But play is also about freedom from all but self-imposed rules. Playing statues, trying not to blink in staring contests, or avoiding cracks in the pavement are all children's attempts at mastery; they are common for many cultures and periods. Moreover, children need fantasy play to allow them to integrate their inner and outer worlds harmoniously and independently of adults. For children in societies where myth and magical beliefs are a normal part of daily reality, the capacity for creative fantasy is fostered; where adult impatience or the constraints of modern life reduce the long hours of leisure necessary for valuable day-dreaming, this ability may be curtailed.

Middle-class children have always been subject to greater adult control over their play. This was extended to working-class children during the century; for example by the introduction of boy scouts and girl guides and the construction of municipal playgrounds in many countries from the 1920s. Shop-bought toys too, were once the preserve of better-off children. In the interwar years mass-market toy manufacture flourished with the introduction of the cheap clockwork motor, although the wholesale commercialization of children's play was only a feature of the affluent postwar years.

Toys mirror societies' values and technological progress. Television has undermined the importance of books, or so it is often claimed. Walkie-talkies and moon buggies have replaced the lead or tin soldiers of the 1900s and the train sets of the interwar years, while the delicate porcelain dolls of Edwardian times have given way to gregarious plastic teenage "Barbie" and "Cindy" dolls, dressed for the discothèque and the beach. Today there is growing concern about the pressures of fashion and crazes on children's toys and play, largely a result of television advertising which exploits children's need to be accepted by their friends.

▲ ▶ Rather than gardens or playgrounds, urban children often favor streets or building sites as the center of their play, like these girls engaged in a game of hopscotch in the 1950s. Outdoor play such as skipping, ball games, tag and hide-and-go-seek have a universal appeal; many such games endure unchanged for generations of children.

▶ ▲ Teddy bears are an invention of the early 20th century. Soft toys provide children with safe objects of affection which they can alternately cuddle and control. They can act as parent substitutes in the long hours of the night. While real bears might be threatening to children, teddies protect them from harm.

▲ The teamwork of organized sport is often seen as character-building. However, for centuries children such as these young Jamaicans have enjoyed spontaneous ball games with minimal facilities, marking out fields in the dust, using t-shirts for goal posts and sticks for makeshift bats.

◄ Fantasy play allows children to act out past and present relationships, by playing the parent or teacher to dolls and siblings, or experimenting with future roles like these children dressing up in adult clothes.

◄ Above all, children engage in play because it is immediately enjoyable and fun. Enjoyment of play extends into enjoyment of life. Like these boys on Brooklyn Pier, New York, in 1914, children of all ages take as much pleasure in exercising their bodies as their minds and need to have their fill of it.

◄◄ Board games are valuable forms of play, offering children the opportunity for competition within a friendly, reassuring (though sometimes moralistic) framework. Games of skill such as chess reward children for concentration, while games of chance like snakes and ladders put them in a rare position of equality with adults.

Datafile

World War I unleashed rapid social and economic change in parts of the "Third World", which threatened the ultimate breakup of the European empires. The spread of manufacturing and modern communications accelerated the growth of towns. The concentration of workers provided the basis for mass trade unionism, major strikes and the development of mass nationalism, often begun by students in higher education. Where governments had political autonomy – as with Turkey, Mexico and Brazil – the state undertook radical social change. Turkey's reforms foreshadowed the programs of state-initiated development in much of the Third World after 1945.

▼ **Most Indians depended on agriculture, often within an oppressive system of land tenure with great landlords and princes at the top. The structures of land tenancy and subtenancy were complicated. There was usually little return for the actual cultivator. Despite 60 years of industry – particularly the development of an enormous textile industry – only 10 percent of India's 96,623,000 workers were employed in industry in 1921.**

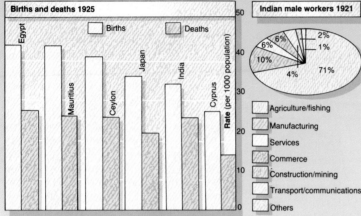
Births and deaths 1925

▲ **Birth rates were beginning to rise in "Third World" countries and rates of population growth to increase, but with great variations between countries. Egypt's rate, for example, was two-thirds larger than that of Cyprus. This in part reflected considerable differences in relative prosperity and diet, influencing how many children survived birth. Death rates also varied widely. Modern medicine had had as yet little effect, and public health measures in the great and growing cities were still limited.**

▶ **The South African economy was boosted by World War I. The Rand became a key supplier of raw materials to Europe, sustained by a continuing inflow of white immigrants. The 2,593,000 workers of 1921 depended on the core activity of exporting minerals. Black and white workers constituted two societies – a high-income white minority and a miserably poor black majority. South African employers purchased white worker loyalty with special privileges, later to be rationalized in apartheid.**

Indian male workers 1921

6% 6% 2% 1%
10%
4% 71%

- Agriculture/fishing
- Manufacturing
- Services
- Commerce
- Construction/mining
- Transport/communications
- Others

S African male workers 1921

8% 3% 3%
10%
10% 62%
4%

- Agriculture/fishing
- Manufacturing/construction
- Mining
- Services
- Commerce/finance
- Transport/communications
- Others

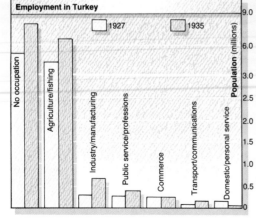
Employment in Turkey

◀ **In 1929 Turkey set out to protect its economy against imports and the effects of the Great Depression in Europe and North America, using the state to foster widespread industrialization and the development of infrastructure (particularly railroads). This approach was embodied in the 1934 Five Year Plan and the declared aim of the state to pursue state capitalism. Perhaps as a consequence, as the labor force grew in a very difficult period for the world economy, Turkish manufacturing employment also expanded.**

World War I was prodigiously demanding in its need for manpower, raw materials and finance. One consequence of this was an economic boom. For the countries of Africa, Asia and Latin America it entailed the creation of an apparently insatiable European appetite for raw materials and, to a lesser extent, men. Furthermore the supply of European manufactured goods to the rest of the world dried up, so overseas countries were obliged to manufacture substitutes. The war thus contributed to a profound breakdown in the 19th-century world division of labor. With this growth came the creation, with remarkable speed, of new working classes, concentrated in a handful of rapidly growing cities. The concentration itself enhanced the potential social power of these work forces, and the 1920s in the area that came to be called the Third World are characterized for the first time by battles between capital and labor.

Urban labor forces around the world

In China, India and much of Latin America the growth in the urban labor force continued, with greater fluctuations, throughout the 1920s. Take, for example, Bombay's textile industry: it had 105,000 workers in 1914 and a peak of 151,000 in 1922. By the early 1920s it was estimated that 11 percent of the city's population was dependent upon the industry. India's textile industry as a whole had become the third largest in the world in the size of its labor force and the second in the volume of production. Only about a quarter of the labor force were born in Bombay, and the rural kinsmen of many immigrant workers called them back to the villages at harvest time or marriage season, or when slump cut employment. The rural base and divisions based upon different origins weakened the capacity to organize trade unions. But the close links between cities and the countryside also provided a channel of refuge against urban disasters, and, as happened in China, a means whereby urban conflicts were swiftly spread to the countryside.

Nonetheless, despite all the divisions, Indian workers did organize. The railroad workers were particularly important here; they were above average in education, and saw the country as a whole. They provided an example for others, particularly as aspirations rose. The Bombay textile workers agitated for a 12-hour day in 1905, and a 9-hour day in 1919. The 1920s saw two general strikes (one in 1928 lasting six months) and an increasingly effective union organization. In the first instance, the work of trade union organizing was not clearly distinguished from general political and social reform or charitable work – "uplift" as it was called by middle-class volunteers in India. Thus some of the leading political figures

THE BEGINNINGS OF MODERNIZATION

were also leading trade union leaders, especially if they were lawyers and could combine trade union work with advocacy of labor's cause in the courts. For example, some of the earliest nationalist work by Gandhi in India was championing the grievances of textile workers in Ahmadabad. Critics, especially the colonial government, argued that the workers could not properly be represented by those who had no direct experience of being workers. But while the outside leadership posed serious problems for workers, in many cases it was the only form of representation they could get against powerful and ruthless employers. Once real mass movements developed, worker leaderships emerged with great speed, as was shown in the 1920s in the Bombay textile industry.

In the turbulence of China, where a republic had replaced the Qing (Ch'ing) empire in 1912, industrial workers made an even more spectacular debut. Their role was the more effective politically because they were so heavily concentrated in a handful of cities (42 percent of modern factories were in Shanghai). Conditions were appalling; impoverished peasants still sold their children into semislavery in the textile mills.

The first major mass movement in China, the May 4th Movement of 1919, was student-led and directed against some of the provisions of the Versailles Treaty, but six years later the May 30th Movement was a workers' campaign. It was initially directed against Japanese factory practices but then spread into protests against all foreign capital. It produced ultimately a long general strike in the south and an effective boycott of British goods which closed Hong Kong. Many workers spread out in the countryside, and one by-product of these events was an extraordinary growth in peasant associations and, later, attempts to seize the land and overthrow landlordism. Membership of the Communist party soared, and trade unions for the first time became effective forces.

When the new armed forces of the Nationalists, the Guomindang (Kuomintang), set out from their southern base in Guangzhou (Canton) on a Northern Expedition to conquer China proper, in 1926, it was the new mass organizations of trade unions and peasant associations that fanned out before the troops, seizing towns, cities and installations along the way. The great trade union federation of Shanghai seized that city in order to present it to the army chief, Jiang Jieshi (Chiang Kai-shek). Those that glimpsed the reality of the violence being unleashed were further horrified when Jiang turned on the unions and the Communist Party to destroy them. In the late 1920s possibly 120,000 union and peasant activists were liquidated or imprisoned.

▼ Evening meal for Indian soldiers, France 1916. Over 3 million served worldwide with the European armies. Possibly 150,000 died in Europe. "Many natives", Albert Schweitzer noted in the Congo, "are puzzled...how... the whites who brought them the Gospel of Love are now murdering each other"

In Africa somewhat similar processes were at work. In South Africa the white working class doubled in size during World War I and emerged radicalized. However, the ferocious competition between poor white and black workers, enhanced by shrewd employers, provided the basis for a racial division of the labor force. Even then, the need for a mass of low-paid migrant labor on the farms and in the mines was beginning to collide with the need of manufacturing for a higher level of productivity in a settled labor force. The slow development of apartheid smothered these tensions. The Urban Areas Act of 1929 sought to segregate the black labor force and control black movement into areas nominated for white occupation. The 1924 Industrial Conciliation Act recognized what were then overwhelmingly white trade unions and set up industrial councils (with representatives of trade unions and employers) with the power to exclude Africans, Indians and Coloreds from apprenticeships and skilled jobs; closed shop provisions further strengthened the power of white unions to exclude black workers.

Elsewhere in Africa the wartime growth of the industrial labor force was less significant. The retention of land rights and the control exercised over peasant production by merchants and their capital meant that the rise of the wage labor force did not generally divorce workers from the land. But incorporation in the cash economy and pressure from the colonial state – taxes were still an important instrument for forcing Africans into employment – threw up an immense migrant population, pressing men (and more slowly, women) into towns to lead a marginal life searching for patrons and work. Resistance involved shirking or desertion rather than strikes, though skilled workers on the Gold Coast or in Senegal began to unionize after the war.

Nationalism and mass movements
World War I and the 1920s offered the first real glimpse of the likely course of future events in what became the Third World: the national assertion of countless peoples who had hitherto been submerged in the misleading uniformity of empire. It still concerned in the main the larger and more advanced countries, but it presaged the

emergence of a host of new sovereign powers. The range of nationalist reactions was wide – from the struggle of independent regimes in Latin America to assert the rights of sovereignty, to limit the role of foreigners, and to use social reform to incorporate a much larger proportion of the population; to the pressure in the Dutch East Indies, in French Indochina or more sporadically in Africa to open government structures to natives; to a war of national unification in China against not only the domestic warlords, but also against foreigners who financed them.

Latin America's independent republics had much greater power to pursue the sorts of reforms already current in Europe. For example, José Batlle y Ordónez as president of Uruguay set about creating what would later be called a welfare state. He instituted an eight-hour working day, pensions for the aged, and expropriated many public services and basic industries; he enshrined in the law the right of women to divorce and abolished capital punishment.

The Mexican government, under a new constitution of 1917, took into state ownership land and water. It assumed powers to control all private

▲ Women workers collect iron ore for the steel works at Jamshedpur in northeast India. The Tata family conceived the project of India's first steel plant in the 1880s; production started in 1911. By the 1920s 53,000 workers were employed in steel production and raw material supply, with 150 Europeans and Americans. Most of the workers were local tribespeople.

▶ World War I blocked imports from Europe so there was a surge in industrial output in the rest of the world. The easiest industry to start was textiles, but steel production opened the way to make machines. The new workers worked long hours for miserable pay. Employers in China purchased the daughters of impoverished peasants and locked them in the mills as virtual slaves. Workers were drawn off the countryside and packed into appalling shanty towns.

property, nationalized all mineral assets, introduced an advanced labor code and excluded the church from education. Much legislation was mere declaration and not implemented, but nonetheless some land was expropriated and redistributed to the cultivators, and rural education was extended. Under President Plutarco Elías Calles – a Bolshevik monster to the shareholders of North America – foreign holdings in the oilfields were converted into 55-year leases (a measure superseded by nationalization in the 1930s). More land was expropriated and redistributed. In Argentina, in 1916, the first radical president proposed to limit working hours and institute a minimum wage level. Throughout Latin America reform was part of the process of incorporating a much larger proportion of the inhabitants into the nation – and in doing so, embracing where relevant a mythical pre-Columbian history rather than Spanish roots.

In India World War I saw the issue of home rule become almost universally accepted as an aim. B.G. Tilak with his band of energetic nationalists took control of the Indian National Congress and reached, for the first time, an alliance with the Muslim League in the Lucknow Pact that seemed likely to frustrate British attempts to divide followers of the two religions. With the arrival in India of a famous Indian agitator and lawyer from South Africa who was to become known as Mahatma Gandhi, a quite new style of politics was promised which would go well beyond the urban middle class to reach out to the mass of the peasantry. Gandhi abandoned the mark of the lawyers who had hitherto run Congress, formal European dress, for an Indian

dhoti and shirt. The great upsurge of feeling towards the end of the war, the belief that India had earned its right to self-government, all added to the sense that a new age was dawning.

Gandhi's role in welding together the contradictory social forces of Indian nationalism – tenant cultivator and landlord, borrower and moneylender, worker and employer – now became vital as the movement of agitation expanded. But it was brief. The economy floundered, stamina was exhausted. The British through the 1920s were slowly able to reestablish their position. They were helped by Congress disunity, by the growing pessimism about the prospects for home rule, by communalism (adherence to antagonistic religious groups) and

▲ **The other India.** Machine-made textiles threatened village spinners like this one. Mahatma Gandhi, the independence leader, opposed modern industry because, he said, it enslaved the workers and made impossible *swaraj* or "self-rule" on an individual as much as a social level. His followers met their own need for clothes by spinning yarn.

The Spread of Industrialization 1929

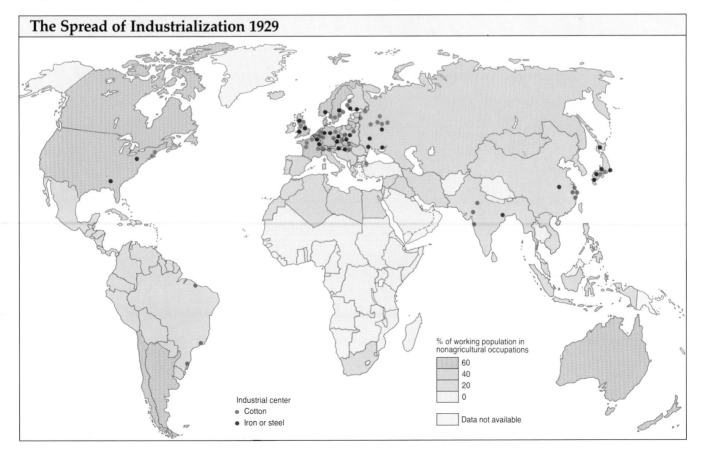

% of working population in nonagricultural occupations

60
40
20
0

Data not available

Industrial center
● Cotton
● Iron or steel

its periodic terrible blood-letting. The British emloyed reform judiciously to strengthen their support – mildly protectionist tariffs to limit imports for businessmen, more public works and education and the promise of extensions of the franchise. By the late 1920s the upsurge in feeling in the immediate postwar years had been dissipated.

Unlike India, where a national industrial and commercial bourgeoisie began to flourish in the 1920s, in Africa – outside South Africa – such a bourgeoisie was barely discernible. Petty commerce was extremely important, and those who were higher up in the labor hierarchy – railroadmen and clerks – often sought to use their jobs as a means of entry to trading. But except in some parts of West Africa – notably the Gold Coast – there was little development of an African bourgeoisie and little interest in entering into capitalist production. The educated elite, created by the need of colonial states for a substantial class of petty bureaucrats, was at best only an incipient bourgeoisie, though it began to become an important group of power-brokers. This class started to form associations reflecting its members' sense of belonging to a distinct interest group. The National Congress of British West Africa was briefly influential in the 1920s, agitating for improved education, especially at higher levels, and for promotion of Africans in the civil service. But it failed to link up with the working masses who sometimes organized to resist colonial rule. The East African Association, an intertribal group formed in Nairobi by a telephonist, Harry Thuku, was briefly more threatening to colonial rule in 1920-21. But the educated elite, as the historian Bill Freund has put it, "remained too deeply rooted in the colonial structure to question the colonial order very profoundly".

Social change in Turkey

A new style of politics, social change and economic policy was being shaped in the 1920s which was to achieve full expression in the newly independent regimes of Asia and Africa in the 1950s and 1960s. It became known as "economic nationalism". The policy presupposed a mass popular basis to government, a nation, and a governmental responsibility for popular welfare. Government embodied, it seemed, the single clearcut interest of the nation, and on that basis could intervene in all fields, particularly the source of popular livelihood, the economy. Because there was only one national interest, only one political party was required and possibly only a single leader.

The carving out of a new Turkish Republic from the domains of the Ottoman Empire provided new opportunities to experiment with social and economic development. The new and overwhelmingly powerful president Kemal Atatürk (elected in 1923), with his successors, undertook a wide-ranging series of measures to create a modern European state and society in Turkey. A new single political party, the People's Party of the Republic, was established in 1919. In 1934 women were given the vote and permitted to hold public office; by 1935 there were 17 women members in the National Assembly.

In a country where over 80 percent of the population was dependent upon agriculture, agrarian reform and improvement were vital. Atatürk established an agricultural bank to provide credit for agricultural exports, and later encouraged credit cooperatives for farmers. He set up a purely Turkish bank, the Ish Bank, in 1924, designed to finance public works, manufacturing, construction and commerce. (It was followed by the foundation of the Sümer bank in 1933 and the Eti bank in 1935.) During the 1920s and 1930s Turkey developed cotton and woolen mills, sulfur and coal mines, iron- and steel-making, and many other industries.

The government eliminated the old religious primary school system and through a newly created ministry of education endeavored to spread a secular educational system. The Arabic script was changed to roman (rendering much of the old order illiterate), and a system of adult night schools was introduced to reduce the level of illiteracy (92 percent of the population). Sports education was begun for the first time and Turkey began to participate in international sporting events. Women's ordinary and professional education was encouraged.

Many of these measures collided directly with an Islamic inheritance and had the potential to promote much discontent. Religious reform was therefore a necessary part of the program from forbidding women public employees to wear anything but Western dress (without the veil), banning for all men anything but Western dress (and allowing ecclesiastical dress only in places of worship), to the abolition of the Caliphate and of Islamic Shariat law. A modern legal system was introduced and all references to Islam removed from the constitution; Sunday, not Friday, became the weekly day of rest.

In sum, the reforms constituted, the governing party decided in 1935, a "Turkish form of State socialism". The appearance of Turkey was transformed and the Turkish model of economic policy persisted up to the great liberalizing and privatizing swing of the 1970s and 1980s.

▲ Boys at school, Turkey 1934. Atatürk's regime made education a priority – to the point, in principle, of punishing adults who remained illiterate. The alphabet was romanized and religious education abolished. Atatürk's theses – on History (that the Turks of Central Asia were the source of the world's great civilizations) and on the "Sun Language" (that modern languages were descended from Turkish) – made education the basis for a new Turkish nationalism.

◀ Turkish women greeting the government's grant of rights to women to vote and hold office in municipalities, 1930. The same happened later for national elections and office (by 1935, 17 women sat in the National Assembly). The women wear Western dress, which was strongly encouraged in Atatürk's Turkey as a means to modernization; it was compulsory for women in government jobs. Women were also encouraged to gain education and enter the professions; there were women judges, lawyers, bank directors, etc. Polygamy was abolished and the right to divorce established. The strongest progress was made among urban educated women. Many in the villages experienced little change.

THE
MODERNIST
WORLD

"Of all the arts the most important for Russia is, to my mind, that of the cinema."

V.I. LENIN, 1919

"What is the meaning of the riot of nudity into which the world of womanhood has plunged so frantically?…The war has profoundly disturbed the feminine mind…There are not enough men to go round…The vogue of the jazz dance is the symptom of this frenzy. The violent outbursts of vehement colors in feminine raiment is another. The hysterical eccentricity of feminine attire is another…But the climax of effrontery is the vogue of the bare back… And the tide of corruption flows more and more strongly every day. The decadent and degenerate poisons of Paris infect our fashions."

JAMES DOUGLAS, 1920

"Let's refresh ourselves ourselves with things that are not Art: the bathroom, the WC, the bathtubs, the telescope, the bicycle, the auto, the subways, the flatiron."

T. VAN DOESBURG, 1920s

"Style is a unity of principle animating all the work of an epoch, the result of a state of mind which has its own special character. Our own epoch is discovering day by day its own style. Our eyes unhappily are as yet unable to discern it."

LE CORBUSIER, 1923

"Before a child of our time finds his way clear to opening a book, his eyes have been exposed to such a blizzard of changing, colorful, conflicting letters that his chances of penetrating the archaic stillness of the book are slight."

WALTER BENJAMIN, 1925-26

"…This is what Vitaphone has done. Metropolitan Opera stars spreading their artistry to the far-flung corners of the world for untold millions to hear and enjoy…Can there be any doubt that a momentous event has come to pass in the industry?"

FILM DAILY, 1926

"Design will now take more advantage of the power of the machine to go beyond what the hand can do and will give us a whole new art."

HENRY FORD, c. 1927

	1919	1920	1921	1922
Film	• *The Cabinet of Dr Caligari* (Erich Pommer) (Ger) • 17 Apr: United Artists Corp founded by Chaplin, Pickford, Fairbanks and Griffith (USA) • 27 Apr: National Association of the Motion Picture Industry agreed to submit films to censorship (USA)	• Marriage of Mary Pickford and Douglas Fairbanks (USA)	• First full-length feature talkie, *Dream Street* (dir DW Griffith) produced by United Artists (USA) • *The Sheik*, with Rudolph Valentino (USA)	• 5 Mar: Premiere of *Nosferatu* by FW Murnau (Ger) • 21 Apr: Lee De Forest invented device to record voice and image on the same film (USA)
Media		• Feb: First public radio station set up by Marconi (USA)		• Sound effects fir used on radio • 5 Feb: *Reader's Digest* magazine first published (USA) • Oct: Foundation of the British Broadcasting Company (licence given 18 Jan 1923
Music	• Rise in popularity of jazz in Europe, after end of the war	• *Whispering/The Japanese Sandman*, by Paul Whiteman, became the first record to sell one million copies (USA) • Disk autochanger first devised by HMV (UK)	• 2 Aug: Death of Enrico Caruso (It) from pleurisy, at 48 • Opening of first public record-lending library, in Detroit (USA)	• Dance marathon a craze (USA)
Fashion and Design	• Europe's first mass-produced car, Citroën Type A, launched (Fr) • Bauhaus design school opened in Germany, with architect Walter Gropius as its first director • Suzanne Lenglen (Fr) shocked Wimbledon by wearing designer Jean Patou's short sleeveless tennis dresses	• Commercially viable acetate fiber made by British Celanese Ltd (UK) • First rib-knit elasticized one-piece bathing suit made by the Jantzen Co. (USA) • French edition of *Vogue* launched • Avant-garde magazine *L'Esprit Nouveau* founded by architect Le Corbusier (Fr)	• Charles Jourdan (Fr) set up shoe workshop • Coco Chanel (Fr) introduced her No. 5 perfume	• Discovery of tomb of Pharaoh Tutankhamun, increasing the popularity of Egyptian motifs in design • *Le Jardin des Modes* fashion magazine first published (Fr) • V Marguerritte's novel *La Garçonne* idealized the androgynous gamine (Fr)
Sport	• Mechanical hare perfected for greyhound racing (USA) • Jack Dempsey (USA) won world heavyweight boxing title for first time, with record ticket sales of $1 million	• Jul: Suzanne Lenglen (Fr) became the first player to win all three Wimbledon tennis titles • Aug: Opening of Antwerp Olympic Games (Belg)		• Aug: Unofficial women's Olympic Games held in Paris (Fr)
Misc.		• Jan: Beginning of Prohibition (USA) • Aug: Women given the vote in USA		

1923	1924	1925	1926	1927	1928	1929
● Release of *The ... Commandments*, ...CB de Mille (USA)	● 4 May: Opening of *Men*, with Pola Negri (USA) ● May: American Society of Composers, Authors and Publishers (ASCAP) denounced film and radio as "parasitic" (USA)	● *Battleship Potemkin*, directed by Sergei Eisenstein, released (USSR) ● Aug: *The Gold Rush*, starring Charlie Chaplin, released (USA)	● Release of *Metropolis*, directed by Fritz Lang (Ger) ● Release of *Ben Hur*, directed by Fred Niblo (USA) ● 23 Aug: Death of Rudolph Valentino, aged 31 (USA) ● Aug: *Don Juan* talkie released by Vitaphone, the film synchronized with phonograph records (USA)	● Clara Bow achieved fame as the It Girl (USA) ● *Napoleon*, directed by Abel Gance (Fr) ● 5 Jan: Movietone introduced by Fox (USA) ● 19 Apr: Mae West imprisoned for indecency in her film *Sex* (USA) ● May: *They're Coming to Get Me*, first film with dialog, released (USA) ● 6 Oct: Release of *The Jazz Singer* starring Al Jolson, the first widely seen talkie (USA)	● Walt Disney created his first Mickey Mouse cartoon, *Steamboat Willie* (USA) ● 21 Jul: Release of the first full-length all-talking movie, with sound on film: *The Lights of New York* (USA)	● Douglas Fairbanks Jnr married Joan Crawford (USA) ● Opening of *Pandora's Box*, starring Louise Brooks, directed by GW Pabst (Ger) ● First Academy Awards ceremony (USA) ● 5 Mar: Opening of *Broadway Melody*, the first film musical (USA)
...oundation of *Time ...*magazine (USA) ...Mar: Daily weather ...ecast first broadcast ...BBC (UK) ...ep: Foundation of ...*dio Times* magazine ...K)	● Feb: Radio used for educational purposes by Columbia University (USA)	● Feb: First issue of *New Yorker* magazine	● 27 Jan: John Logie Baird demonstrated television in London (UK) ● 30 Apr: Opening of radio picture service between London and the *New York Times*	● 1 Jan: Incorporation of British Broadcasting Corporation (UK) ● 25 Mar: First outside sports broadcast, of the Grand National, by BBC (UK) ● Oct: Fox's *Movietone News*, the first sound newsfilm, released (USA)	● 4 Jan: NBC organized a broadcasting hook-up covering 48 states and dozens of well-known entertainers (USA) ● 8 Feb: Television pictures broadcast by JL Baird from London to New York	● Color television demonstrated at Bell Laboratories (USA) ● Tintin cartoon first appeared in *The 20th Century* newspaper (Belg)
...2 Feb: Premiere ...*Rhapsody in Blue*, ...George Gershwin ...SA) ...Rise in popularity of ...Charleston		● Josephine Baker (USA/Fr) danced in *La Revue Nègre* in Paris	● Opening of *Gentlemen Prefer Blondes* on Broadway (USA) ● Soundtrack for *Don Juan* produced on the first 33⅓rpm disks (USA)	● 27 Dec: Broadway opening of *Showboat*, directed by Florenz Ziegfeld (USA)	● Opening of *The Threepenny Opera*, by Kurt Weill and Bertolt Brecht (Ger) ● Columbia (EMI) took over Pathé (UK)	● *Happy Days are Here Again* popular song (USA) ● Jul: Decca launched by Edward Lewis
	● Diaghilev's ballet *Le Train Bleu*, with designs by Chanel, epitomized the fashion for the sporting life (Fr) ● Hairdresser Antoine created fashion for dying gray hair blue (UK) ● Apr: Opening of British Empire Exhibition in London (UK)	● Opening of Exposition Internationale des Arts Décoratifs et Industriels Modernes in Paris (Fr) ● Fashion designer Madeleine Vionnet (Fr) began to use the bias cut, and female curves returned to vogue	● Wide range of synthetic colors for paint launched by Du Pont (USA) ● Anthropometric survey results used in Berlei Co's underwear designs (Aus)	● Prototype factory-assembled house, the Dymaxion House, designed by Buckminster Fuller (USA) ● Architect Mies van der Rohe organized the first postwar Deutscher Werkbund exhibition, launching the International Style (Ger)	● Ecole de la Chambre Syndicale de la Couture established to teach the craft of fashion (Fr) ● Harley Earl (USA) put in charge of General Motors new Art and Color section ● Design magazine *Domus* founded, edited by Gio Ponti (It)	● Raymond Loewy designed streamlined duplicator for Gestetner Co. (USA)
...Wembley Stadium, ...first national ...lti-sport center, ...ened in London ...K) ...Yankee Stadium ...ened in New York ...SA) ...First speedway race ...eeting held, in New ...uth Wales (Aus)	● Jan: First Winter Olympic Games held, at Chamonix (Fr) ● Jul: Paris Olympics attended by 42 nations (but not Germany) ● Jul: American Johnny Weissmuller became the first man to swim 100m in less than 1 minute		● First Central American and Caribbean Games held, in Mexico City (Mex) ● Women's Cricket Association formed (UK) ● Aug: Gertrude Ederle (USA) became the first woman to swim the English Channel	● 20-21 May: Charles Lindbergh made the first nonstop solo flight across the Atlantic (USA) ● First Ryder Cup held in golf (USA) ● Sep: Babe Ruth hit his 60th home run of the baseball season, a record that stood for 34 years (USA)	● Feb: Winter Olympics held in St Moritz (Swi) ● Aug: Women's athletics included in Olympics for first time, at Amsterdam (Neth)	● 11 Mar: World land speed record set at 223.2 mph (359 km/h) by Henry Segrave at Daytona Beach, Florida, in his streamlined car, Golden Arrow (USA)
					● Women in UK gained equal voting rights with men	● 25 Oct: Wall St Crash ushered in the Depression (USA)

Datafile

The 1920s saw the emergence of the United States as the country with an undisputed lead in the economics and business of modernism. Although Paris remained the world artistic center, New York was the city in which the leading advertising agencies were situated, and its rapidly rising skyline exemplified the spirit of the age. The effects of advertising, both economic and cultural, spread throughout the industrial world.

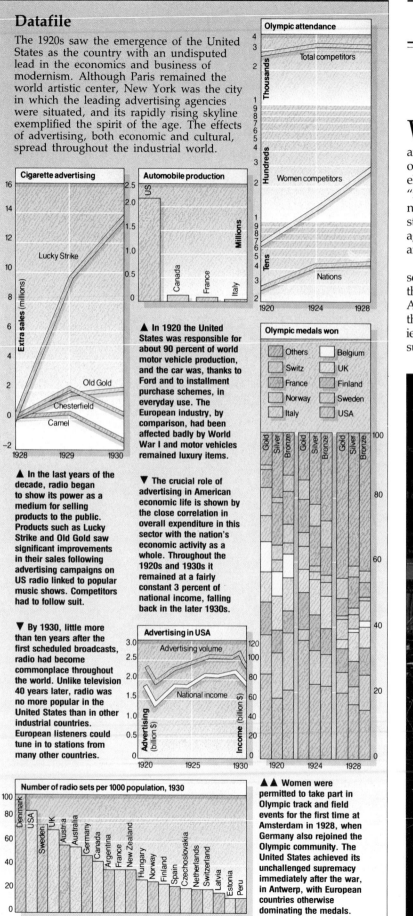

Cigarette advertising

(chart: Extra sales (millions) vs years 1928–1930, showing Lucky Strike, Old Gold, Chesterfield, Camel)

Automobile production

(chart: Millions, US, Canada, France, Italy)

Olympic attendance

(chart: Thousands/Hundreds/Tens, Total competitors, Women competitors, Nations, 1920–1928)

▲ In 1920 the United States was responsible for about 90 percent of world motor vehicle production, and the car was, thanks to Ford and to installment purchase schemes, in everyday use. The European industry, by comparison, had been affected badly by World War I and motor vehicles remained luxury items.

▲ In the last years of the decade, radio began to show its power as a medium for selling products to the public. Products such as Lucky Strike and Old Gold saw significant improvements in their sales following advertising campaigns on US radio linked to popular music shows. Competitors had to follow suit.

▼ The crucial role of advertising in American economic life is shown by the close correlation in overall expenditure in this sector with the nation's economic activity as a whole. Throughout the 1920s and 1930s it remained at a fairly constant 3 percent of national income, falling back in the later 1930s.

Olympic medals won

Legend: Others, Switz, France, Norway, Italy, Belgium, UK, Finland, Sweden, USA

(bar chart: Gold/Silver/Bronze for 1920, 1924, 1928, scale 0–100)

▼ By 1930, little more than ten years after the first scheduled broadcasts, radio had become commonplace throughout the world. Unlike television 40 years later, radio was no more popular in the United States than in other industrial countries. European listeners could tune in to stations from many other countries.

Advertising in USA

(chart: Advertising (billion $) and Income (billion $) vs 1920–1930, Advertising volume, National income)

Number of radio sets per 1000 population, 1930

(bar chart: Denmark, USA, Sweden, UK, Austria, Australia, Germany, Canada, Argentina, France, New Zealand, Hungary, Norway, Finland, Spain, Czechoslovakia, Netherlands, Switzerland, Latvia, Estonia, Peru)

▲ ▲ Women were permitted to take part in Olympic track and field events for the first time at Amsterdam in 1928, when Germany also rejoined the Olympic community. The United States achieved its unchallenged supremacy immediately after the war, in Antwerp, with European countries otherwise dominating the medals.

Whatever else called itself "modernist" in the first quarter of the 20th century – painting, architecture, literature – the great popular apostle of modernism was advertising. It spoke not to an elite of connoisseurs and literati, but to the new "mass man" (in reality, a woman). And it spoke not of adaptations of a literary or architectural style for the new age, but of the engine of that age, the new economy of consumption, pleasure and desire.

Advertising men proudly proclaimed themselves missionaries of modernity, champions of the consumerist esthetics of novelty and progress. Advertising provided the images of aspiration, the vision of a better future. It identified the anxieties of metropolitan life as personal problems such as "halitosis" and "clogged pores", rather

CELEBRITY AND MODERN LIFE

than any wider or deeper social malaise. At this, "the dawn of the distribution age", the art of the advertising agencies of New York's Madison Avenue was, in Michael Schudson's memorable phrase, Capitalist Realism.

The advertisement of education

In about 1914, advertisements began to emphasize the benefits that products brought the consumer, rather than just showing the product itself. In stressing the pleasures and benefits of consumption, advertising started to sell not simply goods, but a whole set of beliefs concerning the good life, and a collection of assumptions about what constituted proper satisfactions and rewards for industriousness. Wholeheartedly embracing their own ideology, advertising men saw

▼ A grand showroom of Model T Fords in 1927.

themselves engaged in a form of public service, educating their readers in the new way of life. Manufacturers, they argued, merely made products. Advertising manufactured customers, by stimulating desire not just for this thing or that, but for a higher standard of living generally. Properly used, advertising could regulate demand and thus keep the balance between production and consumption. Moreover, advertisers were ambassadors for the consumer to the producer; like the press barons, they saw themselves as representatives of public opinion, and missed the ironies implicit in their claims.

Public opinion, however, was regarded as fickle, flighty, and feminine. Recognizing that women were responsible for 85 percent of consumer spending, advertisers defined their mass

market as having feminine characteristics. Persistently complaining that it was not possible to sell things rationally to irrational creatures, they acknowledged the "need" to manipulate consumers for their own good through appeals to their emotions. As one argued, "If exaggeration will induce a million people to brush their teeth every morning, who would otherwise neglect that office, then the end justifies the means."

Unlike the movie mogul, advertising men tended to come from the cultural elite. From the middle-class reformers of the previous decades they adopted the idea that they should raise the masses out of their present condition, and they combined this idea with the 1920s image of business as benign and paternal. They identified their function as raising the intellectual and cultural standards of the mass audience, as well as improving its economic well-being. John Benson, President of the American Association of Advertising Agencies, argued in 1927, "It may be necessary to fool people for their own good. Doctors and even preachers know that and practice it. Average intelligence is surprisingly low. It is so much more effectively guided by its subconscious

impulses and instincts than by its reason."

Given such assumptions, it was not surprising that their audience continued to disappoint advertisers' ambitions for them by repeatedly demonstrating a preference, as commentator Leo Rosten put it, for "the frivolous against the serious, 'escape' as against reality ... the diverting as against the significant." Newspaper readers preferred tabloid pictures and comics to foreign news, radio listeners chose comedy shows rather than classical music. Reluctantly advertisers decided that their readers bought better when solicited by advertisements that imitated these debased cultural forms. Like tolerant fathers indulging their wilful daughters, advertisers accepted the preferences of the masses, so long as they, the rational elite, could regulate them.

The subordination of woman, the feckless consumer, was central to the new economic and ideological system. By endowing her with irrationality, the advertisers explained and even justified any of the system's foibles – for example, its obliteration of the distinction between needs and luxuries. The subservience of woman was assured by her dependence on men for the means

◀◀ Instead of "the drudgery of daily cleaning," new domestic machinery promised more time for leisure and childcare.

◀ At the office, advertisements depicted women decorating office machinery with reverential looks, rather than using it.

▼ Advertising thrived on anxieties; women were told that success in "the beauty contest of life" depended on soap or toothpaste.

Cleans everywhere — more easily.

Electrolux will free your home from dust more rapidly, more easily, and more thoroughly than any other cleaning system. It will pry into all awkward corners and under low furniture. It will slip over the windows, across the walls and ceiling, searching out every particle of dust and grit. This most efficient of all labour-saving devices will clean everything within the four corners of your house, even to the extent of purifying and disinfecting the very air you breathe. Think what this would mean to your home. How your rooms would be brightened and your labours lightened! The drudgery of daily cleaning would be broken. Instead there would be time in your home for the lighter duties and attentions which mean so much to extra happiness and comfort.

Send a postcard for a copy of the new Electrolux Booklet, or ask for a free demonstration in your own home or at our showrooms.

Electrolux
The New Cleanness

ELECTROLUX LIMITED, 153/155 Regent Street, LONDON, W.1 (Gerrard 4947/8) φ
Branches throughout Great Britain and Ireland

"A Miss is as good as her Smile" —

perfects the Smile

Twice a year have the dentist examine your teeth — twice a day brush them with
COLGATE'S RIBBON DENTAL CREAM.
This safe dentifrice cleans the teeth perfectly and polishes them to natural whiteness. You need not be afraid to smile if you use Colgate's.
Sold where you buy your toilet preparations.

COUPON. [Dept. P., 3/29/16.]
COLGATE & CO.,
46, Holborn Viaduct, London, E.C.
Please send me a trial size of Colgate's Ribbon Dental Cream. I enclose 3d. in stamps to defray cost of packing and postage.
Name ....
Address ....

The New Magazines

By 1920 the *Saturday Evening Post* had a
circulation of over two million copies a week,
and, with its mixture of fiction, current affairs
and biographies of public figures, was staple
reading for the American middle-class family.
A newer, brasher style of magazine appeared in
the 1920s. The magazine equivalent of the
tabloid dailies, *True Story* and its imitators
found a new audience of young, working-class
women eager for advice and reassurance. Every
story had to be written in the first person in
simple, homely language, and preach a strong
moral lesson. Perhaps the most enduring
stylistic change was inaugurated by *Time*,
launched by Henry Luce and Briton Hadden in
1922 on the premise that "People are
uninformed because no publication has adapted
itself to the time which busy men are able to
spend simply keeping informed". Individuals,
not governments or mysterious forces, made
Times news: "Since the personalities of politics
make public affairs live...it is important to
know what they drink, to what gods they pray
and what kinds of fights they love."

▲▶ The *Saturday Evening
Post* was for all the family.
Time represented a sharper
journalism attuned to the
modern business age.

to consume, and her duty was to "keep young
and beautiful" through the practice of consumption. Cosmetic advertisements surrounded
women in their boudoirs with mirrors, representatives of the judgmental gaze of a male society,
and advised their readers, "Watch out you don't
disappoint him". Such images emphasized the
importance of appearance in the increasingly
mobile and anonymous culture of the metropolis.
They also endorsed the act of looking at women
as objects of desire.

Increasingly, advertising addressed its readers
as a friend, advisor or coach, more experienced in
the ways of the new world. Companies invented
fictitious characters, such as General Mills' Betty
Crocker, to personalize their products and advise
their use. They adopted a style of presentation
that has been compared with radio "crooning",
an intimate, conversational tone of voice that
belied the nature of mass communications by im-
plying an individual relationship between
speaker and listener, advisor and consumer.
Advertisements reassured readers that the com-
plexities and fragmentations of modern life could
be enjoyed, and that experts in "public service"
would provide them with as much advice as they
needed in the new techniques and arts of personal presentation, appearance, manipulation
and seduction.

Radio, advertising and education

Radio, child of the new technology of electronics,
was the first new medium of the 20th century.
The Marconi Company had begun com-
municating with ships at sea in 1897; the military
applications of radio speeded its development.
Wartime British and American research into the
transmission of speech pioneered the close
cooperation between government and corporate
research in what was later termed the
"military–industrial complex". The United States
government encouraged the major communica-

tion corporations, American Telephone and Telegraph (AT & T) and General Electric (GE), to
create the Radio Corporation of America (RCA) as
the instrument of American technological
preeminence. In Britain, Marconi maintained its
dominance of the radio industry.

All this was undertaken with no thought that
radio would be used principally for broadcasting.
The fact that radio signals could be received by
anyone with suitable equipment was considered
a major handicap by its military users, and a
nuisance by government agencies responsible for
supervising the chaotic confusion of signals in
early radio. Demand for broadcasting came from
amateur enthusiasts who had bought or built
receiving sets to listen in to radio signals. In June
1920 the British newspaper the *Daily Mail* sponsored a broadcast recital by the opera star Dame
Nellie Melba, which was heard by listeners all
over Europe. The publicity this generated showed
the new medium's potential public appeal, but
further developments in Britain were hindered by
official hostility to Marconi and by complaints
from the military that an invention ideally suited
to be a "servant of mankind" was being treated as
"a toy to amuse children".

In the United States Westinghouse, excluded
from the RCA–GE–AT&T combine, recognized
the commercial potential of broadcasting. It opened
its first station, KADA, in Pittsburgh, in the fall of
1920, as part of an aggressive marketing campaign
to sell radio sets. Its success was rapidly imitated,
and by the end of 1922 there were 570 licensed
stations. As with the nickelodeon boom in 1906
(see page 36), radio provided a new means of
consuming leisure. The huge demand for entertainment received directly into the home out-
stripped the manufacturers' capacity to supply
equipment. By 1924 two million receivers had
been sold.

It was far from clear exactly what this new commodity was, or, indeed, how it should be used.

When the world's first radio play was broadcast by the BBC in Britain in 1923, listeners were encouraged to switch their lights out so they could "more easily imagine the scenes". Programming on early American stations was diverse, mixing live and recorded conservatory music with talks, rudimentary news reports and broadcasts of church services. Almost half the stations that were operating in 1922 were run by radio and electrical manufacturers as a way of merchandising their goods. Others were run by newspapers, department stores and other commercial concerns seeking public goodwill.

These stations were the beginnings of commercial radio, but the first problem they had to solve was how to turn broadcasting into a commercial operation. Once the receiver had been purchased, no further transaction took place between the supplier of home entertainment and its consumer. As John Reith, first Director General of the British Broadcasting Company explained, "The broadcast is as universal as the air ... It does not matter how many thousands there may be listening; there is always enough for others, when they too wish to join in ... It is a reversal of the natural law that the more one takes, the less there is left for others." What, then, could be sold?

The solution devised by commercial radio in effect involved selling nothing to the listeners, but rather selling the listeners themselves to advertisers, who paid for the opportunity to persuade listeners to buy whatever they were selling. The first commercial was broadcast in August 1922, but such a solution to the financing of radio was widely regarded as undesirable, even by advertisers themselves, who saw radio as "the great genteel hope" for the cultural redemption of the masses through the "public service" of business paternalism. In the first years of American radio, one in every eight stations was operated by an educational institution, but by 1925 it was clear that radio was commercially too useful to be left to educationalists. With the passage of the Radio Act in 1927, American airwaves were dominated by three networks supplying local stations with packages of programs: two were fed by the National Broadcasting Company (NBC), a subsidiary of RCA, and the third was the Columbia Broadcasting System (CBS).

To an even greater extent than the movies, radio became both a commodity and an instrument of consumer culture. By 1930 there were 13 million radio sets in use in more than 40 percent of American households, who listened to a mixture of variety shows, based on the format of vaudeville, drama (predominantly comedy, with the blackface duo of Amos 'n Andy, minstrel show characters adapted to radio, the most popular individual program in the late 1920s and early 1930s), news, recorded and live music.

The first priority for any government was to organize the allocation of frequencies. The method used in practice dictated the shape of the national broadcasting system. From the outset, British broadcasters looked aghast at the American experience and insisted that they would learn from and avoid American mistakes. To prevent the chaos of too many competing stations, the British

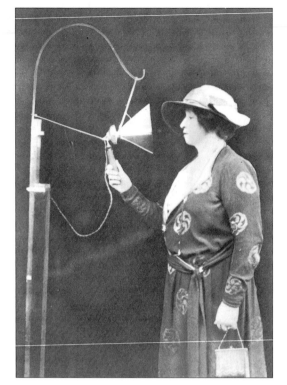

Post Office proposed that equipment manufacturers should form a consortium, the British Broadcasting Company (BBC), to provide regular transmissions. Advertising was prohibited, and the company was to be financed through an annual licence fee on each receiving set – an entirely different principle from the American system, in that it charged listeners for what they heard. The BBC's monopoly over the airwaves meant that it could adopt a very different attitude toward its audience and programming than that produced through commercial competition in the United States. In 1926 it became the British Broadcasting Corporation, "a Public Commission operating in the National Interest".

The BBC was an organization formed by the British establishment in its own self-image, reflecting the values and beliefs of the professional middle class. Under its first and most influential Director General, John (later Lord) Reith, it became almost a domestic diplomatic service, representing "the best of British" to the British themselves. It fervently rejected American influence: Reith and his class saw the products of American mass culture such as Hollywood movies as childish, vulgar and false – a demonstration of why British broadcasting must avoid "giving the public what it wants". British and American broadcasting evolved into their different forms, and provided the two prototypes for other countries, because of the different attitudes of their culturally dominant upper middle class to the new consumer culture. In the United States the middle class were firmly in its vanguard, defining themselves around its material precepts. In Britain, however, older modes of class definition, which were critical of the materialism of American culture, still operated.

Reith was the architect of the BBC's notion of public service broadcasting, but in expressing it

◄ Dame Nellie Melba's broadcast concert of opera music from eastern England in 1920 reached an audience across Europe. Radio's earliest years were marked by confusion about its purposes, content and audience. For many people the pleasure lay in the skill required in the "DX-ing", getting good reception from the most distant stations possible. But as a columnist of *Wireless Magazine* complained in 1925, "Every woman must have noticed how different her point of view about wireless is from that of her husband or son. To women, wireless is a joy, a distraction, a companion, or an excitement; but it is never what it is to men – a toy. They want to play with it and fiddle with it incessantly, just as they do with their cars."

► By mid-decade, the radio was on its way to becoming a center of domestic life in the middle-class households of North America and Europe, as here in Britain.

▲ As "listening-in" became more an everyday activity, radio sets, such as the British design of about 1930, ceased to be just assemblies of electrical components and came to look more like pieces of furniture.

It is occasionally indicated to us that we are apparently setting out to give the public what we think they need – and not what they want – but few know what they want and very few what they need... In any case it is better to overestimate the mentality of the public than to underestimate it.

JOHN REITH 1924

You cannot underestimate the taste of the American public.

ARTHUR BRISBANE

Fads of the Twenties

▲ Atop a flagpole in New Jersey

The 1920s were years in which there were fads more numerous – and in general sillier – than at other times. Fueled by the dare-devil mood of the age and largely sponsored by a tabloid press in search of sensations, some of these fads were both dangerous and shortlived. One of the most unlikely was flagpole sitting – where some individuals managed to survive for 10 days or more living on a tiny platform atop a pole supported by nothing but stirrups. Sitters took short breaks every hour, but otherwise ate, slept and lived on their poles. The most famous, Shipwreck Kelly, claimed to have spent 145 days on various poles during 1929.

Marathon-dancing, in which couples competed for endurance records, was also more entertaining for its spectators than its performers. Couples would dance for days with breaks of only a few minutes each hour, until exhaustion or injury overcame them. One marathon in Chicago lasted 119 days.

A less dramatic but more enduring phenomenon was the sudden craze for crossword puzzles that began in 1924. Roller-skating, yo-yos and parlor games like contract bridge and Mah Jongg were also promoted through newspaper columns.

he acted as a spokesman for the politically powerful, the great and the godly of the nation. When it was established, a dominant version of "national" culture was already firmly in place among the small and cohesive British ruling class, who administered the country through systems of appointment and delegation rather than through centralized state control. The BBC inherited the idea of "public service", defined as the paternalist responsibility of the upper class, as part of the ideological baggage of the British Empire.

The BBC made available the full heritage of English high culture, previously the preserve of a privileged minority, to every member of the nation, at virtually no cost. This *was* a great cultural transformation. However, no-one suggested that the lower classes themselves should be permitted access to the airwaves. Sports, popular music and entertainment were certainly broadcast; by 1934, indeed, the BBC was broadcasting more light music, comedy and vaudeville than any other European station, but the manner in which they were presented, like the voices of the announcers, remained indomitably upper-middle-class.

This attitude of uplift was part of Reith's idea of the BBC as a kind of national church. He argued that it should use the "brute force of monopoly... to instruct and fashion public opinion, to banish ignorance and slavery, to contribute richly and in many ways to the sum total of human wellbeing." Much of the BBC's effort in its early years went towards achieving respectability among the cultural establishment, by avoiding controversial material as well as by educating its audiences and preserving the proprieties of Sunday by broadcasting only church services and serious music.

While the BBC's success in establishing itself as a national institution led other nations – Japan, for example – to imitate its system of government control, it was nevertheless accused of failing to provide for large sections of society.

In the 1930s as much as half the radio audience in Britain tuned to European commercial stations, Radio Luxembourg and Radio Normandie, on Sundays. Resistance to the BBC was not simply a matter of content. Radio entered peoples' daily lives in an immediate and intimate manner. In its content and financial organization, commercial radio was part of a larger notion, the promotion of a consumer society – giving America's businessmen, as one executive said, "a latchkey to nearly every home in the United States".

The BBC and its government-run imitators in other countries had to enter people's homes not as one instrument in a shared culture of consumption, but in the name of a common national culture, which they, almost alone, were creating. National radio was an agency of cultural centralization at a time when many local communities retained their diversity and a tight-knit resistance to intrusion. The national culture of the BBC reflected the elite culture of southern England; it was inevitable that this culture would meet regional and class-based resistance. Broadcasting would be a powerful instrument in the erosion of the cultural independence and diversity of the regions; not until World War II was there a real need for national unity for the BBC to serve.

"Never before in all the black history of slumland has such a light shone upon the darkness of human ignorance and domestic wretchedness... Imagine what it must mean to East London when the Queen's Hall Orchestra floods its foul courts and dark alleys with the majestic strains of the Fifth Symphony... Imagine, too, what it must mean to the minds of those men and women whose only serious mental effort hitherto has been to grasp the rights and wrongs of their economic condition when a man of science speaks to them of the stars."

RADIO TIMES, UK 1924

Sport and the mass media

Throughout all of Europe and the United States, changes in work patterns and new expectations of leisure in the interwar period fueled a demand for leisure that manifested itself in a growing variety of sporting activities. More people had more time for leisure, which was increasingly viewed as something they had a right to enjoy. Many also experienced a genuine rise in disposable income, and although some sports remained socially exclusive, increasing numbers of people enjoyed spectating and more working-class people found themselves able to participate in a range of sports. As one commentator observed of Britain in the 1920s: "The majority of working people, even those in poor material circumstances, were not entirely powerless in the face of external change to shape their own destiny and to gain a sense of well-being from their own spare-time experiences."

The hedonism that marked the 1920s was accompanied by notions of achievement and challenge, record attendance, and the rapid acceleration of commercialized sport. Between 1919 and 1926 Jack Dempsey, the heavyweight boxing champion of the world, drew crowds totalling over one million. The first luxurious sports areas were built such as London's Wembley Stadium,

◄ One of the earliest uses of radio for entertainment beyond music and news was in the field of sports commentating. In the United States in particular, the new skill of describing a fast-moving sporting event as it happened did much to spread enthusiasm for both sport and radio. This outside broadcast is reporting on a rifle shooting contest.

◄▲ Motor racing was one of the sports popular with the rich in the 1920s. The fascination was technical as much as sporting and the masterpieces of engineering and design produced by the Italian Ettore Bugatti (1881–1947) epitomized the esthetic appeal of the sport. Their handbuilt cars remained luxury items to be enjoyed by those with taste. Bugatti built fewer than ten copies of his classic mid-twenties model, Type 41.

which opened in 1923 and was designed to hold 100,000 spectators. In the 1920s Wembley hosted many types of sporting event, including soccer, tennis, boxing, ice hockey and greyhound racing. Throughout the decade attendance records were broken at professional and elite amateur events. Newspapers and radio brought distant events to a public primed for news, and, for the media, sport had the distinct advantage of taking place, and making news, according to an established calendar of events fixed well in advance. For its spectators, the predictability of sporting events provided a stable element in an unstable world. Sporting events enacted essentially optimistic dramas – there was always a victor (whether as hero or villain), a result, a decision, a definite outcome, and always another game in which wrongs could be righted or triumphs repeated.

Sport as a central interest for many people has sometimes been explained in terms of the backcloth it provided for accommodating the larger and less predictable world beyond. Sport became a celebration of human achievement, constructed around individual sportsmen and sportswomen whose personalities were publicized and manipulated by the media. Although they were not the creation of this period, by the 1920s the notions of sporting records and achievements resonated with the cultural values of capitalism. The statistics, totals and averages of a sport such as American football – the "earned run average", or the "yards gained rushing" – bore marked similiarities to the economic statistics, such as the Gross National Product or the Grade Point Average, that were beginning to enter everyday consciousness at this time.

The obsession with records

In the United States there was particular fascination with records. Two uniquely American games, baseball and football, lent themselves to detailed quantification and established a framework for other sports. Interest was mobilized by the press, but radio broadcasting transformed it into a new home-based entertainment. Matches and results were analyzed and players' techniques discussed long before the press could report on them. Through this process sports personalities emerged, their identities developed and embellished by the media, the celebration of their accomplishments part of the entertainment industry's invention of celebrity. Heroic figures in the culture of industrial capitalism, sportsmen and women were recognized as maximizers of performance and output.

In the 1920s the names of Babe Ruth and Red Grange became familiar because of their prowess in baseball and American football respectively. Babe Ruth was the first modern athlete to be "packaged" and "sold" to the American people, not only for his sporting prowess but also for his character. He became a national celebrity who helped to make professional baseball America's number one pastime. Red Grange has been regarded as one of the greatest college football players of all time. His evasive running earned him the title of "the Galloping Ghost" and when he signed for the Chicago Bears in 1925 not only

did he secure a contract worth $3,000 per game but also, in the eyes of many, conferred respectability on professional football itself. From this time on, it was clear that money could be made in the game by college graduates.

Women in sport

In the interwar period, the sport of lawn tennis proved to be a platform for female achievement. Suzanne Lenglen dominated the game from 1919 to 1926, and redefined what could be achieved by women. One historian said of her: "Her gifts were supreme. Her biting accuracy, coupled with divine balletic grace, dominated the game for so long without real challenge, that her immortality is unquestioned."

Lenglen was unbeaten in seven years of tournament play: she won six Wimbledon Championships, six French Championships and two Olympic gold medals at Antwerp in 1920. The combination of her tennis-playing ability and radically different clothing on court attracted considerable comment. In her last Wimbledon triumph Lenglen won the 1925 Championships, losing only five games in the process. A year later she withdrew from Wimbledon after a disagreement over playing schedules and turned professional, for a reported sum of $100,000.

In the 1920s American players were preeminent in men's tennis. "Big Bill" Tilden treated the

▼► Foremost among the heroes and heroines of the 1920s were the achievers and record breakers of the sporting world. As a growing enthusiasm for sport drew ever larger crowds of spectators, these men and women became increasingly marketable, not simply for their sporting prowess, but also for their personalities. The darlings of the American public were the legendary baseball player Babe Ruth (right center) and footballer Red Grange (right top). Atlanta-born golfer Bobby Jones (below) achieved international fame, as did Frenchwomen Suzanne Lenglen – six times winner of the Wimbledon tennis tournament (left).

game as a science, and developed theories of stroke-play, the power-game, tactics, and the crowd-puller. The enormous public appeal of Lenglen and Tilden helped tennis to develop a mass following.

Tennis was becoming a more active game for women, if only in a form that implicitly accepted that women were physically weaker and therefore played a "ladylike" version of the men's game, though to some extent players like Lenglen threatened such assumptions. In most sports women continued to suffer opposition and discrimination. Women's athletics was one of the last sports to be organized, and throughout the 1920s antagonists of women's sports viewed athletics as indecent, unsuited to women's physiques and in danger of producing "an unnatural race of Amazons". The struggle over the inclusion of women's athletics in the Olympic Games came to a head when the International Olympic Committee (IOC) refused to include them in the Games of 1920 and 1924. In defiance of IOC policy Alice Milliat organized the first Women's Olympics in 1922, which were also held in 1926, 1930 and 1934 under the new title of the Women's World Games. These events were unexpectedly successful, attracting large numbers of competitors and spectators from western Europe, the British Empire and North America, and athletics became a growth sport for women.

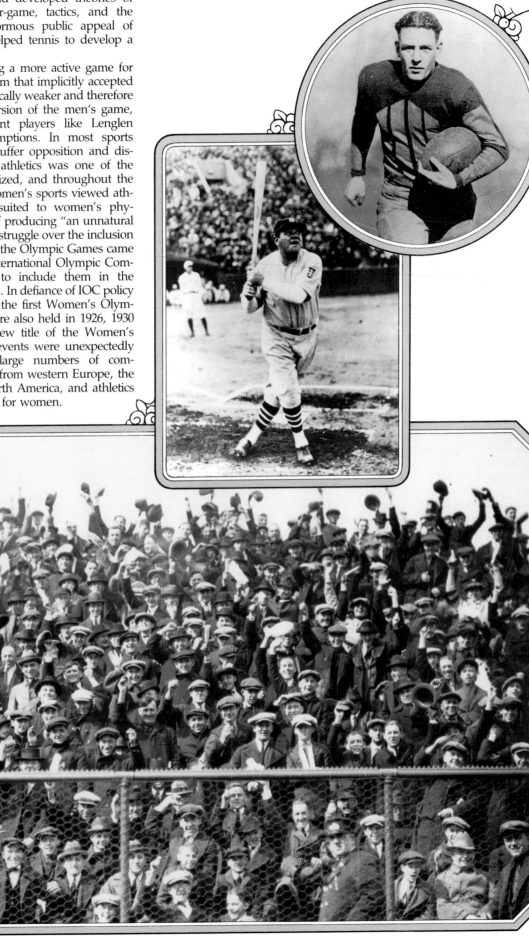

THE CHALLENGE OF THE AIR

Flight was the adventure of the interwar years as developing technology briefly made aviation a competitive sport, in search of new speed and endurance records. None captured the popular imagination of the media so much as Charles Lindbergh's nonstop solo flight from New York to Paris in 1927. Competing for a prize of £25,000 which had claimed six lives in the previous year, 24-year-old Lindbergh took off in a Ryan monoplane he called "The Spirit of St Louis" from Roosevelt Field, Long Island on the morning of 20 May. Thirty-three and a half hours later he landed at Le Bourget, Paris.

Lindbergh's flight seemed to have an esthetic purity about it. Unlike his rivals, he flew alone. Although he had financial backing, his plane was built on a shoestring budget. It had no navigational system, and Lindbergh memorized his route. His exploits fed the hunger to discover new objects of attention, new sensations, new people. Christened "Lucky Lindy" and "the Flying Fool" by an already enthusiastic press before he took off, Lindbergh's story sold a record number of newspapers. After the flight, he appeared to confirm his heroic status by remaining aloof from movie offers and requests for testimonials. But in 1932 his baby was kidnapped, and Lindbergh again became front-page news for the weeks of the prolonged hunt for the child and then the trial of the alleged kidnapper Bruno Hauptmann. It offered the press and public another opportunity to gawk at a celebrity's private life; one imposter who claimed to know where the child was, confessed that he had made his story up to "become famous". Later in the 1930s Lindbergh's open support for the Nazis led President Franklin Roosevelt to denounce him as a Fascist.

▲ Charles Lindbergh and "The Spirit of St Louis", the Ryan monoplane in which he made his first nonstop flight across the Atlantic. Stripped to its essentials and with only minimal stores of food and water, the plane carried almost its own weight in fuel, and barely cleared the telegraph wires on take-off. Lindbergh's flying position was so cramped that he could only look out of the front of the cockpit through a periscope. His description of the flight expressed the extreme solitariness of his flight into the unknown.

▼ Barnstorming flyers provided spectacles of all kinds for fairground audiences in the 1920s, including this unlikely game of tennis. They also offered rides to the public – "Your money back if you get killed".

◀ Lindbergh's return to New York in June was a moment of high optimism. The 1800 tonnes of paper in his ticker-tape parade recorded stock prices at record levels. More than a million people cheered.

▼ Lindbergh's achievement was commemorated in every imaginable way. A town in Texas, was named after him. Songs were composed for him, and a new jazz dance was called the "Lindy hop."

LUCKY LINDY!

Words by
L. WOLFE GILBERT
Music by
ABEL BAER

LEO. FEIST NEW YORK

▲ A crowd of 100,000 was waiting to greet the *Spirit of St Louis* when it arrived at Le Bourget airport thirty-three and a half hours after Lindbergh had taken off from Roosevelt Field, Long Island. In just under two days he had become the most famous private citizen in the world.

135

Datafile

No other decade – except perhaps the sixties – can rival the twenties in its typical image as a "golden age" of popular music.

The first commercially-made electrical recordings appeared in 1925 and set in motion a transformation both in sound quality (therefore also in people's expectations) and in performance style. The most immediate benefits, however, were felt by radio, the successful expansion of which depended very much on its ability to broadcast popular dance music live, from studios or from clubs and ballrooms.

Music proved extremely useful in the commercialization of radio in the twenties, as program sponsors used popular themes or, more often, the sound of individual bands, to give themselves an identity in the public mind. By the middle of the decade, too, the network system was fully operational, permitting the same music to be heard simultaneously across the country – in cars as well as homes.

Phonograph manufacture

21%
Total value 28.2 million $
1914

28%
Total value 158.5 million $
1919

Cost of materials
Value of products

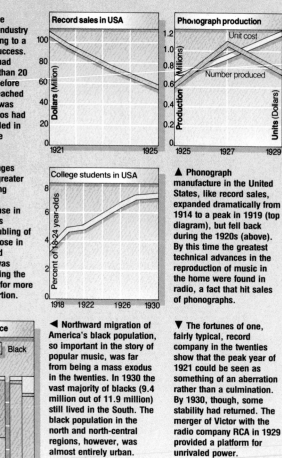

▶ At the start of the decade the record industry seemed to be looking to a future of assured success. Yet by 1921 sales had peaked, and more than 20 years would pass before such levels were reached again. The reason was radio. Sales of radios had more than quadrupled in the first years of the decade.

Record sales in USA

▶ Among the changes which explain the greater prominence of young people in Jazz Age America, the increase in college education is significant. The doubling of the proportion of those in the 18–24 age-band attending college was important in providing the solid underpinning for more confident self-assertion.

College students in USA

Phonograph production

▲ Phonograph manufacture in the United States, like record sales, expanded dramatically from 1914 to a peak in 1919 (top diagram), but fell back during the 1920s (above). By this time the greatest technical advances in the reproduction of music in the home were found in radio, a fact that hit sales of phonographs.

US population by race

White Black Others

◀ Northward migration of America's black population, so important in the story of popular music, was far from being a mass exodus in the twenties. In 1930 the vast majority of blacks (9.4 million out of 11.9 million) still lived in the South. The black population in the north and north-central regions, however, was almost entirely urban.

▼ The fortunes of one, fairly typical, record company in the twenties show that the peak year of 1921 could be seen as something of an aberration rather than a culmination. By 1930, though, some stability had returned. The merger of Victor with the radio company RCA in 1929 provided a platform for unrivaled power.

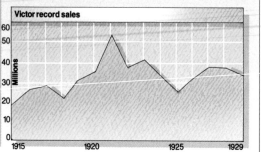

Victor record sales

On 9 August 1920 in a New Jersey recording studio, Paul Whiteman, a symphony orchestra musician-turned-dance-band leader from Denver, Colorado, made the first of several attempts to record some newly-minted Tin Pan Alley tunes. The band's first record (*Whispering/Japanese Sandman*), released four months later, rapidly sold two million copies, emphasizing the ascendancy now enjoyed by records over sheet music, and propelling the portly figure of Paul Whiteman to fame and fortune, and to leadership of a new musical dynasty as King of Jazz. In the judgment of posterity he was an imposter; the true royal blood flowed in darker veins. But Whiteman's bland music, with its careful orchestration and its occasional "hot" moments, was real jazz to a large proportion of its listeners who had never been exposed to black music in undiluted form.

Whiteman himself was more opportunist than rebel. He had grown, he said, "listless, dissatisfied, despondent" with the life of a classical musician and had seen the chance of greater rewards in popular culture. The music of which he was a leading exponent was in fact to become the focus of a collision between the old standards of behavior and the new. In the 1920s appropriation and assimilation of black culture continued; the blandness of Whiteman's music seemed more comfortable, staking out a neutral ground amid the furore. There had been collisions between opposing standards before; what took place in the twenties can be seen as a culmination of a long-term process. But new factors had added an undertow of unease to the American scene. The end of the war and the failure of the peace brought a declining interest in world affairs, a shriveling of idealism and a growth in the attraction of pleasure and entertainment. Labor problems, the fear of communism and the rise of the racist Ku Klux Klan each in its own way signified an alliance between a narrow "respectability" and repression.

Prohibition and the Jazz Age

Then there was Prohibition, the policy which made the manufacture, sale and consumption of alcoholic drinks illegal throughout the twenties. F. Scott Fitzgerald's familiar phrase, the Jazz Age, summed up the spirit of the period; Prohibition was the most potent symbol of its lifestyle. A nostalgic view of the period presents jazz and Prohibition as expressions of the triumph of the pleasure principle. Historians on the other hand may see the hedonism of the era as a mask for alienation, and the conservative backlash as a reminder of the power of the establishment. Both jazz and Prohibition make most sense when seen as outstanding examples of the continuing struggle in mainstream American

THE JAZZ AGE

culture between two pronounced tendencies, which have been called the "ecstatic" – celebratory, immediate, implicit – and the "didactic" – controlled, predictable, explicit.

The evidence of the twenties suggests that it was a complex encounter, rarely clear-cut. The Volstead Act, which initiated the era of Prohibition, had more than one ironic consequence. The practices it sought to curb were made more desirable, as behavior hitherto thought of as mildly antisocial now became deliberate revolt. Criminal elements shed some of their marginality and found themselves the center of attention in the tabloid press. The sinister social evil of organized crime was seen to foster and encourage another marginal group - the black subculture, whose music and dance provided the bulk of the entertainment in the gangster-run clubs.

The motives and actions of the predominantly well-to-do urban white Americans enticed by the thrill of "slumming" in Harlem were not unequivocal, either. In part they were reacting against the restrictions of Victorian morality, but there was also a sense in which they felt their wealth required them to consume: something, anything. Often to their intense discomfort, they found that

- The appeal of jazz
- Prohibition and the Jazz Age
- Jazz and decadence
- White and black culture
- White popular music
- The lost generation
- Flappers and the new fashion
- The influence of art deco style

► Tin Pan Alley, West 28th St, New York, the center of the song-publishing industry in its heyday, was so called because of the cacophony of songpluggers' pianos.

▼ The success of the white Original Dixieland Jazz Band, who took New York by storm in 1917, inspired imitators. Some combined novelty effects with suggestions of southern carnivals.

what was fundamental to the pleasure principle by which they lived at night, was anathema to the principles of personal gain around which their daytime economic world was constructed. As an added twist, the world towards which the pleasure-seekers gravitated was one where pleasures were made available purely as hard-nosed business responses to demand. Organized crime, "the bastard son of corporate capitalism", sold illegal pleasures, providing a perfect metaphor for the contradictions in the businesses of entertainment and leisure.

The argument over jazz, which raged for most of the decade, can be seen as an expression of the conflict between the ecstatic and the didactic. Opposition to the new popular music was mounted, as before, on two fronts: esthetic and moral. The attack was greatly intensified in response to what was perceived as the increasingly rapid spread of degenerative influences. The object of condemnation, collectively known as jazz, included various related styles: the "raggy" music of white New Orleans musicians such as the Original Dixieland Jazz Band and their imitators (music that was itself a limited imitation of the black music most closely associated with the Crescent City), the syncopated dance bands, the Charleston craze, the songs of George Gershwin or Irving Berlin, and the "symphonic" jazz of Paul Whiteman. Equal censure was not applied to them all, but at the start of the decade at least few distinctions were made. Esthetic criticism ranged from the sardonic (Thomas Edison said he preferred jazz records played backwards) to the loftily dismissive. Moral criticism was more strident: jazz, savage, primitive, appealing to the basest instincts, rotted moral fiber, spread a whorehouse culture, polluted children, caused illegitimacy and all manner of unspeakable crimes. A *Ladies Home Journal* article of August 1921 revealed the phobia that lay at the root of the antagonism: "Jazz originally was the accompaniment of the voodoo dancer, stimulating the half-crazed barbarian to the vilest deeds."

There were other reasons for the attack, among them the confusion felt in small-town America over the rapidly changing morality of the big cities. At their core was a perceived threat to white Anglo-Saxon supremacy which found in the sensualism of black America the obverse of all its cherished self-images, and heard in jazz the approaching menace of physical and mental defilement.

Those enticed by the new music reacted in the opposite way to the same perception. Beneath the romantic image of freedom from convention, of individual self-gratification in a return to a more instinctual life, lay stereotypes of black culture as "primitive", sensual and culturally naive. Even among those few members of white society who were familiar with "real" jazz and blues, the fascination of discovery was tinged with paternalism and exoticism.

To these stereotypes of black America were added others; the threat posed by the former slave was complemented by that offered by the more recent immigrant. White ethnic groups had mediated earlier in the popularization of black-

▲ Floorshows such as this in a 1920s Chicago nightclub reflected the public's ambivalence to black culture. While all gradations of color were permitted in male performers, a policy of employing only light-skinned girls ("high yallers") persisted in the 1930s.

▶ Buyers of sheet music did not want for choice of styles or subjects. Love ballads dominated the market, but songwriters were not slow to incorporate current fashions into their "jazzy" numbers. More significant for the future of the industry was the lure of the movies, which claimed many song-writers by 1930.

derived dances (see page 42), and they now contributed to the dissemination of jazz. Jewish songwriters such as Irving Berlin and George Gershwin, who had previously been bracketed with ragtime composers, were now included under the new label; the phenomenal success of their music, and in particular of Gershwin's attempt to blend jazz-derived rhythms and sounds with classical techniques in his *Rhapsody in Blue* (1926), caused consternation among some cultural guardians. This was not attributable solely to concern for the *musical* tradition being challenged; the threat was also one of blood, all the more ominous because the music symbolized an alliance between the erstwhile marginal groups of Jews and blacks.

Among songwriters, Gershwin was one of

▶ For young socialites such as these in Berlin the new fashions in music and dance were experienced at several removes from their roots in black Amerca. The naiveté of the European gaze across the Atlantic has been overlaid by awareness of the momentous political and social developments taking place much closer to home.

▲ One thing at least united all record buyers; the need to change the needle. Access to the world of recorded sound depended entirely on these humble but essential objects. The diamond stylus of Edison's *pièce de resistance*, the Blue Amberol cylinder, was far superior to the steel needle required to play discs; but cylinders had been almost entirely replaced by discs.

those most clearly interested in Afro-American music. Most interesting of the white ethnic performing musicians who gathered around jazz were the Chicago-based players, influenced by both black and white New Orleans musicians. Responding in a way that would be echoed in the fifties by many young whites as they encountered rhythm & blues, Bix Beiderbecke, Mezz Mezzrow, Hoagy Carmichael and others behaved as they did in embracing a new-found way of life that offered an escape from the constraints of their own inherited culture.

Popular music now enjoyed an importance in the debate about culture that was probably without parallel. One has to look back as far as the controversy which raged in 18th-century New England over congregational singing styles to find anything like a precedent. That argument had derived, fundamentally, from the clash of literate and orally based cultures. In the 1920s the players had changed and the plot was more complex, but the underlying antithesis was the same. The gradual "blackening" of white America offered a fundamental challenge to the status quo, and music was in its vanguard. This "blackening" was also taking place in speech, in sport, in dance, but the immediacy of the performance-based black music made it clear that the challenge was not one only of esthetics or morals, or even of racial purity. Jazz was the sound of an orally-based subordinate black culture striking at the basic machinery of control used by the dominant white culture – literacy.

Jazz, blues and the black audience

Within black culture itself music was perceived rather differently. Through the recording industry, the blacks' vernacular culture was made

available to them as a result of mass production becoming part of the popular culture industry. On 10 August 1920 (a day after Paul Whiteman's first studio session), Mamie Smith became the first black singer to record a "blues". *Crazy Blues*, her second record, was actually more of a pop vaudeville song but its commercial success revealed to the record companies the existence of an unsuspected market, and resulted in the so-called "race records" – labels recording and marketing blues, jazz, gospel and other, less readily definable styles for the black audience.

Whatever the particular style – from the guttural dialect of the Mississippi bluesman to the incipient star quality of Louis Armstrong – black music spoke to black society with a confident awareness of its distinctiveness. Immediacy, implicitness and the endless possibilities of the off-beat when removed from the grip of regular rhythm – these features were fundamental, but jazz and blues, in all their wide variety, were principally about emotional and social self-management in American society. As elsewhere in this decade, however, it is a story marked by ambiguity. The music was grounded not in the purity of an oral tradition, but in the interplay between black- and white-derived elements. Black music was based on a dynamic exploration of the tensions between rhythm and harmony, between performer and creator. White popular music's tendency, by contrast, was to assimilate, compromise and thus to neutralize; black music indicated the possibility of a separate co-existence in which there can always be alternatives.

In spite of its distinctiveness, commercially recorded black music of the late 1920s was greeted with reserve by black, as well as by white, society. The greatest hostility came from the black middle class, who most aspired to the level of the white bourgeoisie and detested all manifestations of the subcultural status that might retard their upward progress. Among black intellectuals opinion on jazz and blues was marked by considerable ambivalence. While some writers praised them, others preferred the piety of the spirituals.

An important part of the target audience for this music was now to be found in northern cities close to the mainspring of American society. However, white America's familiarity with styles of black music, as performed for black society, remained very small. Blues singers such as Bessie Smith were known only to a select few, whose influence on popular taste was not great. Only those whites living in some kind of proximity to blacks in the south knew the more rural styles. Among jazz musicians the names of King Oliver, Louis Armstrong and Earl Hines were gradually spread by the enthusiasm of popularizing performers such as Beiderbecke. For most of the decade black bands could be heard in New York's Harlem nightspots (Duke Ellington's stint at the Cotton Club from 1927 to 1932 being the most celebrated example), but this exposure, limited to a small section of society, did not spread the word very far. Those who frequented the clubs seldom bought the bands' records. The prevailing taste in record-buying was for Tin Pan Alley tunes in recordings by Broadway stars such as Al Jolson and Sophie Tucker and white dance bands such as Fred Waring's Pennsylvanians.

White popular music

The white audience was also far from homogeneous. "Hillbilly" music began to be recorded in 1923, and again surprised the record industry by showing that there was a market for the distinctive regional styles of white America. The music of non-English language groups also began to be recorded. The social effects of these developments were complex, but the hostility of the poorer, often fundamentalist rural communities to urban culture was to some extent deflected by this opportunity to become consumers of their own vernacular culture in mass-produced form.

It was through recordings that each social group acquired a public voice, which was both used within the group and also formed part of a larger pattern of cultural communication, of a type not known before. Marketing policies aimed particular products at particular audiences, so wider familiarity with the different musical styles would never have taken place if records had been the only means of communication. It was through radio, broadcasting "music in the night every night, everywhere" and recognizing few barriers, that music of different kinds reached new audiences. The staple fare of radio was provided by the dance orchestras of Vincent Lopez, Guy Lombardo and others who could be relied on to behave respectably in the nation's homes. The studio band system on which radio depended in effect excluded black musicians, but the practice gradually grew of placing "radio wires" in certain New York nightspots. In this way a few black bands were provided with a much wider

The Lost Generation

In the 1920s Paris became the Mecca for every young American who aspired to artistic or literary genius. As the cultural center of the Western world, it popularized a bohemian way of life that was not so much in opposition to bourgeiois philistinism as in advance of it. In the past, bohemian or counter-cultural fashions had often been created as a critique of high fashion. In the 1920s high fashion itself expressed the daring of the artistic avant-garde.

Yet the women in these expatriate circles; seemingly free spirits, were often as exploited as any middle-class housewife, their sexual libertarianism often of more benefit to their lovers than to themselves. American author Scott Fitzgerald's own wife, Zelda, suffered repeated mental breakdowns; Nina Hammett, a promising artist in her own right, became an alcoholic. Nancy Cunard, to many the epitome of 1920s womanhood, could not, as a result of botched abortions, have children.

Emblematic of the period's love of the exotic was Nancy Cunard's armful of African ivory bangles. African art influenced Picasso, Diaghilev and many others in the early decades of the century.

▲ Nancy Cunard was a convention-flouting society beauty of the 1920s, with a genuine interest in things African.

▼ The American black dancer Josephine Baker was well aware of the danger of being caught up in white preconceptions about "primitive" art, and brought an irony to her costumes and performances that was often lost on her audiences.

exposure and areas of America were given their first taste of a black jazz band, and something of the accompanying thrill. In areas where "hillbilly" music was popular, radio stations began to broadcast non-networked "barn dance" programs featuring fiddlers and string bands.

The safer experiences offered by the white dance bands and vocalists remained popular. However, before the end of the decade outright opposition to new styles of popular music had modified considerably, principally because bands such as Paul Whiteman's succeeded in convincing the public – if not the various custodians – that with its more "offensive" and "raucous" elements removed the music was no longer a threat. Whiteman had been as irritated as anyone by traditionalist opposition, but his response had been to seek a compromise. By blending techniques derived from classical music (especially in scoring), he sought to show that some of the well-known morally uplifting qualities of that music had been absorbed. He wanted his music to be thought of as "art".

It was to be an art that depended on the successful incorporation of "native" American elements, but the effect, at least superficially, was rather different. Greater rhythmic freedom, individualistic sound, the hint of bodily emancipation – these qualities were still controlled by pre-regulated harmony and rhythm. The question that lurked beneath the surface, however, was whether these new elements could ever be truly assimilated or whether they would refuse to shed their identity or their power to challenge.

▶ The image of the "flapper" and of the "Bright Young Things" is a part of the myth rather than the reality of the 1920s. Only a very few rich young women had the independence, leisure and daring to enjoy love affairs outside marriage. Skirts never rose above the knee, and this suggestive glimpse of suspender would have been an embarrassment to a real-life young woman – though such awkwardnesses did indeed occur.

Jacques leclerc

The new woman and the twenties

Although the fashions gaining ground before World War I prefigured the "modernism" of the 1920s, it was only in the hedonism and boom atmosphere of the Jazz Age that the revolution in women's clothing begun before 1914 was finally accomplished. The wartime experience of young European women from the middle and upper classes in situations where they could no longer constantly be chaperoned, and the casualty toll that devastated a whole generation of young men, meant that with the dawn of the 1920s a new kind of single woman – independent, self-sufficient, adventurous – stepped on to the social stage. World War I had also expanded employment opportunities for women in the affected nations. Women munitions workers, better paid than working-class women had ever been, appeared on the streets wearing makeup and dressed in seal and musquash fur coats. The mutilations caused by the war itself advanced plastic surgery, and indirectly promoted makeup as well.

In the 19th century painters had arranged their female sitters in static poses in gorgeously elaborate plumage; the wives and daughters of rich men almost became luxury objects to be looked at. By the 1920s a more typical fashion image was the photograph, which captured the model as she sprang across a puddle in the street, or disported herself in a bathing suit or at the races. The fashionable woman of the 1920s was associated with speed, daring and travel. Movement was the key to the new fashions. In a few short years, from being enveloped in yards of material that was buttoned, laced and hooked to swaddle and constrain, women's bodies were set free in the simplest of shifts that left arms, legs and necks shockingly bare, while hair was cropped and brilliantined. Faces, by contrast, were openly and brightly painted. Women smoked, drank, swore and made love in a manner that would have ruined their reputations 30 years earlier.

The influence of sportswear on fashion was even more obvious at this period than before World War I; Suzanne Lenglen, the dynamic French tennis star of the twenties, was dressed both on and off the court by Jean Patou, and her ordinary clothes looked hardly different from her on-court outfits (see page 67). Brief pleated skirts, thin stockings, simple strap or laced shoes, a long straight cardigan and plain shirt was one version of the new uniform for women.

Among the fashion designers, more influential even than Patou or Mmes. Vionnet and Lanvin, who revolutionized the cut of clothing (Madame Vionnet invented the bias cut) was Gabrielle "Coco" Chanel. Her designs dominated the fashion esthetic of the decade, but her work also bridged the prewar and postwar epochs, for she had already been experimenting with sports designs and materials before 1914. She, like Redferns (see page 31), had sensed the possibilities of women's riding wear, but she went much farther. She seized upon materials previously used only for male sporting garb and underwear – locknit, jersey and grey flannel – as a revolutionary new medium for her designs. By 1913 she was devising cardigans and sweaters (until then

◄ Many women now wore cosmetics; it was no longer the sign that you were of easy virtue, or an actress. The movies further popularized makeup. Firms such as Max Factor (from Hollywood), Elizabeth Arden, Helena Rubinstein and Yardley were becoming household names.

◄ These real-life women in Berlin do not look as seductive as the "garçonne" of *La Vie Parisienne* (opposite). Nevertheless, it is hard for us today to imagine the shock that the exposure of stockinged leg would still have caused many spectators in the mid-1920s, not to mention the careless, "unladylike" postures the new freedom encouraged.

▼ The bobbed haircuts of the 1920s, and the lifestyle that went with them, won converts far from the cities of the West where they arose. This group of Korean girls, photographed in 1927, showed a brave allegiance to the styles of New York and Paris, although their clothes retained an oriental flavor.

worn only by fishermen and agricultural laborers) as fashion garments, and by the 1920s she had created an entirely new mode: she replaced the gorgeous colors and yards of silk with beige cashmere, black wool crêpe and men's suitings.

Simple fashions for the wealthy

At this period Chanel's designs were for the leisured rich, the new international set who traveled Europe and the United States in a restless search for seasonal diversions; and the irony of her fashions was that she gave the richest women in the world a look that was indistinguishable from that of a shop girl or office worker. Dressed in this ultra-chic "poor look" – in a simple black dress either with a demure white Peter Pan collar, or, more likely, completely unadorned – the society women who affected it paid everything for a fashion that looked like nothing and reduced women's dress to a minimalist uniform of understatement. Chanel even designed necklaces of uncut diamonds and emeralds that looked as though they were made of common glass.

This, then, was an inversion of values in the so-called democratic century. Dress was no longer a matter of direct display; instead, fashion adopted the language of the streets and of the common man (man, not woman, for both sexes). Chanel flung a trenchcoat around her shoulders and it became the latest thing; jersey, corduroy and tweed, once used to make only workmen's or country clothes, were transformed into high fashion. The concept of casual wear was born.

By this time high fashion was an international movement. Paul Poiret had already toured the United States, where he had been horrified to find his exclusive designs pirated everywhere. By 1930 Seventh Avenue (the New York City garment district) was adapting Chanel's designs for the mass market – and their simplicity meant that they were highly suitable for mass production. In the following year Chanel was invited to Hollywood by Sam Goldwyn. The "poor girl" look that Chanel had made her own was similar to that popularized by Louise Brooks on the screen, where she played ordinary city girls, "good sorts" and tomboys. Goldwyn invited Chanel to dress his stars because she was the most prestigious of all dress designers, but as it turned out her designs were too understated for Hollywood. After designing Gloria Swanson's wardrobe for *Tonight or Never* (1931) she returned to Paris, unenthralled by the celluloid capital, which in turn had no use for her little-or-nothing clothes.

Fashion and modernity

Chanel's collaboration with the Parisian artistic avant garde had been much more successful. As early as 1922 she worked with Jean Cocteau, Picasso and the composer Arthur Honegger on a production of the classical Greek play *Antigone*; and from 1923 to 1927 she worked with Sergei Diaghilev and Cocteau on ballet designs. For the

first of their joint works, *Le Train Bleu*, a fantasy about the Riviera, the dancers were costumed in bathing suits, pullovers and tennis or golf shoes, and the leading female role was a tennis player.

So fashion, sport and the artistic avant-garde united to celebrate the modernity of modern life, and Chanel's little black dress (American *Vogue* called it the "Ford of fashion") became the epitome of modernist style. The modernist movement in art transcended both national boundaries and those of artistic form, influencing all the arts from architecture to the novel. Visually, it was the embodiment of the ideal of speed, science and the machine. It was a love affair with a rationalist, utopian future, and in architecture and design this led to an ascetic functionalism that considered houses and flats as machines for living, furniture and household artefacts as items for use, not ornament, and even human beings as machines.

More than almost any other aspect of mass culture, high fashion acted as a conduit for this esthetic, translating it into a popular language of pared-down design and understated chic. In architecture, the Bauhaus movement created buildings that used glass to reveal the inner workings of the design. They stripped away the superfluous ornament that had cluttered 19th-century architecture with what was now regarded as the sentimental idealization of a past recreated in pastiche. In dress, too, the watchword was now functionalism; clothing was simply an envelope for the body, which it impeded as little as possible. If there was to be adornment of any kind, it was to be of the art deco variety. Art deco was so called after the *Exhibition des Arts Décoratifs*, held in Paris in 1925. This exhibition had in a sense inaugurated the idea of a lifestyle, though the expression was not then used. It included a Pavilion of Elegance, in which the fashion designs of Chanel and Poiret, among others, were displayed. They complemented the furniture, ceramics and architecture – throughout, the few ornamental motifs and bright colors permitted were definite, clean-cut and jazzy.

In literature and painting, part of the modernism of modern art had been that the work of art interrogated its own intentions and questioned its own form. Perhaps what Cecil Beaton was to describe as the "nihilism" of the Chanel look was modernist too: it not only mocked the vulgarity of conspicuous consumption but, in inventing a look that was universal, international and reduced to the minimum, it almost sought to abolish fashion itself, creating instead a classic look that defied the one essential of fashion – change. At the same time the geometric, angular design of women's clothing imitated the clean, spare lines of modern abstract art and design. Woman was no longer treated as a voluptuous animal; she had become a futurist machine.

Fashion thus disseminated the new esthetic of the modernist avant garde across two continents, and radically altered the way in which erotic beauty was conceived. Fashion became, superfiicially at least, classless, and the great thing for a woman was no longer to look grand, but simply to look modern.

▼ Swimwear became more streamlined (two-piece costumes came in in the 1930s), and although a holiday abroad was the privilege of the few, lower-middle-class and even some working-class families were beginning to have holidays in their own country. The French Riviera and Venice Lido were the chic spots for the international idle rich.

◄ Skirts were only really short (knee-length) in 1925–27, and these graceful frocks of 1924 show that the more girlish, less garçonne look of the early 1920s was quite romantic. The swirling patterns show the influence of the abstract art of the Delaunays.

▲ Art deco crystallized as a style from 1925. It was modern style for the 20th-century, but drew on many influences; among them Cubism, the Bauhaus and orientalism, and traditional Mexican, Aztec and North American Indian art. These pieces were by Cartier.

For the first time the New World and the Old engaged in a mutual cultural exchange of style and imagery. Although Paris still led the way, the vamps and innocents of Hollywood – Theda Bara, Gloria Swanson, Mary Pickford, Louise Brooks – constructed new tastes in beauty, while the "lost generation" of American expatriates settled in Paris and the south of France. Some of these hoped to create a new art and a literature that would reflect the often excessive and even tragic pleasure-seeking of the postwar generation. Ernest Hemingway, Scott Fitzgerald and many others tried to be as well as to describe a modern breed of sexually free beings, women and men whose minds, hearts and bodies were as untrammeled by traditional notions of morality as their bodies were by constricting clothes. Fitzgerald's characters "discovered" the Riviera in summer – until then it had been only a winter resort – and the suntan became another sign of working-class toil to migrate up the social scale. It became the status symbol of the globetrotter, who need never work and whose wealth permitted this inversion of established tastes. Society ladies took care to become brown as navvies, and Fitzgerald's heroine wore only pearls and a low-backed white bathing suit to set off her iodine-colored skin as she lay on the Mediterranean sands.

Datafile

The 1920s was the decade of the great picture palaces, the grandiose and luxurious movie theaters. It was also a period of consolidation and organization within the American film industry. A trade association was founded to supervise the industry's public relations and its dealings with government. The leading companies expanded into large corporations by buying and building movie theaters in the most profitable city-center sites. The coming of sound in the late 1920s extended the industry's boom period by providing a new novelty to attract audiences, but it also brought unemployment to the musicians of the orchestras which accompanied "silent" movies.

Films released with sound

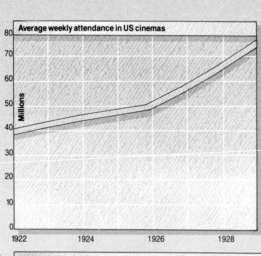

1928

1929

Silent

Part sound

Talking

◄ **Warner Bros. released their first film with a synchronized music accompaniment,** *Don Juan*, **in 1926, and the part-talkie feature,** *The Jazz Singer*, **in 1927. The other companies agreed on which sound system to adopt, and negotiated favorable terms with Western Electric. This achieved, the conversion to sound was very rapid.**

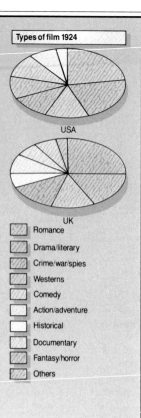

Types of film 1924

USA

UK

Romance
Drama/literary
Crime/war/spies
Westerns
Comedy
Action/adventure
Historical
Documentary
Fantasy/horror
Others

▼ **American films earned 20–40 percent of their revenues from foreign sales. By far the most important foreign market was Britain, which accounted for half the European earnings for most films. The Depression, and government regulation of American imports to protect domestic film production, accounted for most of the fall-off in Hollywood's share of films shown abroad (below right)). Until the 1930s Mexico was the only country to attempt to control imports from Hollywood, because of their derogatory representation of Mexicans.**

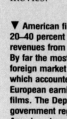

Average weekly attendance in US cinemas

Millions

► **Romance was the staple commodity in almost every film; nine out of ten Hollywood movies featured it as the main plot or an important sub-plot.**

◄ **Movie attendance figures are notoriously unreliable because of the movie industry's tendency to exaggerate. Some sources claim that 90 percent of the American population went to the movies every week in 1929. These figures are more conservative, but still indicate a weekly attendance equivalent to 60 percent of the population.**

Hollywood export revenue

UK
Others
Germany
Australia/N. Zealand
Scandinavia
Argentina
Canada

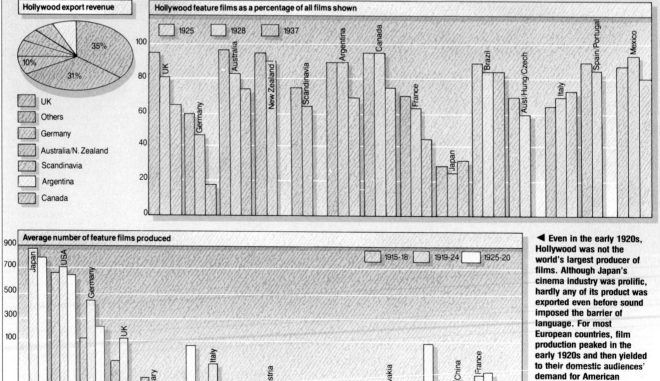

Hollywood feature films as a percentage of all films shown

1925 1928 1937

Average number of feature films produced

1915-18 1919-24 1925-20

◄ **Even in the early 1920s, Hollywood was not the world's largest producer of films. Although Japan's cinema industry was prolific, hardly any of its product was exported even before sound imposed the barrier of language. For most European countries, film production peaked in the early 1920s and then yielded to their domestic audiences' demand for American product. In retaliation, many European governments imposed quota limits on American films. India and China began to develop their industries in the 1920s.**

CATHEDRALS OF PLEASURE

As the United States became an increasingly child-centered culture, concern grew about the moral effects of popular culture on the young. This was not simply a matter of its content: many educationalists shared philosopher Charles Horton Cooley's disquiet about its "expressive" function in stimulating emotions. The "rapid and multitudinous flow of personal images, sentiments, and impulses", he feared, produced "an overexcitation which weakens or breaks down character". Such criticisms of the media's failure to fulfil the great educational and cultural mission that reformers had prescribed for them voiced Victorian dissatisfactions with the social developments of the 20th century. This critique is still echoed in contemporary concerns about the effects of television on children.

Hollywood and American taste

Hollywood continued to educate American audiences in the new pleasures of consumption,

▼ Director Cecil B. De Mille (sitting on running board) and his cast in one of the first feature-length Westerns, *The Squaw Man* (1914). Between 1920 and 1960, more than a quarter of all films produced in Hollywood were Westerns.

increasingly justified as a form of therapy for modern life. As psychologist G. Stanley Hall argued, "Everyone, especially those who lead the drab life of the modern toiler, needs and craves an occasional 'good time' ... Indeed, we all need to glow, tingle, and feel life intensely now and then." Intensity and escape were closely bound together. Cecil B. De Mille's films of the early 1920s made it clear that the real escape was from the confines of a personally and sexually unfulfilling marriage. In *Why Change Your Wife?* (1920) and *Forbidden Fruit* (1921), De Mille depicted couples discovering passion as the savior of their marriage. Both might dally with other, often foreign, lovers in the process of discovery, but they were always reunited in a "happy ending" that contained woman's newfound sexuality within the safe boundaries of the private, leisured home.

Later in the decade, Hollywood incarnations of the "flapper girl", most memorably Clara Bow in

The Plastic Age (1925) and *It* (1927), portrayed restless young women escaping from a restrictive home to the city, where short skirts and innocent flirtatiousness represented independence, and the object was to catch a desirable man without losing your virtue. While these movies suggested new attitudes, they did not challenge the proprieties of conventional morality. Instead, they showed how the modernist hedonism of metropolitan life could be contained within the established social order.

These stories attached desire to youth, newness, and the personality that combined them, the star. Young movie heroes and heroines repeatedly broke with the past, experimenting with identities and styles in new stories and the newest clothes and decor. The stars themselves were ephemeral, subject to change for no greater reason than the producers' realization that a commitment to novelty was a commitment to images that came and went, and thus to a kind of planned obsolescence among their star personalities. Hollywood's lesson was that the *frisson* of novelty could be bought, and thus the illusion of freshness, progress, and constant renewal could be acquired without disrupting the status quo.

The projection of overt sexuality was far more difficult for male stars than female. Rudolph Valentino's screen performances were often ridiculed by American men who either accused him of being a gigolo or questioned his masculinity because he consciously made himself appealing to women. His gaudy, stage-managed funeral after his death from peritonitis in 1926 epitomized the public excesses of the decade.

Despite the complaints of moralists, it was an unthreatening rebellion, with its tensions resolved in the cult of youth. Stars encouraged their fans to make the private world of leisure a refuge from somber public concerns. They offered no challenge to economic inequalities, routine work, or the continuing separation of sexual roles in public life. As work came to occupy less of peoples' energies, leisure became an egalitarian arena where imitating the spontaneity of adolescence brought personal fulfillment. The business world was no longer a moral testing ground, but a supply house for new desires. Scandal became an epidemic in Hollywood at this time, as an inevitable part of the process of publicity for the studios and their stars, but it had unfortunate effects on the careers of its victims, notably Roscoe "Fatty" Arbuckle.

The twenties saw some of Hollywood's most exotic epics, including *The Thief of Baghdad* (1924) and *Ben Hur* (1926). Taking a theme that was close to home, in James Cruze's *The Covered Wagon* (1923) and John Ford's *The Iron Horse* (1924) it also produced the first epic enactments of the Western myth. Here the pioneer endeavors of an earlier generation of Americans were seen as laying the heroic foundations of the 20th – the American – century. The worldwide popularity of these films indicated the extent to which the Western was coming to be seen as a myth of origin not just for Americans but for the emerging Western culture of consumption as a whole.

◄ Fritz Lang's *Metropolis*, made in Germany in 1926, was set in the modernistic, mechanical world of AD 2000. Its technological nightmares were combined with a Gothic horror story in a style typical of the German expressionists. Lang went to Hollywood in 1934.

Russian Revolutionary Cinema

"Of all the arts", said Lenin, "for us the cinema is the most important." The energy of the Russian Revolution was closely attached to the impact of rapid industrialization, and nowhere were the effects of that conjunction more firmly felt than the arts. For a brief period in its early years, the October Revolution produced an atmosphere in which, it seemed, the nature of perception itself had changed. Revolutionary artists endorsed the polemical purposes of new art forms for the people – poster art, popular theater and poetry, but most of all film. Newsreels not only spread the new regime's propaganda message but also revealed the vast diversity and resources of the Soviet Union to its people for the first time.

In their technique, too, Soviet filmmakers enthusiastically adopted the machine esthetic. A chronic shortage of filmstock during the Civil War made necessity the stepmother of Lev Kulushov's inventive theory of montage, but he took the main part of his inspiration from the automobile-factory assembly line. He maintained that two film pieces of any kind, edited together, inevitably combined into a new concept arising out of their juxtaposition. Soviet filmmakers used montage to produce a cinema which rejected Hollywood's conventional construction of space and time and celebrated the fragmentary perception of modern life in the metropolis.

In *Strike* (1924), *Battleship Potemkin* (1925) and *October* (1927), films which mythologized the Revolution for the general public in Soviet Russia, Sergei Eisenstein assembled his images in dynamic collision. He insisted that a film should be constructed in the spectator's imagination, through an association of ideas generated by the clashing of shots.

► Still and poster of *Battleship Potemkin*.

I am the cinema eye. I, a machine, can show you the world as only I can see it. From today, I liberate myself for ever from human immobility. I am in perpetual motion, I approach and move away from objects, I creep up to them, I climb on to them, I move alongside the muzzle of a running horse, I tear into the crowd at full speed, ...I ascend with aeroplanes...My way leads to the creation of a fresh perception of the world.

DZIGA VERTOV 1929

▶ Polish film star Pola Negri was one of the first Europeans to be lured to Hollywood, in 1923. Foreign players provided a sense of the exotic for American audiences, but Hollywood's talent-poaching did nothing to strengthen European film.

European cinema

The idea that the foreign was exotic was a Middle American assumption to which Hollywood happily pandered. In De Mille's films and in those of Erich von Stroheim, Europe represented a half-admired, yet half-condemned sophistication. Europeans were daring but decadent, sensual but self-destructive, charming but dangerous and even evil. They sought, in other words, to do exactly what Hollywood recognized was not permitted to Americans in the new culture of consumption: to enact their desires rather than to sublimate them. While Parisians and Londoners might not recognize themselves easily in such Hollywood-constructed Babylons, a good deal of European silent cinema enacted aspects of the American fantasy. Toppled from its position of world dominance by the war, the French cinema retreated into the parochial concerns of Parisian high culture. In films like *L'Inhumane* (1924) and *Le Brasier Ardent* (1923) it revealed a concern with self-conscious experiment, often in a Cubist-inspired style.

Many German and Scandinavian films sought to contrast the complacency of bourgeois life with the precarious yet imaginatively richer community of artists, entertainers and prostitutes. The decadence that Hollywood imagined was echoed in many of these films, with their assumption that passion's choice of love-object is arbitrary and often, as in G.W. Pabst's *Pandora's Box* (1928), linked to a wish for self-destruction. In other respects German cinema shared with the French a greater concern for technique – the almost constantly mobile camera of F.W. Murnau's *The Last Laugh* (1925), for example – than for character, psychology or politics. Many of the contradictions of European cinema derived from its attempts to define a commercial position for itself, both

within its own culture and in the world market, in the face of the dominance of Hollywood products and styles. But they also resulted from unresolved tensions about the uncertain status of cinema in Europe. Its commercial appeal and its melodramatic plots, frequently derived from pulp fiction, denied it elitist "artistic" value on any quasi-literary grounds of narrative or thematic complexity. Instead, directors like Murnau or Fritz Lang achieved their cultural status as artists in the way that painters did, through displays of technical virtuosity.

For many foreign audiences, the lure of Hollywood movies had much to do with the physical genius of Americans. In Eric Rhode's phrase, "They held the secret of movement, and Europeans went to American movies to learn the secret." In the process, they found themselves seduced into desiring the American things they saw on the screen. Using the maxim, "Trade Follows the Films", the movie industry and the State Department promoted Hollywood as an advertiser of American culture.

For Hollywood the European film industries were a source of talent, a means by which they could import new ideas and faces. Directors such as Murnau and Ernst Lubitsch, and stars such as Pola Negri and Greta Garbo were lured by American money and facilities. There they found that Hollywood's narratives did not have time for the complex characterization of the realist novel or naturalist drama; nor did they draw attention to their techniques. Instead, they focused attention on individual characters and their motivations, and aimed to make the workings of cinematic narration as "invisible" as possible. Typically, a Hollywood narrative would create a problem for characters to solve, show them attempting to solve it, and provide a definite resolution. One action triggered the next in a chain of cause and effect; each scene depicted one event and advanced the narrative one step nearer the climax.

The coming of sound

By 1920 the industry had embarked on a second phase of monopoly control. It was organized not around patents but around the economies of scale permitted within large companies involved in production, distribution and exhibition. Under its president, Adolph Zukor, Paramount developed some of the basic mechanisms of monopoly control such as block booking, by which exhibitors could buy films only in groups, whether they wanted all the films or not. Other companies, including Metro-Goldwyn-Mayer (MGM) and Fox, enlisted Wall Street finance in following Zukor's example. In 1922 they formed a trade association, the Motion Picture Producers and Distributors of America, Inc. (MPPDA). As its president, and "spokesman for the industry", they hired Will H. Hays, then Postmaster-General, and the man who had run Warren Harding's successful presidential campaign in 1920. While the Hays Office, as the MPPDA was popularly known, was most famous for its involvement in film censorship, it was also much less publicly involved in a wide range of political and legal activities on behalf of its members.

◀ Charlie Chaplin's 1920s comedies continued to be immensely successful. But increasingly he placed his tramp in settings removed from the everyday world: a circus, or the Klondike of *The Gold Rush*. Harold Lloyd (seen center in *Safety Last*, 1923) and Buster Keaton belonged to a modern, mechanical age, and accepted its absurdity as a fact of life. Much of their acrobatic comedy arose from their attempts to restore order to a chaotic world. Of all the silent comedians, however, only Stan Laurel and Oliver Hardy (below) really negotiated the change to sound successfully.

▶ Released in October 1927, *The Jazz Singer* was the first "part-talkie"; four of its sequences used the Vitaphone sound system to record vaudeville star Al Jolson's singing.

▼ In 1928 MGM's Leo recorded his roar.

The major companies cooperated with each other on such major issues as censorship, legislation and the introduction of sound. Warner Bros pioneered sound movies as part of a planned program of expansion which included extensive theater purchases. In August 1926 they assembled their first package of sound films, containing six musical performances and the John Barrymore feature *Don Juan*, which had recorded musical accompaniment. Initially uncertain of the long-term profits in sound, the larger companies agreed to spend a year jointly investigating all the available systems. Meanwhile, Warners continued to produce short sound films featuring the biggest stars of vaudeville, including Al Jolson. In 1928 the other companies opted for the Vitaphone system used by Warners. In order to exploit RCA's rival Photophone system which they had rejected, David Sarnoff, head of RCA, organized a series of mergers to create the last of the great Hollywood companies, RKO (Radio Keith Orpheum). A year later, RCA took over the Victor Talking Machine Company, making itself the first entertainment media conglomerate, with interests in broadcasting, recording, movies and vaudeville.

Warner Bros. Supreme Triumph
AL JOLSON
THE JAZZ SINGER
Price 25 cents

THE PICTURE PALACE

From the early 1910s, going to the movies became an event in itself. As Adolph Zukor explained, middle-class audiences demanded better facilities: "The nickelodeon had to go, theaters replaced shooting galleries, temples replaced theaters, and cathedrals replaced temples". By 1925, the United States had nearly a thousand picture palaces.

The cathedrals of the movies were to be found in the business and shopping centers of large cities. Their elaborate exteriors, featuring exotic motifs from ancient, oriental or European culture, were massive outdoor advertising displays. At night they were lit by multicolored electric signs, sometimes three storeys high. Inside, the foyers were large enough to hold the audience waiting for the next show. There might even be a small orchestra playing to keep them entertained. The two-hour show included a live orchestral overture and stage show, a comedy short and newsreels as well as the feature film.

Despite their grandeur, the American picture palaces were insistently egalitarian, places where the architectural and decorative styles of the wealthiest estates and hotels were made available to all. "Movies", declared William Fox, "breathe the spirit in which the country was founded, freedom and equality. In the motion picture theaters there are no separations of classes ... the rich rub elbows with the poor and that's the way it should be. The motion picture is a distinctly American institution." Indeed, the picture palace was perhaps the only legitimate arena in which the classes and sexes mingled. The "Million Dollar Theaters" sought to convince all their clientèle that, as viewers, they could become part of the glamorous life they watched on the screen. Many cinemas provided free baby-sitting. Mirrors encouraged patrons to recognize themselves amidst the chandeliers and fountains, so they could feel that escaping from the cramped anonymity of the office or the apartment house into these gilded mansions of romance should not be an occasional luxury, but a necessary regular respite from all that was oppressive in metropolitan life.

This idyll proved enormously seductive. Imitating the business strategies of chain stores, the industry looked for ways to present a more standardized product. One of the reasons for introducing sound was that it would reduce the cost of musical entertainment by replacing the theater orchestra and stage shows with recorded music and filmed vaudeville shorts.

▶▶ The 5th Avenue Theater in Seattle, opened in 1926, typified the extravagant decor of the picture palaces based on Chinese motifs.

▶ The theater organ of New York's largest picture palace, the Roxy, which seated 5,889 people. It was named after its manager, Samuel Rothafel, who led many of the trends towards ornate luxury.

▶▲ As well as their luxurious surroundings, cinemas offered voyages into the exotic: the spectacular epics like *Ben Hur*; the amorous orientalism of Rudolph Valentino, or the rich, flapper world of Clara Bow. As an advertisement for Paramount explained in 1925, "All the adventure, all the romance, all the excitement you lack in your daily life are in – Pictures."

BIOGRAPHIES

Adams, Walter Sydney 1876–1956

US astronomer. He graduated in arts in 1898 and then read mathematics. He gained his first astronomical experience under G.E. Hale at the Yerkes Observatory, and returned there from Europe in 1901 before moving on in 1904 to the Mount Wilson Observatory, where he remained, latterly as director (1923–46). He was a skillful observer with interests ranging from sunspots to interstellar gases and planetary atmospheres. He is chiefly remembered, however, for the first observation of a "white dwarf", and for devising a method for measuring the distance of stars.

Adrian, Edgar Douglas 1889–1977

British neurophysiologist. He entered Cambridge University in 1908: graduating in natural science, he was a fellow from 1913, professor of physiology (1937–51) and master (1951–65). His first research was on responses in muscle-nerve preparations, but the special problems created by World War I led him to examine the clinical problems of nerve injury and war neuroses. In 1925 he began a study of the encoding of sensory information to the brain by impulses in nerve fibers. Using the cathode-ray oscilloscope, he began in 1930 to investigate the "brain waves" discovered by Hans Berger. Finally his research extended to the brain itself. In 1932 he shared a Nobel prize with C.S. Sherrington. He was later president of the Royal Society (1950–55).

Armstrong, Louis 1900–71

US jazz trumpeter, vocalist and composer. The greatest jazz trumpeter ever, he joined Joe "King" Oliver's band in 1922, leaving for New York in 1924. By 1930 he was a star with some great recordings (including *Potato Head Blues* and *West End Blues*) behind him and he had invented scat singing. In 1935 Mafia man Joe Glaser became his agent, and until 1947 he played with big bands. His final line-up, the six-piece All Stars, produced classic albums such as *Plays Fats* and *At the Crescendo*. He appeared in several hit movies.

Arp, Jean (Hans) 1887–1966

German-born French sculptor, painter and poet. After studies in Strasbourg, Paris (where he encountered modern art) and Weimar, Arp took up poetry. In 1909 he met Klee in Switzerland, and in 1912 exhibited with the *Blaue Reiter* group. In 1914, in Paris, he mixed with the avant-garde, and showed "abstract" paintings. He was a founder member of the Zurich and Cologne Dadaists. From 1926 to 1930 he was with the Surrealists, and then turned increasingly to sculpture; he founded the Abstraction-Création group. He had a sense of fun, reflected in subjects like *Fork and Navel* (1927), and *Head with Three Annoying Objects* (1930). His forms are smooth, and quasi-organic; he believed the forms of art should arise spontaneously: "Art is a fruit that grows in man".

Aston, Francis William 1877–1945

English physicist. A graduate in chemistry, he entered the Cavendish Laboratory, Cambridge, in 1910 to work under J.J. Thomson, investigating the streams of positively charged particles emitted when electricity is discharged through a tube filled with gas at low pressure. Using electric and magnetic fields it was possible to separate the particles according to their mass:charge ratio. From this it appeared that neon consisted of two isotopes. In 1913 he succeeded in enriching the gas in respect of the rarer isotope, neon 22. On his return from war service he devised, on the same principle, his mass spectrograph (1919) by which the mass of isotopes could be deduced from a photographic image. With this he investigated the isotopic composition of some 50 elements. He was awarded a Nobel prize in 1922.

Atatürk, Mustafa Kemal 1881–1938

Soldier, and first president of modern Turkey. During World War I, as a general, Atatürk commanded the Turkish forces at the Dardanelles and opposed German control of Turkey. After the war, he opposed the Sultan's surrender to the Allies and the intended partition of Turkey and in 1919, as president of the National Congress, organized resistance against the Greek occupation of Smyrna. In 1920 he was elected president of a new National Assembly he had helped to form, and virtual head of state. In 1922 he abolished the sultanate and replaced the pro-Allied government with a new republic. He expelled the Greeks from Asia Minor and, by the 1923 Treaty of Lausanne, gained recognition for Turkey from the Allies. He was elected president in 1923, and created a dictatorship. He modernized Turkey, adopting the Latin alphabet, Western-style surnames and Western dress, reformed the legal and educational systems, and gave women the vote. He promoted nationalism over religion, nationalized foreign industry and created national banks. Under Atatürk, Turkey joined the League of Nations.

Atlas, Charles 1893–1972

Italian-born body builder. He was the creator of a popular body-building course marketed by mail order. A young, skinny immigrant, he suffered the famous sand-kicking humiliation when a lifeguard stole his girl at Coney Island, but by 1922 he had improved his physique so much he was described as "America's Most Perfectly Developed Man." In 1929 he and a young advertising man, Charles Ronan, began marketing a program of isotonic exercises and advice on nutrition.

Baird, John Logie 1888–1946

British pioneer of television. Ill health prevented his completing an electrical engineering course. After several unsuccessful business ventures, and a complete breakdown, he retired to Hastings. There he became interested in the possibilities of television and on 26 January 1926 gave the world's first public demonstration of it, using a crude electromechanical system. In 1927, using a telephone line, he transmitted from London to Glasgow, and in the following year to New York. From 1929 to 1935 he gave regular television broadcasts with the British Broadcasting Corporation (BBC). Baird's system was then superseded, and abandoned.

Baker, Josephine 1906–75

US-born dancer and singer. A flamboyant entertainer whose beauty and vivacious personality made her the toast of Paris in the late twenties and thirties. Daughter of a washerwoman, she joined a touring company at 16, later working in Boston and New York. On Broadway she rose through the ranks of *Chocolate Dandies*, also making an impression in the floor show at Harlem's Plantation Club. In 1925 she went to Paris for *La Revue Nègre*, found international success, and stayed, taking French citizenship in 1937; at the height of her success she was the highest-paid entertainer in Europe. She joined the World War II resistance, and later marched with Martin Luther King.

Balfour, Arthur J. 1848–1930

British prime minister. In 1874, Balfour was elected to parliament as a Conservative. From 1878 to 1880 he acted as aide to the foreign secretary Lord Salisbury at the Berlin Congress, and served as secretary for Scotland during 1886–87. He was secretary for Ireland from 1887 to 1891, and strongly opposed Home Rule, which he attempted to "kill by kindness", whilst crushing any potential uprisings. In 1891, he became First Lord of the Treasury and leader of the Commons, and in 1902, prime minister. Domestically, he introduced reforms in education, defense and Irish absentee landlordism, and internationally he secured the Anglo-French Entente in 1904. The party had split, however, in 1903 over the question of tariff reform versus free trade, and this led to Balfour's resignation as prime minister in 1905, though he remained party leader until 1911. In 1915 he became First Lord of the Admiralty in Asquith's coalition. As foreign secretary (1916–17), in 1917 he issued the Balfour Declaration, expressing British support for a Zionist homeland in Palestine, and in 1919 was involved in the Versailles settlement. He represented Britain at the first congress of the League of Nations in 1920, and the Washington Naval Disarmament Conference in 1922. Also in 1922 he was granted an earldom. He served during 1925–29 under Baldwin, and was involved in the negotiations which led to the Statute of Westminster (1931), whereby self-governing dominions of the empire gained autonomy, but continued to owe allegiance to the Crown.

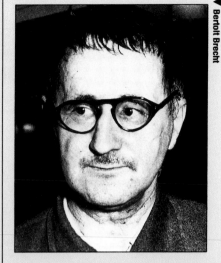

Banting, Frederick Grant 1891–1941 and Best, Charles Herbert 1899–1978

Canadian medical research workers who first isolated insulin and successfully used it for the treatment of diabetes. After war service, Banting practiced as a surgeon in London, Ontario. In 1921, with his research student Best, he succeeded in preparing a pancreatic extract from dogs which was active against diabetes. With the aid of a chemical colleague, J.B. Collip, and the Professor of Physiology, J.J.R. Macleod, they succeeded in preparing much larger quantities of active extract from animal pancreas (sweetbread). Clinical trials were highly successful and a pharmaceutical firm began manufacture in 1922. Banting and Macleod shared a Nobel prize in 1923: believing that the contributions of Best and Collip had been gravely underestimated they insisted on sharing it with their younger colleagues.

Bara, Theda 1890–1955

US film actress. Her first big role, as a femme fatale in *A Fool There Was* (1915), brought instant stardom. Born Theodosia Goodman of Cincinnati, she was marketed as the child of a French painter and his Egyptian mistress, born in the Sahara and named after an anagram of "Arab Death". From 1914 to 1919 she appeared as the vamp in more than 40 films.

Beckmann, Max 1884–1950

German painter. Beckmann studied in Weimar, Paris and Florence until 1906, after which came several exhibitions of his work. In 1915, after serving as a medical orderly, he was discharged with a nervous breakdown. At this point his work became a symbolistic critique of a corrupt world: painting had become a moral rather than an esthetic imperative. He continued to exhibit internationally and in 1925 became professor at the Frankfurt Städelschule. In 1933, however, the Nazis dismissed him and he painted the triptychs *Departure*, and then *Hölle der Vögel* (Birds' Hell). He moved in 1947 to the USA, where he taught in Washington and Brooklyn art schools. In 1950 he won the first prize for painting at the Venice Biennale and received an honorary doctorate.

Beiderbecke, Bix 1903–31

US jazz cornet player, pianist and composer. Jazz's first great lyricist and the first white jazzman admired by black musicians, his style, with its delicate, thoughtful phrasing, was influential after his death. His most famous solo is *Singing the Blues*. He began playing cornet at 15, influenced by riverboat music, and worked in New York, Chicago, St Louis and Detroit, before joining Paul Whiteman (1928–30). He also played with Louis Armstrong and "King" Oliver. His piano composition was influenced by Debussy, the most famous piece being *In a Mist*.

Birdseye, Clarence 1886–1956

US businessman and inventor. As a fur trader in Labrador (1912 and 1916) he was inspired by the practice of freezing food during the winter owing to a lack of fresh food. During the 1920s in the US Birdseye developed a method for quick-freezing food, and in 1924 helped form the General Seafoods Company. In 1929 he started to sell his quick-frozen foods, including fish, fruit and vegetables, and soon became wealthy. He was not the first producer of frozen foods but his method, using two refrigerated metal plates to freeze packaged food, was efficient, quick, and preserved the original flavor. In 1929 the company was sold for $20 million and became the General Food Corporation, with Birdseye continuing as a consultant. He was president of Birds Eye Frosted Foods (1930–34) and of Birdseye Electric Company (1935–38). He continued to invent and owned 300 patents when he died, including a superfast dehydrating technique suitable for most foods.

Bjerknes, Jacob Aall Bonnevic, 1897–1975

Norwegian meteorologist. He entered Christiania (Oslo) University in 1914 and in 1920 was appointed director of the Weather Forecasting Center in Bergen and subsequently (1930) professor of meteorology in the university there. He established an international reputation and in 1940 – happening to be in America at the time of the German invasion of Norway – became professor of meteorology in the University of California, Los Angeles. Under his direction UCLA became one of the world's great centers for teaching and research in meteorology. From the records of a network of observing centers established in Norway during World War I he developed in 1919 the concept of vast air masses – cold polar ones and warm tropical ones – which keep their identity for long periods and are separated by fronts. A lifetime of experience was summarized in his *Dynamic Meteorology and Weather Forecasting* (with C.L. Godske) (1957).

Boeing, William Edward 1881–1956

US aircraft designer and founder of The Boeing Company. He entered aircraft manufacture in 1916 with the establishment of Pacific Aero Products Company, renamed the Boeing Airplane Company in 1917. Boeing helped to design the company's first plane for the US Navy. The company produced a variety of military aircraft. In 1927 he also helped to form Boeing Air Transport which became part of United Aircraft and Transport Corporation, until 1934 when it was again incorporated as Boeing. During World War II Boeing produced such planes as the B-17 Flying Fortress. The 1950s saw production of commercial as well as military aircraft, including the Boeing 707, the first US jet airplane, which went into service in 1958.

Bow, Clara 1905–65

US film actress. Winning a fan-magazine beauty contest took her to Hollywood, but her break came in 1925 when the producer she was under contract to joined Paramount. Molded by the studio publicity machine with her swinging bob and cupidbow lips, she became the ultimate flapper: vibrant, liberated. *It* (1927) confirmed her status, but scandal, a shift in taste, mental instability and the coming of sound put an end to her career as quickly as it had started.

Brecht, Bertolt 1898–1956

German playwright. Brecht won the Kleist prize for his first play, *Drums in the Night* (1922); he was given a post as artistic advisor to a theater in Munich, and then, from 1924, to one in Berlin: 1928 saw the production of his great popular success, *The Threepenny Opera*, written with Kurt Weill, with whom other work followed. From 1929 to 1936 Brecht embraced Communism, finally becoming disaffected with party organization. *Galileo* (1938), written in exile in Scandinavia, resulted. In the USA during World War II Brecht wrote *Mother Courage* (1941), *The Good Person of Setzuan* (1943), and *The Caucasian Chalk Circle* (1944). In 1949 he settled in East Berlin, founded the Berliner Ensemble, and developed his dramatic theory of "alienation" – preventing the audience from identifying unconsciously with characters by narrative devices and interpolated songs.

Broglie, Prince Louis-Victor de 1892–1987

French physicist, pioneer of the wave theory of matter. He originally studied history and turned to physics only after radio service during World War I, enrolling in the Sorbonne: he was professor of theoretical physics in the Henri Poincaré Institute (1928–62). In his doctoral thesis of 1924 – later published in the *Annales de Physique* – he suggested that in addition to waves sometimes behaving as particles, particles could also behave as waves. This was demonstrated experimentally by G.P. Thomson in 1927. This particle-wave duality was the basis of the quantum mechanics of E. Schrödinger. De Broglie was awarded a Nobel prize in 1929.

Bugatti, Ettore 1881–1947

Italian automobile manufacturer. A designer for several small companies before setting up a factory at Molsheim, Alsace, in 1909, his first production model, the Type 13, was raced successfully in 1911. Two of his other racers, the Brescia and the Type 35, were outstanding, the latter being the only car capable of winning grand prix while priced for amateurs. A passionately meticulous man, his great folly was the Type 41 (La Royale), designed to be the ultimate supercar: only six were ever built and three sold. He used the redundant engines in high-speed railcars in the thirties.

▲ Alexis Carrel

▲ Coco Chanel

▲ André–Gustav Citroën

Bukhárin, Nicholas Ivanovich 1888–1938

Communist leader, economist and Marxist theoretician. He studied economics at Moscow University but did not graduate. In 1906 he joined the Bolshevik party and was made a member of Moscow Bolshevik Committee in 1908. He was imprisoned and then deported in 1911. Bukhárin returned to Russian after the 1917 Revolution, becoming editor of *Pravda*, 1917–29, and being elected to the executive committee of the Comintern. In 1920 he published *The Economy of the Transitional Period* and strongly supported Lenin's New Economic Policy (NEP). A member of the Politburo from 1924, he supported Stalin after Lenin's death, despite distrusting him; but when Stalin abandoned the NEP in 1928 Bukhárin tried in vain to move party opinion against him. He opposed Stalin's industrialization policy and argued against his brutal collectivization program. Bukhárin was expelled from the Politburo in 1929, and, although briefly (1934) editor of *Izvestia*, and one of the authors of the 1936 Constitution, his political career had ended. In 1938, after a show trial, he was executed for high treason.

Capone, Al 1899–1947

US gangster. Son of an Italian barber, Capone forsook school early for the mean streets. An associate, Johnny Torrio, went to Chicago to run a brothel network, and in 1919 sent for Capone to help; Prohibition, in 1920, brought them the lucrative possibility of bootlegging. In 1925, injured in a battle, Torrio retired, and Capone, aka Scarface, inherited his empire, becoming underworld king, first of Chicago and soon of the USA, expanding his operation by violence and bloodshed, including the notorious St Valentine's Day Massacre of 1929. His annual take in 1927 was around $100m.; and his political influence was great. In 1931 he was given an 11-year jail sentence for tax evasion; but he was released in 1939, paralysed from advanced syphilis. He died a recluse, in Florida.

Carrel, Alexis 1873–1944

French pioneer of organ transplantation. A qualified surgeon, he joined the Rockefeller Institute, New York, in 1906, and examined problems of organ transplantation. Here a major task was to reconnect the blood vessels of the transplanted organs. With new micro techniques for suturing the severed vessels, he successfully removed organs and replaced them in the same animals. Transplantation from one animal to another was unsatisfactory, however, as the new organ was usually rejected. His suturing techniques found further application in vascular surgery. Carrel is also remembered for his pioneer research on tissue culture. He was awarded a Nobel prize in 1912.

Cavafy, Constantine 1863–1933

Greek poet. Cavafy wrote early, in English, French and Greek. Being out of touch with the Greek literary tradition due to living in England (1872–77) and Istanbul (1882–85), and out of tune with its contemporary poets, Cavafy matured as a writer late, about 1911. He wrote on the ancient Greek period, and wrote homoerotic pieces; the two modes often combined. He also used a mixture of "high" and demotic Greek, influencing other writers worldwide.

Chanel, Coco 1883–1971

French couturier. She persuaded women to look for casual, understated elegance and introduced several classics, including the jersey dress, trench coat, turtleneck sweater, and little black dress, as well as costume jewelry and bobbed hair. Her empire grew from a tiny hat shop opened in 1913 and included a textile business, perfume laboratory and jewelry workshop. The perfume Chanel No.5 was introduced in 1922 and financed many of her enterprises. She retired in 1938 but made a comeback in 1954, introducing another classic, the cardigan suit.

Chaplin, Charlie 1889–1977

British actor, director, producer and screenwriter. A childhood music-hall artiste, he created one of the world's greatest screen clowns, Charlie the Tramp – pathetic, heroic, naively full of impossible aspirations and yet finally triumphant – pantomimic performances of balletic delicacy. His masterpieces include *The Tramp* (1915), *The Kid* (1921), *The Gold Rush* (1925), and two silents made after sound *City Lights,*(1931) and *Modern Times* (1935).

Citroën, André-Gustave 1878–1935

French engineer and industrialist. After convincing the French Army of the need to mass- produce munitions during World War I, he was appointed to construct a munitions plant which became his automobile factory after the war. He began mass-producing a small car, the Citroën, when hostilities ended. Using Henry Ford's production methods, he built one of the largest automobile manufacturing companies in France. He introduced the Citroën Seven in 1934, despite the Depression. However, the company went bankrupt in 1934, and Citroën lost control of it. Also a financier of scientific and geological expeditions, Citroën provided the lighting for the Arc de Triomphe and the Place de la Concorde as gifts to the city of Paris.

Clair, René 1898–1981

French film director and screenwriter. One of the innovators of early sound, he explored ways of using sound, image and movement, writing or collaborating on almost all his films. His sequence

of musicals – *Sous Les Toits de Paris* (1930), *Le Million* and *A Nous la Liberté* (both 1931) and *Quatorze Juillet* (1932) – were among the most original early sound films. His second film, *Entr'acte* (1924), demonstrated a brief involvement with surrealism, but many of his films were fantasies: he was a humanist, using satire or irony to make his points.

Clemenceau, Georges 1841–1929

French premier. After a radical student career and four years in the USA, Clemenceau, now a doctor, became mayor of Montmartre (1870) and entered the National Assembly (1871), resigning from both positions after involvement in the Paris Commune. In 1876, re-elected to the Assembly, he became leader of the far left. In 1880 he started a radical paper, fiercely denouncing colonialism as debilitating to France. His opposition brought down two premiers, gaining him a reputation as a powerful antagonist who would not take office himself. His unpopularity grew and he was defeated in the elections of 1893. He became an outstanding political writer. In 1902 he became senator for the Var, and then interior minister (1906), breaking with the left when he ordered out troops against striking miners. He served as premier from 1906 to 1909 and again during and after World War I. He inspired popular resistance to Germany and in 1918 secured a unified Allied command under the French officer Ferdinand Foch. Known as "The Tiger", Clemenceau presided at the Paris Peace Conference (1919), defending French interests and pressing for German disarmament. The concessions made by France to Germany in the Treaty of Versailles were seized upon by the right wing, and in 1920, having failed to gain the presidency, Clemenceau resigned.

Cocteau, Jean 1889–1963

French writer, film-maker, and artist. Although a poor scholar, Cocteau soon mixed with the artistic-literary-musical talents of his time. After driving an ambulance in World War I, he met *Les Six* and worked with them: his first ballet, *Parade*, was created with Satie and Picasso. Such glittering cooperation, and virtuosity, was a keynote of Cocteau's life. In 1923 his first novel, *Thomas L'Imposteur*, appeared. It dealt with his war experiences; also in this year he turned to opium, following the death of his 21-year-old protégé, Raymond Radiguet. Cocteau made fine films, including *La Belle et la Bête* (1941) and *Le Testament d'Orphée* (1950). His novels included the famous *Les Enfants Terribles* (1929), which he later filmed, and *La Machine Infernale* (1934) was his best-known play; he worked in glass, ceramics, and illustrated books, decorated public buildings, and wrote libretti, yet he called himself a poet in all these media. He saw the artist's task as the "rehabilitation of the commonplace"; the weakness

of his work may be that he tended to subsume ethics in esthetics. In 1955, Cocteau became the first person ever to be elected to the Académie Française without paying court to its members.

Coolidge, Calvin 1872–1933

30th president of the United States. Republican governor of Massachusetts in 1919, Coolidge came to national attention when he called out the state guard to restore order during a police strike. In 1921 he became vice-president, and on the death of Harding in 1923, president, then winning the elections of 1924. He reduced government intervention in the economy (although high, protectionist tariffs remained), cut taxes and paid off a large proportion of the national debt. Coolidge successfully opposed farm relief, but his opposition to bonuses for World War I veterans was defeated by Congress. He retired in 1929.

Curzon, George 1859–1925

British politician and Viceroy of India. Elected to parliament as a Conservative in 1886, Curzon became under secretary for India in 1891, and under secretary for foreign affairs and a privy councillor in 1895. From 1898, as Baron Curzon, and Viceroy of India (the youngest ever), he reformed taxation, created the Northwest Frontier Province, partitioned Bengal and restored the Taj Mahal, although there was personal rivalry and intrigue between him and his military commander, Lord Kitchener. In 1905 Curzon tendered his resignation, as a gesture. It was accepted, however, and, now an Earl, he entéred the House of Lords, and in 1915 became Lord Privy Seal in Asquith's coalition government. He went on to become a member of Lloyd George's war cabinet in 1916, and from 1919 to 1924 served as foreign secretary under Lloyd George, Bonar Law and Baldwin. In 1919, he proposed the "Curzon Line" across Poland, which formed the basis of the Polish-Soviet border after World War II. He was instrumental in the conclusion in 1923 of the Treaty of Lausanne, and he helped to rebuild Anglo-German relations after World War I.

Dalí, Salvador 1904–89

Spanish painter. Suspended (and imprisoned) for subversion during his studies at Madrid Fine Art School, he was expelled in 1926. He went to Paris, where he met Picasso and Miró, and studied Freud's work. In 1929 he joined the Surrealists and had a one-man show. During this time he collaborated with Luis Buñuel on two films, *Un Chien andalou* and *L'Age d'or*. Dalí's "paranoiac-critical" method of invoking quasi-hallucinatory images while retaining a critical consciousness of the imaging process, coupled with his brilliantly realistic style of execution, produced work like *The Persistence of Memory* (1931) and made him the most popular of the Surrealists. In the 1930s, he

began to emulate Raphael; he also flirted with Fascism, and this led to a rift with the Surrealists, although he continued to exhibit with them. From 1940 until 1955 he lived in the USA, during which period his work drew more and more on his Catholicism, as in *The Crucifixion of St John of the Cross* (1951) and *The Last Supper* (1955). After returning to Spain he spent much of his time decorating the museum of his works in Figueras.

Davis, Stuart 1894–1964

US painter. Davis studied with Robert Henri, and exhibited five paintings in the 1913 Armory Show, causing some outrage. His work was of the New York Ashcan School; he was influenced in color by the Fauves, and in construction by Cubism. In the 1920s he produced abstract paintings featuring juxtaposed shapes and mass-produced objects – *Lucky Strike* (1921). He also painted the 1927 *Eggbeater* series. A visit to Paris in 1928–29 boosted his confidence. In 1932 he painted murals in Radio City. His work was influenced in theme and manner by jazz – *Swing Landscape* (1938), and *The Mellow Pad* (1951). He used stronger color and texture in the 1940s, and his paintings of the 1950s were large and striking – *Little Giant Still Life* (1950). Before Warhol, Davis was producing icons of the waste products of a consumer society.

Dawes, Charles Gates 1865–1951

Chicago banker and US Republican vice-president. Dawes was initially in banking but during World War I he became the outspoken purchasing agent for General Pershing's Expeditionary Force in France. In 1919 he resigned as brigadier general. He was appointed the first director of the budget bureau in 1921 and in 1923 became chairman of the Allied Reparations Commission. The Commission produced the Dawes Plan in 1924 which, with the help of US loans, reorganized German finances. The plan prevented immediate economic collapse in Europe but did not solve the wider question of world economic dislocation. Dawes was vice-president from 1925 to 1929, having played a powerful and positive role in the election campaign. He later served as ambassador to Britain (1929–32) and as president of the Reconstruction Finance Corporation in 1932. In that year he resigned and returned to banking. He was awarded the Nobel Peace Prize in 1925.

De Mille, Cecil B. 1881–1959

US director, producer and screenwriter. A co-founder of the Lasky company, later to become Paramount Pictures, he pioneered the switch to feature-length films, developed his own regular players and concentrated on improving production values. His early romantic comedies and later epic spectaculars such as *The Ten Commandments* (two versions: 1923 and 1956) demonstrate the same

successful formula: explicit visual detail allied with verbalized Christian values. De Mille was also an entrepreneur in commercial aviation.

Dempsey, Jack 1895–1983

US boxer. World heavyweight champion between 4 July 1919 and 23 September 1926, he attracted bigger gates than any previous fighter. He began boxing professionally in 1914 and took the title at the first attempt, knocking his opponent down seven times in round 1. His title defense against Firpo in September 1923 was typical of his courage: knocked out of the ring in round 1, he came back to win in round 2. He failed to recover his title, retiring in 1940. He won 62 of his 84 bouts, 31 of them by knockouts.

Dirac, Paul Adrien Maurice 1902–84

Swiss-British theoretical physicist, who made major contributions to quantum theory and predicted the existence of the positron and other antiparticles. After studying electrical engineering and mathematics in Bristol he took his doctorate in Cambridge in 1926. In 1932 he was appointed Lucasian Professor of Mathematics, a post he held until retiring in 1969. A talk by Heisenberg in 1925 aroused his interest in what was to be quantum mechanics and in the winter of 1927–28 he formulated the celebrated "Dirac Equation", a relativistic theory of the electron. This led on to his prediction of a positvely charged "anti-electron", experimentally observed by C.D. Anderson in 1932. In 1933 he shared the Nobel Prize for Physics with E. Schrödinger.

Dix, Otto 1891–1969

German painter. Dix was apprenticed to a painter (1905–9), and then studied art in Dresden (1909–14) and Düsseldorf (1919–22). In 1923 he joined the *Neue Sachlichkeit* school. He was professor of art at Dresden from 1927 to 1933, when the Nazis dismissed him. His paintings had pseudo-Romantic traits and a Mannerist-Realist style deriving from 16th-century art. This slightly distorted despairing hyper-realism is exemplified in *The Artist's Parents* (1921). His finest works were portraits painted in the 1920s, and his lithographs of World War I after Goya's *Horrors of War*.

Earl, Harley 1893–1969

American industrial designer. He was born into a Hollywood coach-building family which produced customized car-bodies for the stars and even supplied the film industry with chariots for epics. When the firm was bought out by Cadillac, he introduced the now-standard method of sculpting body-work designs in clay. He was invited to join General Motors in 1925. His major success were the 1927 la Salle and the 1937 Buick Y Job, but he also introduced two-tone paint, chromium painting, and tail-fins.

Ebert, Friedrich 1871–1925

German president. Elected to the Reichstag in 1912, in 1916 Ebert became chairman of the Social Democratic party (SPD). His support of World War I led to the breaking away of the left wing. In November 1918, revolution broke out, and the Kaiser was deposed. Ebert was made chancellor, but immediately transferred power to the Council of People's Representatives, where an SPD-USPD coalition formed a provisional government. In 1919, elections under the Weimar constitution were held. The SPD formed a coalition with the Center party and the Democrats, known as the black-red-gold coalition, and Ebert became president. He engaged in a civil war with revolutionary socialists. Owing to the harsh terms of the Treaty of Versailles the coalition lost their majority in 1920. In 1923, when German payment of war reparations to France ceased, French troops occupied the Ruhr. A general strike followed in the area, severely damaging the Germany economy, and Hitler led an attempted coup in Munich. The reparations question was eventually settled, and inflation was brought under control, but Ebert still took much of the blame, and was accused of treason, technically speaking, for supporting a munitions strike during the war. He died in 1925.

Eisenstein, Sergei 1898–1948

Russian film director and theorist. Originally a theater director, he was influenced by the Japanese Kabuki theater. His reputation derives from a vigorous editing technique based on the theory of montage – that two conflicting images produce a third element, and that such elements can induce predetermined emotions in an audience. His first film, *Strike* (1925), *The Battleship Potemkin* (1925) and *October* (1927) explored and developed this line of work. *Alexander Nevsky* (1938) and *Ivan the Terrible Pt I* (1945) and *Pt II* (completed 1946), eased and confirmed his reprieve after a period out of favor for his deviation from Socialist Realism.

Eliot, Thomas Stearns 1888–1965

US British poet, playwright and critic. Eliot read philosophy at Harvard, then studied under Bergson and Alain-Fournier at the Sorbonne. He absorbed Laforgue's writing, and Indian philosophy. *The Love Song of J. Alfred Prufrock*, written in 1910, revolutionized poetic diction, imagery, and tone. Ezra Pound encouraged and supported him, editing *The Waste Land* (1922), his major work. Eliot founded *The Criterion*, a literary journal, and in 1925 became poetry editor of Faber and Faber the publishers. In 1927 he became a British citizen and an Anglican. He received the 1947 Nobel Prize for the *Four Quartets* (1935–44), a long meditation on time, and history both personal – there are elements of autobiography – and collective. Eliot's verse drama is not great, except for *Murder in the Cathedral* (1935). His criticism is;

he brought about the revival of Elizabethan and Jacobean drama, and of the Metaphysical poets, through his influential critical essays, and coined phrases like "dissociation of sensibility", and "objective correlative" – which became literary-philosophical stock in trade. Eliot fused layers of allusion and literary reference, achieving a directness and clarity in expressing the transcendent which is unsurpassed in modern poetry.

Eluard (Grindel), Paul 1896–1952

French poet. Eluard, after running away from home and traveling the world, started writing poetry in 1917. He was a co-founder of Surrealism. *Capitale de la Douleur* (1926) explores the dream world; *L'Immaculée Conception* (1930), poems written with Breton, runs the gamut of mental disturbances. In 1938 Eluard left the Surrealists; in 1942 he became a Communist, and joined the Resistance, expressing his hatred of the Occupation in *Poésie et Verité*, and two further volumes; these books were parachuted to Resistance fighters. His erotic poetry is arguably even better than his political work, as in *Poésie Ininterrompue* (1946). Passion, and a lyrical esthetic, marked Eluard's work.

Epstein, Jacob 1880–1959

US British sculptor. In 1901, while working in a bronze factory, he took evening classes in drawing, and then studied in Paris; the Louvre's primitive sculptures impressed him. He finished his first major commission, of 18 figures for the British Medical Association, in 1908. Showing Rodin's influence, this work caused a furore, because of its nudity, and expressive exaggerations. Epstein was branded controversial, and was heavily criticised. Epstein's meeting with Brancusi at this time confirmed and speeded him in his artistic direction. Epstein produced serene pieces like doves and marble Venuses; he also approached abstraction, as in *The Rock Drill* (1913); he produced religious work, in a primitive style, like *Risen Christ* (1919), but he was still widely scorned: some pieces were bought for a seaside freak show. He is best remembered now for his realistic bronze busts, like *Einstein* (1933) and *Shaw* (1934).

Ernst, Max 1891–1976

German-born French painter. Reading philosophy and psychology at Bonn University, Ernst neglected his studies for painting, and investigating the art of the insane. In 1911 he met *Der Blaue Reiter* group, and exhibited with them in Berlin in 1913, the year he first visited Paris. After World War I, Ernst was a leading Cologne Dadaist, "Dadamax". In 1919 he made his first collages and in 1925 developed the *frottage* technique, taking rubbings of leaves, paper or wood. He also used the reverse, *grattage* – scraping paint off over

objects under the canvas. A much-loved central figure in Surrealism until he left after a quarrel (1938) with Breton, in 1934 Ernst produced a superb book of collages, *Une Semaine de Bouté*. In 1942, now in New York, he dripped paint on to the canvas in executing *Man Intrigued by the Flight of a Non-Euclidean Fly*. In 1953 he returned to France, and won the 1954 Venice Biennale first prize.

Fairbanks (Ulman), Douglas 1883–1939

US actor. Despite an on-off early career as a stage actor, he was starring on Broadway by 1910. A contract with Triangle took him to Hollywood in 1915. He found instant success: cheerful, athletic, courageous – the American male ideal – he played tongue-in-cheek comedies, then swashbuckling roles. In 1916 he set up his own production company, joining other big names to form United Artists in 1919. Among these was Mary Pickford, Hollywood's darling, and Fairbanks' wife from 1920 to 1935. His appeal survived the coming of sound but not of age; he retired from acting in 1936.

Feuillade, Louis 1873–1925

French film director. He directed over 800 films, scripting many of them and writing about 100 others, but he is most remembered for the dreamlike quality of fantasy serials such as *Fantomas* (1913–14), *Les Vampires* (1915–16) and *Judex* (1916). His ability to create mystery and suspense from the most everyday surroundings commended him to the surrealists.

Fitzgerald, F. Scott 1896–1940

US writer. *This Side of Paradise* (1920), a popular success, made Fitzgerald, an advertising copywriter, rich enough to marry Zelda Sayre. Despite his continued success, with both short stories and novels, including *The Great Gatsby* (1925), Fitzgerald lived beyond his means, and became part of the French Riviera's "jet set". In 1930 Zelda suffered a schizophrenic breakdown, and was hospitalized in 1935, the year after the publication of *Tender is the Night*, perhaps Fitzgerald's finest novel, which deals with his married life. In 1937 Fitzgerald, ill with heart problems and incipient TB, tried film-writing. Although his life seems marked by a deficiency in commitment to his art, Fitzgerald was a superb writer, drawing on the pain, mania, and tragedy of his own existence. His writing style, nerved by his intense sensitivity, is exemplary – beautiful and lucid.

Fleming, Alexander 1881–1955

British bacteriologist. A small legacy allowed him to qualify in medicine at St Mary's Hospital where, save World War I, he spent the rest of his working life as a bacteriologist. He was appointed professor in 1928 and on retiring in 1948 continued as

principal of the Wright-Fleming Institute of Microbiology. During these years he made two major discoveries. The first (1922) was lysozyme, an enzyme present in nasal and other bodily secretions which has the power of digesting (lysing) certain types of bacteria. This demonstrated the existence of substances which could destroy bacteria and be harmless to human tissues, and he soon observed the similar lytic action of a mold which had accidentally contaminated a staphylococcal culture (1928). He rightly attributed this to the production of an antibacterial substance, pencillin. However, he failed to recognize penicillin as a uniquely powerful chemotherapeutic agent, and by 1934 had lost interest in it. It was left to H.W. Florey and E.B. Chain to establish penicillin in clinical medicine in the early 1940s. All three shared a Nobel prize in 1945.

Foch, Ferdinand 1851–1929

French general. During World War I, Foch helped stop the German advance at the first battle of the Marne (1914), and was at the battle of Ypres (1915). He coordinated French troops at the battle of the Somme (1916), and in 1918 he was given command first of Allied troops on the Western Front, and then of all Allied troops. After the war, Foch was made Marshal of France, and England made him an honorary field marshal. He broke with the prime minister Clemenceau, by insisting on French control of the Rhineland.

Forster, E. M. 1879–1970

British novelist and critic. After a closeted upbringing, and a boarding-school education he hated, Forster enjoyed the freedom of thought and action he found at Cambridge. After graduating, he traveled Greece and Italy, and wrote short stories, and in 1905 *Where Angels Fear to Tread*, a novel set partly in Italy. The fine *Howard's End* (1910) counterposes the increasing commerciality of the modern world with a life lived in touch with the earth. After a visit to India in 1912, Forster produced *Maurice*, a novel showing an "ideal" homosexual relationship; it was published posthumously. His best-known novel, *A Passage to India* (1924), followed another trip to the subcontinent. It deals, characteristically, with the conflict between human culture and convention, and an imaginative "earthy" life. "Only connect" a commonly quoted Forster exhortation, urges the resolution of this conflict. In 1927 Forster delivered the prestigious Clark lectures at Cambridge; they were published as *Aspects of the Novel* (1927). He had a reputation as a literary and social critic, speaking for the virtues of honesty and kindness, whose demise he feared among the shibboleths of materialism. He was the first president of the National Council for Civil Liberties. In 1946 he was made an honorary fellow of his old college, King's.

Fox (Fried), William 1879–1952

Hungarian-born film executive. Starting with the purchase of a penny arcade in 1904, by 1915, after spearheading the victory gained by the independent distributors over the Motion Picture's Patents Company's attempt to impose a monopoly, he had set up the Fox Film Corporation, merging a production company, motion-picture theater chain and distribution business. The business grew and by the end of the twenties the company (estimated value $200m) was making about 50 films each year. Two of his coups were the introduction of the cinema organ and the creation of Theda Bara as a star. On the brink of a series of important takeovers, the stockmarket collapse, the cost of converting his cinemas to sound, anti-trust laws and a car crash forced him into sale and eventual bankruptcy.

Gandhi, Mohandas K. 1869–1948

Indian nationalist leader. Born in India, in 1893 Gandhi went to work as a lawyer in South Africa, where he campaigned vigilantly against the discrimination suffered by his fellow Indians, developing the concept and using the technique of *satyagraha* (nonviolent resistance). Returning to India in 1914, Gandhi identified himself with the plight of the poor. During World War I he recruited Indians into the armed forces, but became disillusioned with British rule after the war when civil liberties were still restricted. In 1919 he began the first Indian campaign of nonviolent noncooperation and called a strike, which he called off after the British had massacred unarmed demonstrators at Amritsar. In 1920 Gandhi, now India's foremost leader, called for Indians to boycott British cloth, and in 1921 supervised the burning of imported goods. Once again he ended the campaign, in 1922, after the eruption of violence. That year he was imprisoned until 1924, when for a short time he was president of the Congress party. From 1924 to 1927 he campaigned for the rights of untouchables and of women, for unity with the Muslims, for cottage industries and for education. In 1928 he demanded dominion status for India. In protest against the salt tax, in 1930 he walked more than 300 kilometers to the sea and there illegally distilled salt. The salt tax was lifted in 1931. In 1932 he was again imprisoned, and fasted in protest at the new constitutional status of untouchables. In 1934 he resigned from the Congress party. Gandhi launched his last campaign in 1942, calling on the British to quit India. Imprisoned again from 1942 to 1944, he was involved, in 1946, in independence negotiations. He opposed the partition of India. When rioting broke out in Bihar and East Bengal, Gandhi traveled there in an effort to bring peace. After partition, he fasted to appeal for an end to rioting. He was assassinated by a Hindu nationalist on 30 January 1948.

Garvey, Marcus 1887–1940

Black leader and organizer of the first major US black nationalist movement. Founded the Universal Negro Improvement Association (UNIA) in Jamaica but, unable to attract support, moved to the USA (1916). Establishing UNIA headquarters in New York, Garvey also founded branches in the main black communities of the North. He held the first UNIA convention (1920) with delegates from 25 countries present and spoke on Negro rights, achievements and culture, setting a precedent in encouraging blacks to be proud of being black. Garvey also advocated Negro economic independence and began various enterprises to forward this aim. However, his belief in racial purity and separation (which led him to endorse the Ku Klux Klan) and his dubious business practices brought him enemies. Garvey's influence declined and he was convicted of fraud (1925). His sentence was commuted by president Coolidge (1927) and he was deported. Despite attempts, Garvey could not revive support abroad and he died in obscurity.

Goddard, Robert Hutchings 1882–1945

US physicist. He was educated at Worcester Polytechnic Institute and Clark University, where he remained, as professor of physics. His interest in rocketry derived from a desire to investigate the physics of the upper atmosphere. In 1929 he launched a liquid-fueled rocket carrying camera, barometer and thermometer. For the next ten years he worked mostly at a research station in New Mexico. By 1935 his rockets had achieved heights of 2.3km (1.5mi). He lodged over 200 patents, from which he gained little reward, but in 1960 the US government paid his widow a handsome indemnity for the use they had made of them in developing the space research program.

Gramsci, Antonio 1891–1937

Italian Marxist. Gramsci joined the Socialist Party (1914) and turned to Marxism after the Russian Revolution. He formed a leftwing group within the Party and founded the Socialist newspaper *L'Ordine Nuova* (1919). He became disillusioned with the Socialist Party and in 1921 left to found the Italian Communist Party (PCI). Gramsci then worked in the Soviet Union before returning to Italy to become leader of the PCI (1924) and an elected member of the Chamber of Deputies. In 1926 he was arrested and imprisoned by the Fascist government. Released in 1937 because of ill-health, he died in the same year. Gramsci developed the concept of hegemony, in which the domination of one class over others is attained by both political and ideological means. While in jail he recorded his thoughts, which were published posthumously and helped him gain his reputation as one of the most important and influential Marxist thinkers of the twentieth century.

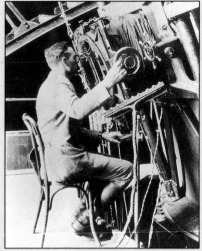

Griffith, D.W. 1875–1948

US film director, the first to use film techniques creatively. This showed even in his earliest shorts for Biograph – using close-ups, full shots, dramatic lighting, camera movement, parallel action, intercutting and rhythmical editing to convey narrative. He also sought a subtler style of performance, establishing a stock company. His major works were the epics *The Birth of a Nation* (1915) and *Intolerance* (1916).

Gropius, Walter 1883–1969

German architect. Gropius studied architecture, and was assistant to Peter Behrens before setting up a practice in Berlin, in 1911 designing, with Adolf Meyer, the Fagus shoe factory in Alfeld-an-der-Leine, an innovative structure introducing the use of curtain-wall glass. In 1918, head of Weimar Academy and School of Arts and Crafts, he made them into the Bauhaus. He propounded the essential unity of art and architecture, and in 1925 designed the new Bauhaus in Dessau, perhaps his *chef d'oeuvre*. He also wrote *Internationale Architektur* this year. Wishing to make well-designed housing universally available, Gropius went into prefabrication. In 1928 he resigned from the Bauhaus, and continued to design prefabricated housing and multistory blocks. He went in 1934 to England, where he produced a single-story school community center. In 1937 he became Professor of Architecture at Harvard University; in 1941 he developed a low-cost housing scheme in Pittsburgh, which generated his "Packaged House System". From 1945 he worked with his "Architects' Collaborative" designing, among other buildings, the US embassy in Athens.

Grosz, George 1893–1959

German painter. After studying art in Dresden and Berlin, Grosz worked as a caricaturist, using *Jugendstil* technique. He developed a powerful drawing style, incorporating Expressionism and Futurism, and, in collaboration with the Herzfelde (and Heartfield) brothers, produced series of prints attacking capitalism, like *Metropolis* (1917). In 1918 he moved to Berlin and cofounded Dadaism there; he produced drawings which violently attacked the Weimar Republic, like *Ecce Homo* (1920); he was often sued for the outrageousness of his work. In 1925 he joined the *Neue Sachlichkeit* movement. In 1933 he moved to New York, taught there, and produced more romantic pieces until World War II, when grim images returned. Grosz's sardonic work vibrates with anger and bitterness, and was cuttingly satirical.

Hagen, Walter 1892–1969

US golfer. Almost single-handed, he changed the status of the professional golfer: dressing and living well, he demanded to be treated like a gentleman. A caddie at nine, he gained his first major championship title when 21. He won the US Open twice (1914 and 1919), the British Open four times (1922, 1924 and 1928–9) and the US PGA five times (1921 and 1924–7). He led the US Ryder Cup team six times and played over 2500 exhibition matches worldwide.

Heisenberg, Werner Karl 1901–76

German physicist, founder of quantum mechanics. He studied physics in Munich and then lectured under Max Born and Niels Bohr (1924–26). Back in Germany, he was professor of theoretical physics at Leipzig 1927–41; director of the Max Planck Institute in Berlin, 1941–45; and professor of physics in Berlin. He considered Bohr's atomic theory to be inadequately supported by experiment and in 1927 formulated the system of matrix mechanics from which the wavelength and intensity of spectral lines – both easily measurable – could be deduced. Also in 1927 he put forward his revolutionary uncertainty principle, according to which it is impossible exactly to determine both the position and momentum of a body at any given moment. He received a Nobel prize in 1932.

Hemingway, Ernest 1899–1961

US writer. Invalided out of the wartime ambulance service aged 18, Hemingway returned to the USA as a reporter, soon becoming a foreign correspondent. He settled in Paris, and *The Sun Also Rises* (1926) and *A Farewell to Arms* (1929) secured his fame. He wrote four more novels, including *For Whom the Bell Tolls* (1940), and some superb short stories. In 1952 he won the Nobel Prize for Literature and the Pulitzer Fiction Prize. Despite his evident flaws – cardboard characters, a self-conscious and sentimental machismo barely concealing an anguished sensitivity – Hemingway's writing is without doubt great. His style is stark and resonant, and his descriptive passages outstanding, compulsively beautiful. He committed suicide.

Henderson, Fletcher 1897–1952

US pianist, arranger and composer. The first to use written arrangements without losing jazz's improvisatory spirit, he became recording manager for a black label after university, working with Bessie Smith among others, but by 1924 he was leading his own band. His contrapuntal use of sections of the orchestra and his technique of setting soloists against an amplified orchestral backing foreshadowed the thirties' big bands. After a serious car crash in 1928, he was known mostly as Benny Goodman's arranger.

Hevesy, Georg (György) von 1885–1966

Hungarian chemist, pioneer of the technique of isotope labeling. After studying at Budapest and Freiburg he worked briefly (1911–13) with Rutherford in Manchester. There he was set the task of separating radioactive Radium-D from ordinary lead: as they proved chemically inseparable he concluded that they were in fact isotopes of the same element. As extremely small quantities of radioactive isotopes can be accurately traced with the aid of Geiger counters, or photographic film, he conceived the idea that they might be used to follow the normal (nonactive) atoms of elements through chemical reactions. This idea he worked out with F.A. Paneth in Vienna in 1913, determining the solubility of lead sulphide and lead chromate in water, too low to be measured by existing methods. Subsequently he made extensive use of such marker elements: for example, to trace the absorption of phosphate in human tissue using radiophosphorus (1934). He was awarded a Nobel prize in 1943.

Hindenburg, Paul von 1847–1934

German general and president. A general during World War I, Hindenburg commanded the German Eighth Army, his forces defeating the Russians at Tannenburg and at the Masurian Lakes in 1914. He then went on to invade Poland. A field marshal by 1916, he was appointed chief of general staff and transferred to the western front. In 1918, having been defeated at Amiens and at the second battle of the Marne, he pulled back his forces behind what became known as the Hindenburg line. Its penetration by the Allies virtually signaled Germany's defeat in the war. In 1925 Hindenburg was elected as the rightwing candidate for the presidency. In 1930, when no party held an overall majority in the German parliament, he held the power of veto to Brüning's government by decree; he then tried to operate a nonparty government under Von Papen. In 1932 he was re-elected in a contest against Hitler, but in 1933, acting on Von Papen's advice, Hindenburg appointed Hitler as chancellor of a coalition government.

Hines, Earl "Fatha" 1903–83

US jazz pianist and bandleader. He rivaled Armstrong as Chicago's brightest star in the twenties: duets like *Weatherbird Rag* (1928) recorded, along with other classics, with Louis Armstrong, are plainly competitive. He got his own band and 12-year tenure at the mob-controlled Grand Terrace in 1928, expanding to big band later. Another big band followed (until 1947) and another unsatisfactory teaming with Armstrong, (until 1951). It was 1964 before concerts for Stanley Dance put him back with the greats. Hines' forceful, free, brassy-sounding piano style prefigured the development of modern jazz.

Houssay, Bernardo Alberto 1887–1971

Argentinean physiologist remembered for his work on the endocrine glands. When he graduated in medicine from the University of Buenos Aires in

▲ Al Jolson

▶ James Joyce

1911 he was already interested in the physiological role of the pituitary gland. This engaged his interest throughout a lifetime of research devoted largely to the endocrine glands. Houssay showed that among the hormonal products of the pituitary is one which increases, and can even induce, the symptoms of diabetes. For his research demonstrating that hormones do not act wholly individually, but are part of a complex interacting system, Houssay was awarded a Nobel prize in 1947. The Argentinean press – controlled by the dictator Juan Perón, with whom Houssay had longstanding differences – was critical, alleging that the award was designed to embarass Perón. Houssay's reputation was restored when Perón was exiled in 1955, and he resumed his career at Buenos Aires University.

Hubble, Edwin Powell 1889–1953

US astronomer. He began life as a lawyer, graduating at the Universities of Chicago and Oxford, but an amateur interest in astronomy led to his making this his life's work, mostly at the Mount Wilson Observatory, California, with its 2.54m (100in) telescope. In 1923 he showed that the nebulous outer part of the Andromeda galaxy in fact consisted of a myriad of individual stars. Turning to other galaxies, he was able by 1929 to measure the speed of recession from the Earth of 18 of them. Analyzing the results, he showed that this speed of recession is proportional to their distance (Hubble's Law). This gave the first positive evidence for the concept of an expanding Universe, advanced some years previously. Calculation of the distance at which the recession reached the speed of light, and calculating backward to the moment of zero speed, led him to put the boundary of the Universe at a distance of 18 billion light years. He estimated its age as two billion years, but later research suggests that this was a tenfold underestimate.

Hull, Albert Wallace 1880–1966

US electron physicist. He graduated in Greek at Yale and taught French and German for a year, then returned to Yale to graduate in physics and after five years teaching joined the General Electric Research Laboratory, Schenectady, in 1914, working initially on electron tubes (valves). In 1921 he published a classic paper on the motion of electrons in a magnetic field between coaxial cylinders. He called this configuration a magnetron. Also in the 1920s he invented the thyratron, a heavy-duty triode for converting alternating to direct current for long-distance power transmission. Independently of Walter Schottky he devised the tetrode tube (valve). In the 1930s his interest turned to glasses and metallurgy. This led to alloys with expansion coefficients similar to those of glass, making strain-free vacuum seals possible.

Ince, Thomas 1882–1942

US film producer, director, screenwriter and actor. Tight shooting scripts, organized production and procedures, spectacular action (using trained horses and buffalo), authentic cowboys and Indians, and a 20,000-acre desert lot won his Westerns at NYMP a fine reputation. In 1915, in partnership with Mack Sennett and D. W. Griffith, he set up a production company. By 1916 he was concentrating on scriptwriting and supervising the studio's stars and directors. In 1918 he built his own studios at Culver City, merging with First National in 1922.

Janáček, Leoš 1854–1928

Czech composer. A choirboy from 1864, Janáček became choirmaster in 1870, when he began to play the piano and compose. He went to teacher training college, and Prague Organ School (1874–75). In 1881 he married and became director of Brno music school. His first published work, in 1886, was choral. He wrote his first opera, *Šarka*, based on a story in Czech folk-mythology, in 1887. Janáček used nature, mythic and folk tales, and speech rhythms, in his music – as in the opera *Jenůfa*, completed in 1903, the year his last surviving child died. In 1904 Janáček became director of the Brno Organ School. Following the theory he had formulated of speech-rhythms as music he continued to compose especially choral and operatic works. He usually wrote his own libretti. His finest period was 1916–28; the superb *Katya Kabanova* (1921), *The Cunning Little Vixen* (1923), and the powerfully religious *Glagolitic Mass* (1926), exemplify the flowering of this work. Janáček, like Smetana before him, was a Czech nationalist; he intended his *Sinfonietta* "to cleave to the simple Czech soul".

Jessel, George 1898–1981

US comedian, actor, composer, writer and producer. A professional at nine, he developed a popular vaudeville act which mixed comedy, nostalgia and sentimentality. Through the twenties and thirties he composed, wrote and produced musicals, starring in several, including *The Jazz Singer* (1925). Moving to Hollywood in 1943, he spent 10 years producing films, among them *The Dolly Sisters* (1945).

Jolson, Al (Asa Yoelson) 1886–1950

Russian-born US singer and actor. Remembered as the star of Hollywood's first sound feature, *The Jazz Singer* (1927), he had been a black-faced Broadway hit in Shubert Brothers' shows since 1911 and in *La Belle Paree*. He found his style earlier in circus, café and vaudeville spots. *Sinbad* (1918) contained "Swanee", the song he made his trade mark; and *Bombo* (1921) featured three favorites, "Toot, Toot, Tootsie", "April Showers", and "California, Here I Come". Films, then rather more stage work,

followed the 1927 success as musical tastes changed. He made a comeback, dubbing Larry Parks's singing in *The Jolson Story* (1946). Jolson also co-wrote many popular songs.

Jones, Bobby 1902–71

US golfer. An amateur player, he was the first to win golf's grand slam: in 1930, the British and US Open and Amateur championships. It was 1973 before his record of 13 wins in those championships between 1923 and 1930 was equaled. He won the US Amateur five times (1924–25, 1927–28 and 1930); the US Open four times (1923, 1926, 1929 and 1930); the British Open three times (1926–27 and 1930), and the British Amateur once (1930).

Joyce, James 1882–1941

Irish novelist. A Dublin University graduate, Joyce, with his wife Nora Barnacle, fled from the circumscription he felt in Ireland in 1904 to Trieste, where he wrote the *Dubliners* stories. In 1916 he produced the autobiographical *Portrait of the Artist as a Young Man*. He moved to Paris in 1920. His great stream-of-consciousness novel *Ulysses* initially appeared chapter by chapter in a magazine. Published in 1922, it was banned in many countries for obscenity, and copies were seized and destroyed. In 1939, the year before Joyce's move to Zurich, *Finnegan's Wake*, a vast iconoclastic, inaccessible, poetic dream-piece, devastated the literary establishment. He drew heavily on myth, using Wagnerian themes, images, and scope; his radical treatment of form and linguistic innovations have revolutionized language and changed the face of literature.

Keaton, Buster 1895–1966

US film actor, director, producer and screenwriter. An accomplished child acrobat, he began making comedy shorts in 1917. *One Week* (1920), *The Boat* (1921) and *Cops* (1922) helped establish his deadpan persona: using only tiny facial movements to indicate emotion, he outfaced chaos. In 1923 he turned to feature-length material, including *Our Hospitality* (1923), *The Navigator* (1924) and *The General* (1927).

Kern, Jerome 1885–1945

US composer. His work often had a melodic, folk quality. He began studying music in 1903 and worked as a pianist and music-publishing salesman from 1905, writing for European operettas. His first musical was produced in 1912. Stage credits include *Oh! Boy* (1917); *Show Boat* (1927), the first "serious" musical derived from a literary source; *Music in the Air* (1932) and *Roberta* (1933). Moving to Hollywood in 1930, he began writing film music. His best-known songs include *Ol' Man River*, *Smoke Gets in Your Eyes* and *They Didn't Believe Me*.

161

Klee, Paul 1879–1940

Swiss painter. Born to musician parents, Klee was a poet and professional violinist before studying art in Munich (1898–1900) under Franz von Stück. After touring Italy, Klee did a series of grotesque etchings, influenced by Blake and Goya. In 1906 he encountered the Impressionists and Post-Impressionists, and began to work from nature. 1911 saw his first one-man show, and meeting with Marc and Kandinsky. In 1912 he exhibited with *Der Blaue Reiter*. In 1914, visiting Tunisia, he dedicated himself to painting, writing: "Color and I are one". Influenced by Delaunay, he turned to Cubism, but always depicted Nature. In 1920 he taught theory of form at the Bauhaus, and wrote his *Pedagogical Sketchbook* (1925). He exhibited as one of the "Blue Four" (1924). The Surrealists admired paintings like *Fish Magic* (1925); Klee admired, but never embraced Surrealism. In 1933 the Nazis closed the Bauhaus, and Klee returned to Switzerland; in 1935 he contracted skin cancer; he painted as prolifically as ever, producing an extraordinary 2,000 works in 1939. Klee's work combined sensitive, childlike images with a sophisticated style and maturity of vision; he saw the artist as a part of Nature, not its observer, and believed that one must attune oneself to Nature, and "be newborn". "Art", he said, "does not reproduce the visible, but makes visible".

Kollontay, Alexandra (1872–1952)

Russian revolutionary and diplomat. Kollontay advocated radical changes in traditional Russian society, including "free love", simpler marriage and divorce procedures, general improvements in the status of women, and the ending of the stigma attached to illegitimacy, policies which influenced the early communist regime. She rejected her privileged status and became an active propagandist among women workers and a member of the Bolshevik central committee when they assumed power (1917). Her prominent role in the Workers Opposition, a group promoting the role of workers within the Communist Party, won her popular support but resulted in an attempt by the central committee to expel her from the party, stopped only by Lenin's intervention. She continued her political career as a diplomat in Norway, Mexico and Sweden.

Kreuger, Ivar 1880–1932

Swedish businessman and financier. Joint founder of Kreuger and Toll (1908) which rapidly became a large international company, and in 1913, with Kreuger's family's match factories, became a base for the construction of a cartel, Svenska Tändsticks AB (STAB), which by the 1920s, controlled nearly three quarters of the world's match production. After 1914 he used his business and his personality to arrange loans for various governments in return for concessions for match monopolies,

subsequently transferring production to the respective countries. He developed an enormous paper financial empire on which he built a corporate structure extending to various types of industry. By 1932 Kreuger was head of a multinational concern, including nearly 400 businesses, was worth hundred of millions of dollars and played a very important role in international finance. His liabilities far exceeded his assets and as the Depression deepened (1931–32) his empire became unstable, his position became increasingly indefensible, and he committed suicide in March 1932. Investigations uncovered frauds, forgeries and financial manipulations; the empire collapsed, a serious setback to the Swedish economy at a time of deep depression.

Krupp family

German industrialists. The Krupp industrial empire, founded by Friedrich Krupp in 1811, became world-famous as a manufacturer of steel and related products. In 1903, under Bertha Krupp, it was incorporated Friedrich Krupp Grusonwerk AG. On Bertha's marriage in 1906, control passed to her husband Gustav, who took the name Krupp. During World War I, Krupp manufactured heavy guns. Gustav, an ardent Nazi supporter, later increased illegal armaments production for Hitler's rearmament program. In 1943 Hitler ordered that the Krupp works be converted into a family holding, and Gustav's son Alfried took control, Alfried, assuming the name Krupp, expanded the massive empire by accumulating property in countries invaded by Germany during World War II. Krupps used prisoners of war and concentration camp internees as slave labor. Alfried was later tried as a war criminal at Nuremberg, sentenced to 12 years imprisonment and the surrender of his property. He was released in 1951, and his property returned. He restored Krupps to prosperity and by the 1960s it was the largest steel producer in the world and worth over one billion dollars. Gustav was never tried, owing to his senility. Alfried's only son, Arndt, relinquished his succession rights and the Krupp name. In 1967, when Alfried died, the company became public.

Kun, Béla 1886–1937

Hungarian politician. Imprisoned by the Russians during World War I, Kun was converted to communism, and trained in revolutionary methods. He returned to Hungary in 1918, and founded the Hungarian Communist party. He was imprisoned until 1919, when the government resigned, after the Allies had ordered them to cede more territory to Romania. The Communist party then formed a revolutionary government in coalition with the Social Democrats. Technically foreign minister, Kun in fact exercised overall control. He was involved in the creation of a Red

Army, which proceeded to attack Romania and Czechoslovakia, in the expectation of imminent assistance from the Soviet Union. This failed to materialize, however, and the collectivization of agriculture angered farmers. Distribution of food deteriorated, and the army mutinied. The government fell, and Kun fled abroad. He eventually settled in Soviet Russia, where he became a member of the Third International and agitated for world revolution. He died in one of Stalin's brutal purges.

Laban, Rudolf 1879–1958

Hungarian dance theorist. Laban moved from painting to the study of dance. In 1915 he set up the Choreographic Insitute in Zurich. In 1928 he perfected *Kinétographie Laban*, now called Labanotation, a system for recording all human movement. In 1930 he became director of Berlin Allied State Theaters. In 1938, with two ex-pupils, he went to Dartington School in England. He remained in England, teaching, and researching industrial efficiency. His theories influenced Central Europeans, like Kurt Jooss, and paved the way for dance Expressionism. Laban advocated the use of "choreography" to increase the efficiency and safety of factory workers.

Lang, Fritz 1890–1976

Austrian-born US film director. Initially a painter, he fled Nazi Germany in 1933 after critical and commercial successes which included *Der Müde Tod* (1921), *Dr Mabuse der Spieler* (1922), *Metropolis* (1927) and *M* (1931). He worked for over 20 years in Hollywood, often frustrated by studio interference. After three social-concern films, *Fury* (1936) being the most powerful, he turned to commercial material. Credits include *Man Hunt* (1941), *The Woman in the Window* (1944), *Rancho Notorious* (1952), *The Big Heat* (1953) *Moonfleet* (1955), *Beyond a Reasonable Doubt* and *While the City Sleeps* (both 1956).

Langmuir, Irving 1881–1957

US industrial chemist, remembered for research on thermionic emission and the properties of surfaces. After graduating in the USA (metallurgical engineering, 1903) and Germany (physical chemistry, 1906) he returned to America and in 1909 joined the research laboratories of the General Electric Company at Schenectady. He remained there for the rest of his working life, later (1932–50) as associate director. He was a versatile research worker, but two particular achievements were outstanding. One was the invention of the coiled-coil filament which much improved the efficiency of electric lamps, especially when coupled with the further improvement of replacing the vacuum with an inert gas. His investigation of the spread of oils and other immiscible liquids to form monolayers on water gave a measure of the

▼ Suzanne Lenglen

▼ Vladimir Ilych Lenin

▼ David Lloyd George

size and shapes of molecules. During the two world wars he was associated with the development of submarine detectors, the improvement of smoke screens and other devices. He was also concerned with stimulating rainfall by "seeding" cumulus clouds with chemicals. He was awarded a Nobel prize in 1932.

Lawrence, David Herbert 1885–1930

British writer. Lawrence, son of a violent-tempered miner and a bourgeois mother, taught from 1902, and attended Nottingham University. He left teaching on the publication of *The White Peacock* (1911) and in 1912 eloped with Frieda Weekley, wife of one of his teachers. *Sons and Lovers* (1913), an exorcism of his childhood, shocked the public with its sexual frankness and its grip on the nettle of class. *The Rainbow* (1915), a story of young woman's self-development against the background of provincial society, was suppressed as immoral after World War I, yet it and *Women in Love* (1922) are his two greatest novels. The Lawrences entered a nomadic exile, living in Italy, Australia and Mexico. He wrote nearly a thousand poems, as well as essays, short stories and travel-writing. Penguin publishers were taken to court in 1960 on account of his last book *Lady Chatterley's Lover* (1928), a tale of passion across class barriers. It was innovative in its sexual explicitness, and in the lovers' dialog, but marred by a characteristic flaw of Lawrence's fiction: a tendency for the author to intrude, expounding a "doctrine" (Birkin in *Women in Love* is just such a "self-portrait"). However, Lawrence is an unquestionably great figure; his expression of the human "life-force" is equaled by few. He died of TB in the south of France.

Léger, Fernand 1881–1955

French painter. Léger studied architecture, and later painting, at various Paris art schools. He was deeply affected by the 1907 Cézanne Retrospective and developed rapidly from an early Impressionist/ Fauvist style. With *Nudes in a Forest* (1909), he began to explore Cubism, using cylindrical, not flat, forms. He exhibited in 1911–12 with the *Section d'Or*. In 1913, he began to produce abstract works, called *Contrasts of Forms*. *The City* (1919) shows his awareness of machine forms, developed during the World War I, and his wish to reconcile them with life; in its depiction of the workers who build and maintain the city, it also reflects Léger's passionate Socialism. He was influenced by *de Stijl* and Surrealism; he also designed for ballet, worked as an illustrator, and, in 1924 made a film, *Ballet Mécanique*. In 1933 his first murals were shown in Paris. He also worked extensively in stained glass. From 1940 to 1945 he was a professor at Yale University. He then joined the Communist party, attending two Peace Conferences. He intended his art to be accessible to all, in its simplicity and clarity of form and color.

Lemaître, Georges Edouard 1894–1966

Belgian cosmologist. He studied at the University of Louvain and was ordained as a Catholic priest. After a period of study in the UK and America he returned to Louvain as professor of astronomy. On the basis of Einstein's relativity theory he deduced – independently of A.A. Friedmann – that the Universe must now be expanding, having begun as a small, very highly compressed unit – the "primal atom". This theory (commonly referred to as the "big bang" theory), was validated experimentally in 1929 by the brilliant US astronomer E.P. Hubble.

Lenglen, Suzanne 1899–1938

French tennis player. A volatile player with enormous flair, she was among the first personality players in tennis. One of the greatest ever women on grass and hard court, she lost only one match between 1909 and 1925. She dominated tennis from 1919 to 1926, winning the Wimbledon singles and doubles championships six times and the mixed doubles three, and the French singles championships six times and both doubles titles twice.

Lenin, Vladimir Ilych 1870–1924

Russian revolutionary leader and founder of the Soviet Union. In 1895 Lenin was imprisoned as an agitator, and in 1897 exiled to Siberia. In 1900 he went to Western Europe, where he became involved with the Russian Social Democratic Labor party. In 1903 he split the party, forming the Bolshevik (majority) wing. He returned to Russia during the unsuccessful revolution of 1905, and left again in 1906. In 1912, he founded the breakaway Bolshevik party, coordinated the infiltration of Russian unions and increased the publication of propaganda. In 1914 he denounced World War I as imperialist and called on workers everywhere to transform the war into civil war. He returned to Russia in 1917, after the overthrow of the czar, and in October of that year used the Red Guard in a successful coup to replace the liberal-controlled Constituent Assembly with the Soviet of Peoples' Commissars, of which he became chairman; he immediately made peace with Germany. While in power, Lenin began the process of nationalization, though in his later years his New Economic Policy (NEP) allowed some small-scale private enterprise. The devastation of World War I was followed by civil war (1918–21) with requisitioning of food for the army and industrial workers and the takeover of industry. By June 1918 all large-scale industry was nationalized without compensation, private trade was officially abolished and strikes declared illegal. Lenin created a secret police and was absolutely intolerant of opposition. His NEP achieved a period of stability and recovery in which industry and agriculture reached prewar levels by 1926 but his repressiveness, as well as

increasing bureaucratization assisted the subsequent rise of Stalin. A prolific writer with a powerful intellect, Lenin is regarded as probably the greatest-ever exponent of Marxism.

Lindbergh, Charles 1902–74

US aviator. He made the first nonstop solo flight across the Atlantic. Experience as a stunt pilot and with the airmails preceded his attempt in "Spirit of St Louis" on 20–21 May 1927. Retained as technical advisor by two airlines (and in World War II), he pioneered many routes. The kidnap and murder of his son in 1932 attracted so much attention that the family moved to Europe. Criticized for his neutrality in 1940–41, he flew combat missions.

Lloyd, Harold 1893–1971

US film actor. His films were often more popular than those of Chaplin and Keaton and he became Hollywood's highest-paid actor. An extra in 1912, his friendship with director Hal Roach was crucial. They developed several characters before finding the go-getting, all-American boy whose dotty optimism saw him through. Slapstick gave way to careful plotting and features such as *Safety Last* (1923) and *Girl Shy* (1924) are classics.

Lloyd George, David 1863–1945

British prime minister. In 1890 Lloyd George was elected to parliament as a Liberal, and later opposed Britain's role in the South African (Boer) War. In 1905, he joined the cabinet as president of the Board of Trade, and in 1908 was appointed Chancellor of the Exchequer. He inspired the Old Age Pensions Act in the same year, and the National Health Insurance and Unemployment Insurance Acts in 1911, and Lloyd George pushed through a package of legislation inspired by the German benefit system. In 1909, he introduced the People's Budget, which proposed supertax and tax on land values. The House of Lords rejected it, however, and this precipitated a constitutional crisis. Their right of veto was removed in 1911. In the same year, Lloyd George confronted Germany over the third Moroccan crisis. He originally opposed British intervention in World War I, but reversed his views after the invasion of Belgium. In 1915, as munitions minister, he mobilized the war industries. In 1916 he served briefly as war minister, and replaced Asquith as prime minister. He introduced merchant shipping convoys to defeat the U-boat blockades, and subverted the influence of General Haig by securing a unified Allied command under Foch. In 1918–19, Lloyd George was one of the three principal negotiators of the Treaty of Versailles. There then followed the Anglo-Irish war of 1919 to 1921, after which he partitioned Ireland. This was very unpopular with Conservative members of his coalition, and after the Anglo-Turkish crisis at Chanak in 1922, they withdrew their support. He left office in 1922.

Lorca, F. García 1898–1936

Spanish poet and playwright. Lorca, also a painter and a musician, briefly studied law at Granada University. In 1921 his "folk-style" *Book of Poems* appeared. *Romancero Gitano* (1928) brought massive popularity. Lorca visited New York, and empathized with black Americans. His trilogy of "folk tragedies", *Blood Wedding, Yerma,* and *The House of Bernarda Alba* (1933–36), crowned his dramatic achievement. Lorca's writing deals always with the magnetic, dark, natural forces – the "*duende*" – and the ethos of Andalusia. He used songs, children's games and Surreal devices in his drama – he influenced Miller, O'Neill, and Williams. His poetry was written for speech – he called the poet "teacher of the five body senses". He was also a painter, friend of Dalí, and musician, collector of folk songs and friend of Falla. Social comment, as in *Mariana Pineda* (1925) gave him a leftwing reputation, and it was perhaps for this, and for his homosexuality, that Francoist soldiers shot him.

Ludendorff, Erich von 1865–1937

German general. Ludendorff joined the army in 1883, and the general staff in 1894, in 1908 becoming head of its operations section. His strategy was deployed in the invasion of France. In 1914, he became Hindenburg's chief of staff in the east, and his planning led to victory at Tannenburg and the Masurian lakes. In 1916, as First Quartermaster General, he was given equal responsibility with Hindenburg, and was sent to the west after the failure of the Verdun offensive. Several unsuccessful operations ensued, and the ineffectual chancellor, Bethmann-Hollweg, was brought down by Ludendorff, who then planned the last major German attack of the war, which was defeated by Foch in 1918. Ludendorff insisted on negotiation rather than surrender, and a short time later resigned his commission. In the same year, he fled to Sweden, but later returned to Germany. In 1920, he was involved in the Kapp putsch, and in 1923, in Hitler's Munich putsch. Ludendorff was a member of parliament during 1924–28, and in 1925 was the Nazi presidential candidate. He broke with Hitler after failing to gain the presidency, and founded a small party of his own.

Machado, Antonio 1875–1939

Spanish poet. A Madrid University graduate, Machado produced his first volume, *Solitudes*, in 1903. He then taught French; tragedy hit him with the death in 1912 of his 19-year-old wife; he returned to his native Andalusia. The 1915 edition of *Campos de Castillo* includes poems of the desolation of widowhood – he identified Castile with his wife. Machado had a strong feeling for the landscape as the soul of a Spain he wished to see great again. He was, with Lorca, one of the greatest modern Spanish poets.

Malevich, Kasimir 1878–1935

Russian painter. Malevich's early work, after studying at a Moscow art school, was Post-Impressionist in style. In 1907, influenced by Matisse, he adopted a vivid, primitive style. He then absorbed influences from the European avant-garde, approaching Synthetic Cubism in *The Knife Grinder* (1912). In 1913 he designed for the Moscow Opera; he began to use black squares, in design, and in paintings, like *Black Square* (1915). He was soon producing paintings dealing purely with the play of force and mass; he believed that *any* image blocked the communication of sensation, and he did not predicate a "spiritual essence". This work reached its ultimate in *White Square on a White Background* (1918). This genre was called Suprematism, and was exhibited in Moscow in 1919. Malevich then taught with Chagall at Vitebsk; he formed the *Unovis* group, and quarreled with Chagall, who left. Malevich did not paint again until 1930, but, with *Unovis*, looked for ideal architecture models ("planity"). His book *The Non-Objective World*, published in 1927 by the Bauhaus, was an important influence on Bauhaus work. Malevich's later paintings were figurative, but primitive, using simple shapes.

Mandelstam, Osip 1891–1938

Russian poet. Mandelstam, a cofounder of Acmeism, aiming at precision and concreteness, and looking back to Hellenism as the supreme cultural expression, produced his first volume of poetry, *Stone*, in 1913. *Tristia* (1922), made him famous; he wrote only prose from 1926, and in 1929 was sent away, and became a provincial journalist. In 1934 he was exiled for writing satirical verses on Stalin, and in 1937 was sent to a labor camp, where he died. His melancholy poetry, using classical underworld and other motifs, addressed the problem of the vulnerability of culture against chaotic forces. It was banned for over 30 years in the Soviet Union.

Mann, Thomas 1875–1955

German novelist. Living in Munich from his father's death in 1891, Mann wrote critical and philosophic essays, but achieved the status of classic writer with his novels, the first of which, *Buddenbrooks* (1901), brought instant success. The elegant *Death in Venice* (1911), on the Apollo-Dionysius conflict, and *The Magic Mountain* (1924), using a Swiss sanatorium as an analog of a Europe menaced by German folly, followed, and he won the 1929 Nobel Prize. He fled Germany in 1933, and took refuge in Switzerland, where he wrote the trilogy *Joseph and his Brothers*, emigrating in 1938 to the USA, where he examined the Third Reich in *Dr Faustus* (1947); in 1952 he returned to Switzerland. His writing pointed to the historical responsibility borne by each human being, the imperative of full consciousness.

Mansfield, Katherine 1888–1923

New Zealand short-story writer. Mansfield went to London in 1903 to study music, and never settled again in New Zealand. A fine collection, *In a German Pension*, appeared in 1911, the year she encountered the Bloomsbury group. In 1915, with her husband-to-be, John Middleton Murry, and D.H. Lawrence, she produced the magazine *The Signature*. The awful trauma of her brother's death that year sharpened her sense of nationality and her desire to put New Zealand on the literary map. The novella *The Prelude* illustrates this. Struck in 1917 by TB, she traveled Europe in search of a cure. Two more collections, *Bliss* (1920) and *The Garden Party* (1922), secured her reputation as a master of the form, writing delicate, subtle, stories, revealing depth of experience through the surfaces of ordinary lives.

Masaryk, Tomas G. 1850–1937

Czechoslovakian president. In 1890, Masaryk, a professor of philosophy, joined the Young Czech Party, and in 1891 was elected to the *Reichsrat* in Vienna, where he campaigned for Czech autonomy. In 1900, he founded the Realist party, and was reelected to the *Reichsrat* in 1907. As leader of the left Slav opposition, he spoke against Austro-Hungarian encroachment upon the Balkans, and the alliance with Germany. In 1914 he fled to Western Europe, and helped to found the Czech National Council, of which he became president. Unlike most of his colleagues, he presented the case for Czech independence to Britain and France, rather than to Russia, which he visited after the overthrow of the czar. In 1918, he visited the USA, and received support both from Slovak immigrants and from President Wilson. Later the same year, the Allies recognized the republic of Czechoslovakia, and Masaryk became president. He held together the different nationalities, and was one of the first to express concern over Hitler's rise. He resigned in 1935.

Mayer, Louis B. 1885–1957

Russian-born film executive. In 1907 he bought a rundown cinema, soon owning New England's largest theater chain. In 1914 he entered distribution. After experience with Alco, he founded a production company in 1918. In 1924 Mayer merged with Metro and Goldwyn, and until 1951 maintained control. A hardworking tyrant, his nose for popular taste, willingness to spend money and ability to pick personnel made him the most powerful studio boss in the Hollywood boom years of the thirties and forties.

Mellon, Andrew William 1855–1937

US financier and politician. Began his career at his father's banking house, eventually becoming its president. Established himself as an industrial magnate and was one of the richest men in

▼ Amedeo Modigliani

▼ Hermann Muller

▼ Pablo Neruda

America by the 1920s. Entering politics as a Republican, Mellon was appointed secretary of the Treasury (1921–31). He introduced controversial fiscal reforms in order to reduce the national debt, decreasing tax and economizing in order to encourage business expansion and stimulate investment. As chairman of the World War I foreign debt commission he influenced policy on the US funding of foreign war debts. His insistence on a high tariff hindered repayment of European war debts, and he failed to foresee the Depression. Mellon was US ambassador to Britain in 1932–33. In 1937 he gave the US government an art collection, and much of the money needed to build the National Gallery of Art in Washington to house the paintings.

Mendelsohn, Erich 1887–1953
German architect. An Expressionist, Mendelsohn produced curving, quasi-organic buildings, like the *Einstein Tower* at Potsdam (1921). He produced numerous factories and stores, before fleeing the Nazis in 1933; he settled in Britain and, with Chermayeff, designed Bexhill's *De La Warr Pavilion* (1934). He moved in 1934 to Palestine, where he designed several hospitals, and in 1941 to the USA. His energetic, sculptural, horizontally focused work can be seen in synagogues there and in the Maimonides Hospital, San Francisco (1946).

Mies van der Rohe, Ludwig 1886–1969
German/US architect. Apprenticed as a stonecutter (1900–02), he later (1908) worked for Behrens; in 1911 he set up a practice. From 1920 he undertook ambitious skyscraper schemes, using the motto "Less is more" in producing good-quality, cheap mass housing. He designed the German Pavilion for the 1929 Barcelona World Exhibition, a modular, largely transparent piece. Director of the Bauhaus (1930–33), in 1937 he went to the USA and became director of architecture at the Illinois Institute of Technology (IIT). His designs included several IIT buildings, apartment blocks, the Seagram Building in New York, and the National Gallery in Berlin. He used simple forms, believing that as a building's use was liable to change, beauty was the priority in architecture.

Miró, Joán 1893–1983
Spanish painter. He studied at Gáli's School of Art in Barcelona (1912–15), after a nervous breakdown. He absorbed many influences, including those of Cubism and Fauvism. In 1918 he had his first one-man show. In 1919, he became friendly with Picasso, and moved to Paris in 1920, meeting Dadaists and Surrealists. As his style developed, his work became very detailed and "fantastic". He joined the Surrealists in 1924, and painted the near-abstract "dream paintings" (1925–27). With Ernst, in 1926, he designed for Diaghilev. Influenced by Vermeer, in 1928 he painted his

detailed "Dutch Interiors". Paintings like *Seated Woman* (1932) show his distress at the rise of Fascism. In 1940–41 he painted the series *Constellations*. 1947 saw his first US visit, though his work had been shown in New York in 1930. He produced only ceramic work from 1955 to 1959, notably a wall design for UNESCO in Paris. He started to sculpt in the 1960s.

Mix, Tom 1880–1940
US film actor. His faster, more exciting format ousted the "authentic" film Western. His military career a publicity fiction, he got early experience in Wild West shows between 1906 and 1910. Selig hired him to herd cattle in 1911, but he was soon starring, directing or producing his own films. By 1917, when he joined Fox, his vehicles were action-packed two-reelers full of stunts he performed himself. Fox's top directors and cameramen made him the silents' cowboy star.

Modigliani, Amedeo 1884–1920
Italian artist. Modigliani studied painting in Rome, Florence, and Venice. He settled in Paris in 1906, met other painters, taking in Fauvism, Expressionism and Cubism, and adopted a dissolute, drug-ridden lifestyle which hastened his death. He was deeply affected by the 1907 Cézanne Retrospective. In 1909 Brancusi, introduced to him by a patron, inspired him to sculpt. In 1911 he produced a series of stylized *Caryatids*, paintings influenced by the primitive sculpture he admired. These features became central to his work. From 1916 to 1920 he produced his most powerful work, including portraits of Gris (1915) and Cocteau (1916). Modigliani was influenced by Cubism, but was atypical, using graceful, elongated lines in his figures, strongly reminiscent of Botticelli.

Mondrian, Piet 1872–1944
Dutch painter. Mondrian came from a Calvinist background. His early works were quiet, dim, landscapes, which become brighter, as in *The Red Tree* (1908), a Fauvist work. In 1909, he took up Theosophy; he turned to Symbolism, then Cubism, but sought more extreme abstraction. From 1913 he moved away from the use of perspective, into compositions, monochrome and color, using lines and rectangles. In 1915 he cofounded *de Stijl*, asserting that natural forms hid "reality". He reduced his technique even further in the 1920s, in Paris, and broke with van Doesburg (*de Stijl*) in 1925 because the latter used diagonals. Mondrian believed that the right angle represented the fundamental polarity of existence, and contained all other relationships. In 1938 he moved to London, and in 1940 to New York, a city he loved for its lines and its jazz music, where he produced some of his finest work, like *Broadway Boogie-Woogie* (1943). His first one-man show was held there in 1942.

Moore, Marianne 1887–1972
US poet. After studying biology at Bryn Mawr, Moore taught shorthand, and worked as a teacher, then a librarian in New York from 1918 to 1925. In 1915, T. S. Eliot published several of her poems, and in 1921, unknown to her, a collection, *Poems*, appeared in England. *Observations* (1924) won the *Dial* award, and Moore became editor of *Dial* till it closed in 1929. Her *Collected Poems* appeared in 1951. Moore's poetry often used remarkable animals to reflect, and later, to prescribe, ways of being human. Although didactic, it is quirky and appealing, commonly using quotations like collage. Her work developed from an early angry stance, into the formulation of an "ethics of the appropriate".

Muller, Hermann Joseph 1890–1967
US geneticist. He graduated in biology at Columbia University, and then studied genetics at Columbia; at the Rice Institute, Texas; in Berlin; in Leningrad and Moscow; in Edinburgh; and finally in the University of Indiana. His great interest was in the production of mutations (sports), both natural and artificial, mainly in the fruit fly *Drosophila*. X-rays, for example, were shown to increase the mutation rate 150 times. This led him to draw attention to the potential danger of such radiation to the human race. He was awarded a Nobel prize in 1946.

Murnau, F.W. 1888–1931
German film director. A director of government propaganda films during World War I, Murnau was one of the most talented of silent directors; his reputation rests on three films: *Nosferatu* (1922), an expressionist film shot uniquely on real locations; *The Last Laugh* (1924), visually so powerful that it needed no titles; and *Sunrise* (1927), his first American film, a lyrical, pessimistic work which suffered a hastily applied moral ending.

Neruda, Pablo (Ricardo Reyes) 1904–73
Chilean poet. Neruda, who changed his name in 1920 to avoid embarrassing his father, started writing poetry in childhood, and was famous at 20, with three books published, including his most popular, *Twenty Love Poems and a Song of Despair* (1924). From 1927 he was Chilean ambassador in various Asian countries, where he wrote *Residencia en la Tierra* (1931). He moved in 1934 to Spain, where he founded a poetry magazine. In 1940 he went to Mexico, where Rivera's work influenced him, and he became a Communist. In 1945, back in Chile, he was made a senator; in 1948 he had to leave for eastern Europe. During this period he wrote the massive, superb *Canto General* (1950) an epic history of the Americas, including *Heights of Macchu Picchu*, on his own spiritual progress and political career. In 1952 he returned to Chile. He won the 1971 Nobel Prize.

▼ Georgia O'Keeffe

▼ W. Heisenberg (centre), E. Fermi (left), W. Pauli (left)

Norman, Montagu Collet 1871–1950

English banker. In 1915 he joined the Bank of England's governors full time. Governor general from 1920, he took the Bank from commercial into central banking and established its authority. During the 1920s' economic crisis Norman worked with the League of Nations and the Dawes and Young committees, helped stabilize foreign currencies and halted British inflation by balancing the budget. The establishment of new central banks abroad was part of his policy and he worked with Strong of the New York Federal Reserve Bank to provide US financial aid. Norman separated economic from political issues and always resisted government intervention. During the Depression, Norman restored confidence in sterling, helped reorganize industry and assisted Austria and Germany. With the outbreak of World War II he planned war finance and exchange controls. Forced to retire in 1944 owing to illness, he was made a peer. Despite the Depression, London never suffered a bank failure during his governorship.

O'Keeffe, Georgia 1887–1986

US painter. After studying art, O'Keeffe worked (1908–12) as a commercial artist, and then as an art teacher until 1918. She studied further from 1912 to 1918; and in 1917 joined Alfred Stieglitz's 291 Gallery group. Stieglitz organized her first solo show in New York in 1923, and they married in 1924. Her paintings were Precisionist, from early flower paintings (often with sexual overtones) like *Black Iris* (1926), to southwestern American scenes like *Ranchos Church Front* (1929). From 1929 she spent much time in New Mexico, settling there in 1945. In the 1940s she approached abstraction, using single magnified or extensive images – *Pelvis Series; Red with Yellow* (1945). She visited Europe in 1953 and then traveled widely; aerial views began to appear in her works.

Oliver, Joe "King" 1885–1938

US jazz cornetist and composer. His skill took time to build but by 1917, with volume and plenty of muted effects, Kid Ory was billing him "King". Shrewdly, he followed the flow from Orleans to Chicago in 1919. His Creole Jazz Band (1922–4) with Armstrong on second trumpet was the hottest thing around, featuring the pair's complex "ad-libs" in classics like *Mabel's Dream* and *Riverside Blues* (recorded in 1923). In 1925 he formed the Dixie Syncopators, with a new saxophone team.

O'Neill, Eugene G. 1888–1953

US playwright. Son of an actor-manager, O'Neill was a sailor, then a journalist before beginning to write in 1912. His first play, written for his company, the Princeton Players, rejected drab naturalism for a drama of poetry and passion. He won a Pulitzer Prize in 1920, the beginning of his most prolific period. *Anna Christie* (1921), *All God's Chillun Got Wings* (1924), *Desire Under the Elms* (1924), *The Iceman Cometh* (1939), *Long Day's Journey into Night* (1939–41) are among the best of his many plays. In 1936 he became the first US playwright to win a Nobel Prize. O'Neill treated drama as high literature; he imitated classical tragedy in *Mourning Becomes Electra* (1931). He revered tragedy, seeing it everpresent in the gap between aspiration and reality.

Orozco, José 1883–1949

Mexican painter. Orozco trained as an agronomist, and studied art intermittently from 1908 to 1914. His early paintings were Post-Impressionist in style. He was a political caricaturist during the Mexican revolution. From 1923 he executed many large, prodemocracy murals in public buildings. His style was now Realistic Expressionism, with the influence of folk art, and in his work he denounced the oppression of ordinary people. *Prometheus* (1930) is an example. From 1927 to 1934 he was in Europe and the USA, painting murals of the same nature. Among his works are the pacifist frescoes for Mexico City's Palace of Fine Arts (1934) and a mural for New York's MOMA (1940). With Rivera and Siqueiros, he was one of the major Mexican muralists.

Pauli, Wolfgang 1900–58

Austrian-born pioneer of quantum mechanics. After graduating at Munich (1921) he studied with Niels Bohr in Copenhagen and Max Born in Göttingen. From 1928 to 1958 he was professor in the Federal Institute of Technology, Zurich, except for the war years which were spent at Princeton, USA (when he acquired American citizenship). On the basis of quantum mechanics he formulated (1924) the exclusion principle, according to which no two electrons in an atom can be in the same quantum state. He also postulated that in addition to the three quantum numbers assigned to electrons in an atom, a fourth – a positive or negative – was necessary to take account of electron spin. For this highly original concept, verified experimentally in 1926, Pauli was awarded a Nobel prize in 1945.

Pétain, H. Philippe 1856–1951

Soldier and president of Vichy France. A general, Pétain led the French defense of Verdun in 1916. In 1917 he became French commander-in-chief, restoring morale after mutinies, and in 1918 marshal of France. He later entered politics, in 1934 became war minister, and in 1939–40 was ambassador to Spain. He then became head of state after the fall of France, and signed an armistice with the Germans. He relocated his government in Vichy, with effective control only in the south, and pursued a secret policy of neutrality. He dismissed his openly pro-German foreign minister Laval in 1940, sent a secret emissary to London, tried to persuade Franco not to give the Germans access to North Africa, and maintained relations with the US. In 1942 the Germans forcibly reinstated Laval and occupied southern France. After this, Pétain's powers became only nominal, but in 1942, while officially denouncing the Allied landing in North Africa, he issued secret orders for Vichy troops to join them. After the 1944 Allied landing in Normandy, he fled to Germany, but later returned voluntarily to France, where in 1941 he received a death sentence for collaboration; this was later commuted to life imprisonment.

Pickford, Mary 1893–1979

US film actress. The most popular film star ever, she had a natural, radiant child-woman appeal: she was "America's Sweetheart" and no one wanted her to change. So she played lovable little girls and was 28 before she insisted on cutting off the curls. Her career went downhill. A shrewd negotiator, in 1909 she was earning $40 a week; in 1916 $10,000, plus bonus and profit share. In 1919 she, Chaplin, Douglas Fairbanks and D.W. Griffith formed United Artists, and in 1920 she married Fairbanks, to the public's delight.

Pirandello, Luigi 1867–1936

Italian playwright. After studying philology at Rome and Bonn universities, Pirandello wrote poetry, short stories, and novels. Success came with his third novel in 1904, the year of his wife's breakdown, which culminated in violent insanity, and her commital in 1918 to an asylum. His shift into drama as primary medium was marked in 1916 by his writing nine plays, including *Right you are (if you think so)*. The Paris production in 1923 of *Six Characters in Search of an Author* (1921) and *Henry IV* (1922) made him famous worldwide. In 1925 to 1928, he extended this success with his own company, "Teatro d'Arte". Pirandello won the 1934 Nobel Prize. He was innovatory in theatrical techniques, employing lighting to point the drama, and in writing, using the "play within a play" in his exploration of "appearances" versus reality. Pirandello uses the theatrical illusion to reveal inner truth, in the cause of human happiness, which he saw as achievable only in conscious connection with reality.

Poincaré, Raymond 1860–1934

French prime minister and president. In 1887, Poincaré was elected to the Chamber of Deputies as a Republican. He served in several ministerial posts, was elected to the senate in 1903, and in 1912, became prime minister, reaffirmed the alliance with Russia, and strengthened that with Britain. In 1913 he was elected president. He tried to unite France during the war years, appointing his adversary Clemenceau as prime minister in

1917. He left office in 1920, and returned to the Senate, where he chaired the reparations committee. He regained the premiership in 1922, and, claiming that Germany had defaulted on war reparations, in 1923 ordered the French occupation of the Ruhr. Fiscal problems resulted, and he lost the premiership in 1924, but regained it in 1926, and resolved the economic crisis he then inherited. He retired in 1929.

Primo de Rivera, Miguel 1870–1930
Spanish dictator. Primo served as military governor of Cadiz during 1915–19, and then became captain general of Valencia. In 1922, he was appointed military governor of Barcelona. He led a military coup in 1923, and then established a dictatorship, through his leadership of the Union Patriótica. He began a program of public works and improved labor relations, but failed to introduce land reforms and curtailed civil liberties in Catalonia. In 1926, he defeated three attempts to overthrow him. Abroad, in 1927 he ended the Moroccan war. By 1929 the economy had seriously deteriorated and Primo lost the support of the army. He resigned in 1930.

Rathenau, Walter 1867–1922
German industrialist and politician. Headed the large Allgemeine-Elektrizitäts-Gesellschaft (AEG) founded by his father, after 1914. During World War I he instigated and directed the war raw materials department (1914–15), vital to Germany's economic mobilization for war. Rathenau then returned to his business empire. In 1921 as minister of reconstruction, he advocated compliance with Germany's obligations under the Treaty of Versailles. As foreign minister (1922) Rathenau sought reconciliation with the Allies, and signed the Treaty of Rapallo with the Soviet Union (1922), which canceled war debts, gave the Soviet government diplomatic recognition, and strengthened Russo- German economic ties. Despite his success he was increasingly detested in Germany as a Jew, a representative of the Weimar government and for signing the Rapallo Treaty with Communists. An advocate of social democracy, he wrote several books, including *New Society* in 1918. He was murdered in Berlin.

Ray, Man (Emanuel Rabinovitch) 1890–1976
US photographer and painter. In 1915, after studying painting in New York, and trying to start an artists' community, Ray met Marcel Duchamp. Both witty and curious, they were lifelong friends, and spearheaded New York Dadaism. In 1918 Ray painted imitation photographs, using an airbrush. He began to produce surreal objects, like *Gift* (1921), an icon with tacks attached. In 1921, Ray moved to Paris, mixed with the Surrealists, and earned money with fashion and portrait photography. He also made films, like *L'Etoile*

du mer (1925). He developed the "Rayograph" (photogram), and "solarization" – introducing light while processing film, which featured in *The Age of Light* (1934). In 1935, Ray collaborated with Paul Eluard on a book of love poetry, *Facile*. In 1940 Ray moved to Hollywood, and in 1951, to Paris.

Reith, John 1889–1971
Scottish creator of British public-service broadcasting. Trained as an engineer, he was appointed general manager of the newly formed BBC in 1922. He aimed to bring purpose and status to broadcasting, including cultural, educational and religious programmes alongside information and entertainment and demanding high standards of behavior from his staff. When the company was made a corporation, he became its director-general, pursuing the same policy while keeping technical standards high. In 1936 he inaugurated British TV. He left the BBC in 1938 to serve as a wartime minister and peacetime adminstrator.

Richards, Gordon 1904–
British jockey. He was the most successful jockey through 26 British flat-racing seasons he rode in from 1925 to 1954. In May 1950 he became the first to ride 4000 winners. His total score – 4870 – was a world record, not broken until 1956. He won the St Leger five times, the 2000 Guineas three times but the Derby only once. He retired after injury to become a trainer and racing manager.

Rivera, Diego 1886–1957
Mexican painter. After studying art in Mexico and Madrid, and touring Europe, Rivera settled in 1911 in Paris, where he met Picasso and others, and took up Cubism. In 1921, returning to Mexico, he embraced its folk art, and became active as a revolutionary. In 1923 he began to execute enormous murals on public buildings, in a realistic manner with a political and historical narrative content, like *Workers of the Revolution*, painted in 1929, the year he became director of Mexico's Central School of Fine Arts. His influence on Mexican art was enormous, and it spread to the USA and Europe; in the 1930s he also painted murals in the USA. It is these monumental works that have left the most enduring mark on 20th-century painting.

Rodchenko, Alexander 1891–1956
Russian artist and designer. After studying fine art, Rodchenko discovered, and was impressed by, Futurism. From 1915 he painted abstracts; spurning the mysticism of the Suprematists, he began in 1917, influenced by Tatlin, to create constructions of wood and iron. In 1918 he became the first director of the Museum of Artistic Culture, and in 1919, co-director of Moscow's Industrial Art workshops. In 1920, he painted *Black on Black*, in

response to Malevich's *White Square on a White Background*; he also made Constructivist hanging pieces, and started to design posters. In 1925 he designed the Russian stand at the Paris exhibition of decorative arts. He also made in this year his only visit to Paris, to set up a Workers' Club.

Rubinstein, Helena 1870–1965
Polish-born cosmetician. She left Poland in 1902 to visit Australia, where she opened a beauty salon, offering free consultation and a cream she had taken with her. An instant success, she studied dermatology in Europe, opening salons in London (1908) and Paris (1912). In 1914 she immigrated to the USA and set up salons in New York and other cities. By 1917 she was distributing products wholesale and after World War II she manufactured on all five continents. Constantly improving and developing new lines in cosmetics, she was the first to introduce medicated skin-care products and cosmetics for men.

Ruska, Ernst August Friedrich 1906–88
German physicist, pioneer of the transmission electron microscope. After studying engineering in the Technical University, Munich, and working as a research student in Berlin University, he became development engineer for Television Berlin (1934–36), an appointment which stimulated his existing interests in electron optics. From 1937 to 1955 he was with Siemens and Halske AG, and was subsequently appointed director of the Institute for Electron Microscopy. His research career started just as quantum mechanics were establishing a duality between waves and particles. In 1928, while still a research student, he collaborated with M. Krull in constructing a microscope in which a beam of electrons was focused by a magnetic coil, analogous to the way in which lenses focus light in a conventional instrument. This gave a modest X17 magnification but by 1933 he had constructed a far more sophisticated instrument giving X12,000 magnification, six times greater than that of the best optical microscope. Magnifications up to one million times were eventually achieved. In 1986 Ruska shared a Nobel prize with H. Rohrer and G. Binnig, of IBM in Zurich.

Ruth, Babe 1895–1948
US baseball player. The holder of a record 60 home runs in a 154-game major-league season (1927), he became a professional in 1914. He pitched 29 consecutive scoreless innings for the Boston Red Sox in the 1916 and 1918 World Series. Sold as an outfielder to the New York Yankees for $125,000 in 1920, he stayed there until 1934. In 1930–31 he was the game's top earner with a salary of $80,000. He led the American League in home runs for 12 years, hitting in 22 major-league seasons a total of 714 from 8399 times at bat.

David Sarnoff

Erwin Schrödinger

Bessie Smith

Sanger, Margaret 1883–1966

Founder of US birth control movement and major influence upon changes in law and public attitudes towards contraception. As a nurse on the Lower East Side of New York City Sanger encountered the poverty, illness and death associated with uncontrolled fertility which, with her belief in a women's right to control her own body, initiated a lifelong campaign to supply women with birth control information and methods. Publishing the magazine *The Woman Rebel* (1914) and writing and distributiing the pamphlet *Family Limitation* led to an unsuccessful prosecution for obscenity. In 1916 Sanger opened the first US birth control clinic in Brooklyn, for which she served thirty days in the workhouse. She also founded the American Birth Control League (1921), organized the first World Population Conference (1927), was the first president of the International Planned Parenthood Federation (1953), and worked for birth control in many other countries, especially India and Japan.

Sarnoff, David 1891–1971

Russian-born US broadcasting pioneer. Using his first wages to buy a telegraph machine, he became a radio operator for Marconi, picking up the Titanic's distress signal at the world's most powerful radio station on top of a Manhattan store in 1912. Promoted to a position of authority, in 1916 he proposed the marketing of home radio-receivers to Marconi; in 1921, by then at RCA, he broadcast the Dempsey-Carpentier bout to demonstrate the idea's potential. In 1926 he formed NBC, launching research into TV in 1928.

Schacht, H.H.G. 1877–1970

German financier. Appointed Reich Currency Commissioner and President of the Reichsbank in 1923. Schacht was largely responsible for stabilizing the German mark when it was near collapse in 1923. By 1928 he had achieved eminence as a financier and was re-elected as Reichsbank president. Shortly after he reluctantly signed the Young Plan in 1929, he resigned and became an outspoken critic of German economic policies. In 1933 he resumed the presidency when called back by the Nazis and became the principal director of the German economy for the next six years. Schacht restored the German trade balance by a system of bilateral trade with a number of smaller countries and undertook an expansionist credit policy. His unorthodox methods financed the large Nazi rearmament and public works programs and supplied work for many unemployed. He resigned as president of the Reichsbank in 1939 over a disagreement with Hitler. Charged with high treason and imprisoned by the Nazis, he was acquitted by the Allies in 1945 of crimes against humanity. He subsequently founded a bank in Düsseldorf and was economic advisor to Persia, Syria, Egypt and Indonesia.

Schrödinger, Erwin 1887–1961

Austrian physicist, founder of wave mechanics. He graduated in Vienna, was professor at Breslau and then Zurich. In 1927 he succeeded Max Planck as professor of physics at the University of Berlin but left for Oxford when Hitler came to power in 1933. He returned to Austria , but in 1938 went to the Institute of Advanced Studies, Dublin. In 1957 he accepted a professorship in Vienna. His great achievement was the Schrödinger Equation (1926) in which he expressed mathematically the simultaneous identification of atoms as both waves and particles, postulated by L. de Broglie in 1924. From this arose quantum mechanics.

Schwitters, Kurt 1887–1948

German painter and poet. After studying art in Dresden, Schwitters at first embraced Expressionism, then, influenced by Arp and Dadaism, began in 1918 to produce abstracts, using torn-paper collage, which he named *Merz* (a meaningless word echoing *schmerz* = pain). In 1920 he built a *Merzbau*, a Dadaistic construction filling his house. The Berlin Dadaists rejected him as a "bourgeois reactionary" for the esthetic content of his work and his assertion that *Merz* was art, and that art was "an arch-principle". Still he promoted Dadaism; in 1923 he published *Merz* magazine. In 1932 he joined the Abstraction-Création group, and in 1937, branded "degenerate" by the Nazis, emigrated to Norway, and built his second *Merzbau*. In 1940 he moved to Britain, where he built his last, unfinished, *Merzbau* (1947).

Sidgwick, Nevil Vincent 1873–1952

British chemist. He graduated at Oxford with first class honors in chemistry and classics. After working in Leipzig he returned to Oxford in 1901 becoming reader (1924) and professor (1935). In 1914 he visited Australia and met Ernest Rutherford, then developing his theories on atomic structure. This led him to attempt to interpret the chemical bonds between atoms in terms of the electronic theory being developed by the physicists, which led to the concept of two different types of bond: the coordinate link, comprising two electrons from one atom, and the covalent link, comprising one electron from each atom. His great *Electronic Theory of Valency* (1927) established his reputation internationally.

Sloan, Alfred Pritchard, Jr 1875–1966

US Chairman and President of General Motors. After graduating in electronic engineering in 1895 he joined Hyatt Roller Bearing Company as a draftsman and became its president in 1897. He led the company's rapid progression, quickly exploiting the increasing market for his product in the expanding automobile industry. Hyatt was purchased by the General Motors Corporation (GM) in 1917 and in 1918 Sloan was appointed a

GM vice-president, director and member of the executive committee. He was soon promoted, eventually becoming president and chief executive in 1928. He resigned as president in 1937 and was elected Chairman of the Board. Sloan was given much of the credit for GM's success and its quick recovery from the postwar slump. During his presidency GM became the largest automobile manufacturer and largest single business organization in the world. Through divisions and subsidies he diversified and decentralized production but simultaneously centralized administration. When Sloan retired in 1956, GM accounted for over half US automobile sales. Sloan also supported many philanthropic ventures.

Smith, Bessie 1895–1937

US jazz vocalist. The greatest blues singer ever, by 1920 she had a show in Atlantic City and in 1923 she moved to New York and signed with Columbia. By 1925 she was star of a hugely successful summer touring show, Harlem Frolics, and in 1927 was earning more than any black artist anywhere. A second show, Mississippi Days, followed in 1928, but tastes changed and her career declined. Her hard-living lifestyle was a prototype for women blues singers.

Smith, Mamie 1883–1946

US blues vocalist. Her second record, *Crazy Blues* (1920), opened the market for black blues recordings aimed at black audiences, selling 7500 copies the first week. It was her big break: she formed the Jazz Hounds and made a fortune. By the mid-twenties she owned three luxury homes in New York. Tastes changed and her career waned through the thirties and early forties. Finally poverty and arthritis overtook her.

Spencer, Stanley 1891–1959

British painter. Spencer attended the Slade School, London (1908–12); his work appeared in London's Second Post-Impressionist Exhibition (1912). Military service in the World War I deepened the visionary quality of his painting; he set religious tableaux, Crucifixions and Resurrections, in scenes of daily life in his home village of Cookham, in works like *The Resurrection, Cookham*, completed in 1927, the year of his first one-man show. He painted the massive mural in the War Memorial Chapel, Burghclere (1926–32). As an official World War II artist, he painted shipyard scenes. From 1945 to 1950 he did a series of *Resurrections*. As well as religious vision, his work's strong eroticism spoke for liberation from sexual guilt.

Stambolysky, Alexander 1879–1923

Bulgarian prime minister and agrarian reformer who moved taxation from the peasantry to the bourgeoisie and urban proletariat; redistributed land to the peasantry; and reformed the judicial

▼ Stanley Spencer

▼ Marie Stopes

▼ Gloria Swanson

system to make it more accessible to the common man before being overthrown in a military coup and executed. After studying agriculture in Germany he returned to Bulgaria, became editor of the *Agrarian Banner* and was elected to the National Assembly as leader of the Agrarian National Union (1908). Stambolysky's opposition to King Ferdinand's decision to enter World War I on the side of Germany resulted in imprisonment (1915) but, released (1918), he led an insurrection which forced Ferdinand's abdication. He became Prime Minister (1919) and, despite signing the unpopular Treaty of Neuilly, gained a majority in the 1920 elections. With virtual dictatorial powers. Stambolysky implemented policies favoring the peasantry, who composed eighty per cent of the population.

Staudinger, Hermann 1881–1965

German chemist, pioneer of polymer chemistry. After studying in the Universities of Halle, Darmstadt and Munich he became professor of chemistry successively at Karlsrühe (1908), Zurich (1912) and Freiburg (1926–51). About 1920 he became interested in polymers. The conventional view was that these were aggregates of small molecules (monomers) but Staudinger demonstrated that they were in fact giant molecules consisting of thousands of atoms. This opened up new possibilities for the synthesis of many new types of plastics and fibers. Belatedly, he was awarded a Nobel prize in 1953.

Stevens, Wallace 1879–1955

US poet. Stevens studied law, and was called to the bar in 1904. He became involved with a Greenwich Village poetry group, publishing poems in little magazines. From 1916 he worked for an insurance company, becoming its vice-president in 1934, and writing secretly. His first collection, *Harmonium* (1923), had poor sales and good reviews. In 1951 a book of essays, *The Necessary Angel*, appeared, and in 1954, his *Collected Poems* won a Pulitzer Prize. Stevens writes about the difference between reality and human perception, and about loss of belief. In 1940 he wrote, in a letter, that his "major poetic idea is the idea of God". Influenced by Japanese art, and haiku – see "Thirteen Ways of Looking at a Blackbird" – his work uses the natural world to achieve Joycean "epiphanies".

Stopes, Marie 1880-1958

Pioneer of birth control clinics. After graduating in three subjects in 1902, Stopes taught and wrote botanical papers, becoming in 1904 Britain's youngest Doctor of Science. The distressing annulment of her first marriage in 1916 caused her to turn her attention to the desirability of birth control as liberating for married women and a factor in a successful and pleasurable marriage. She

began to write on the subjects of sex and contraception, producing in 1918 *Married Life*, which was unprecedentedly direct, and *Wise Parenthood*. In 1921 she and her second husband Humphrey Verdon-Roe founded a birth-control clinic in North London. She wrote many more books, including *Contraception* (1923), the most comprehensive work on the subject. Stopes' frankness, practicality and commitment, romantically tinged by her view of sexual pleasure as the right of all women, were pivotal in the dramatic change of attitude toward women and sexuality which occurred in the later 20th century.

Strong, Benjamin 1872–1928

US banker. Starting as a banking clerk in New York, he became secretary of several companies including the Bankers' Trust Company (1903) of which he became president in 1913. He was involved in the investigation and assistance of New York banks in difficulty in the 1907 crisis and was director of a number of companies, including the General Electric Company. In 1914 Strong was appointed the first governor of the Federal Reserve Bank of New York, the largest of 12 regional banks established under the 1913 Act, and it became the pivot of the new system, with Strong exerting considerable influence. US entry into the war in 1917 put the system under strain but this was alleviated largely through Strong's leadership. His postwar conferences with heads of European central banking systems resulted in the vital measures taken for fiscal readjustment and stabilization. Measures that he initiated included loans to Poland, the German Reichsbank and the Bank of England, and the stabilization of the French and Italian currencies.

Strumilin, Stanisláv G. 1877–1974

Russian economist and statistician. Participated in revolutionary activities as a young man, was arrested, imprisoned and exiled, escaping twice. An economics graduate, he worked as a professional statistician for the government and on the wartime fuel distribution committee (1911–14). After the Revolution he began a long career in Soviet statistical and planning bodies, heading statistical offices for the Labor Commissariat and All-Russian Central Council of Trade Unions (1918–23). He became a Presidium member of the State Planning Commission, Gosplan, from 1921, subsequently being appointed chief of the Central Statistical Administration and deputy chairman of Gosplan. Strumilin was largely responsible for the earlier drafts of the first five-year plan. He left Gosplan in 1937 but returned during World War II (1943–51). In 1931 Strumilin was elected a full member of the USSR Academy of Science, becoming head of its Institute of Economics. He wrote prolifically on economics, receiving two Orders of Lenin and the Red Labor Banner.

Sumner, James Batcheller 1887–1955

US biochemist. He entered Harvard in 1906 to study engineering but changed to chemistry, graduating in 1910. From 1911 to 1914 he was a research worker there before becoming assistant (later full) professor of biochemistry (1914–38) at Cornell University Medical Schooi, where he was soon appointed director of a laboratory of enzyme chemistry. In 1917, convinced that enzymes were proteins, he set out to isolate one (urease) in pure form. In 1926 he succeeded, producing what he claimed to be a pure crystalline product. This was disputed, however, because it was contrary to the views on enzymes of the eminent German chemist R. Willstätter. Not until John Howard Northrop produced crystalline pepsin in 1930 was Sumner's work validated; he went on to produce a number of other crystalline enzymes. In 1946 he shared a Nobel prize with fellow biochemists Northrop and Wendell Meredith Stanley.

Swanson (Svensson), Gloria 1897–1983

US film actress. Romantic comedy and tearjerkers for Triangle filled most of 1916–19. She joined De Mille at Paramount and found stardom in suggestive bedroom farces like *Don't Change Your Husband* (1919). In the mid-twenties, mostly in drama, she was America's ultimate glamor queen. Stroheim's extravagance broke an independent venture, *Queen Kelly* (1928), and she retired in 1934. Of her three comebacks, the second was the most memorable – *Sunset Boulevard* (1950). Her autobiography appeared in 1980.

Tanguy, Yves 1900–55

French US painter. Tanguy came to Vlaminck's attention with some drawings made in 1922; in 1923, inspired by a de Chirico piece, he decided to paint. In 1925 he joined the Surrealists, and painted bleak, eerie dream landscapes with phantom forms; he attempted to paint subconscious contents – *He Did What He Wanted* (1927). Some of his paintings were characterized by flame-like images and rocks, some contained smoother forms, reminiscent of those of Arp. His consciousness of rock formations was deepened after a trip to Africa in 1930. Tanguy proceeded to paint a series with rugged rock formations, backed by distant, hazy vistas (1931–34).

Teague, Walter Dorwin 1883–1960

US industrial designer. The pioneer of industrial design as a profession, he worked first in advertising as a designer. In 1926 he set up an office specifically to design exhibitions, interiors, corporate graphics and product. Important early work included the design of two Eastman Kodak cameras (1927) and the Marmon 16 automobile (1930). He also designed railway coaches, office machines, filling stations and the Boeing 707 interior. He wrote several books.

Tiselius, Arne Wilhelm Kaurin 1902–71

Swedish biochemist, remembered for his use of electrophoretic analysis and chromatography for the purification of proteins. After graduating in science and mathematics at Uppsala, he remained there as assistant professor of physical chemistry (1930–37) and of biochemistry (1937–67): latterly he worked in a new Institute of Biochemistry founded in 1946. Initially his research was with The Svedberg on the purification of proteins and other large molecules by ultracentrifugation but he later developed "the Tiselius apparatus", to be employed in an alternative technique by which such molecules were separated by their different rates of movement in an electric field. He used this technique for many purposes, including the separation of the main blood proteins. He also used chromatographic methods for adsorption analysis. After World War II he took a leading role in formulating Swedish scientific policy. In 1947 he was appointed vice-president of the Nobel Foundation and did much to extend its activities. He received the 1948 Nobel Prize for Chemistry.

Trotsky, Leon 1879–1940

Russian revolutionary and Marxist thinker. Trotsky joined the Russian Social Democratic Labor party in 1896, and was banished to Siberia in 1900. He escaped abroad in 1902, and in 1903 sided with the Mensheviks against Lenin, whom he criticized as a potential dictator. Trotsky returned to Russia, and was prominent in the 1905 revolution. Banished again, he escaped to Europe, and tried to reunite the two wings of the party. He campaigned against World War I, and so was deported from France. He returned to Russia after the February Revolution, joined the Bolsheviks and was appointed to their central committee. During the October Revolution, as chairman of the Petrograd soviet, he organized the seizure of power in St Petersburg. From 1917 to 1918 he was commissar for foreign affairs, negotiated with Germany at Brest-Litovsk, but resigned over the conclusion of the treaty. From 1918 to 1925 he was war commissar, founded the Red Army, and led them in the civil war of 1918–20, afterwards using them as labor in economic reconstruction. He was also a Politburo member from 1919 to 1927. After Lenin's death in 1924, Trotsky seemed his most likely successor. He argued a theory of "permanent revolution" as opposed to Stalin's "socialism in one country", forming the left "combined opposition" with Zinoviev and Kamenev. They were defeated by Stalin and his new comrades on the right, and in 1929 Trotsky was banished abroad. He continued to propagandize against Stalin, who successfully represented him to the Soviet people as a monster. Trotsky attempted unsuccessfully to create a Fourth International to fight fascism and replace the Comintern. He was assassinated in 1940, probably by a Stalinist agent.

Valentino, Rudolph 1895–1926

Italian-born film star. After four years as a Hollywood bit-part player, he won the lead in *The Four Horsemen of the Apocalypse* (1921) and was instantly a star. To his American female audiences he represented exotic sensuality, mystery and illicit eroticism in a potent compound of passion and melancholy. His subsequent box-office hits were *The Sheik* (1921), *Blood and Sand* (1922) and *Monsieur Beaucaire* (1924). News of his death, from a ruptured ulcer, met with unequaled fan hysteria, including several suicides.

Valéry, Paul 1871–1945

French poet and essayist. As a law student he met Louys, Gide, and Mallarmé. Influenced by the latter, Poe and Huysmans, he had produced 200–300 "pure" poems, some published in Symbolist journals, by 1892, when, crossed in love, he "renounced emotion", and wrote only prose, using a character, *M. Teste*, to represent the intellect. He meditated each dawn for the rest of his life, on consciousness and language – his quest was to find "what a man can do". In 1917 *La Jeune parque* appeared, a collection which brought him recognition as the finest living French poet. He followed up with *Album de vers anciens* (1920) and *Charmes* (1922), which contains his best-known poem "Le Cimetière Marin". Valéry's poetry, at once abstract and sensuous, often erotic, bespeaks the tension between contemplation and action he felt in his life.

Vidor, King 1894–1982

US film director. After a feature debut with Universal and a stint with his own studio (Vidor Village), his reputation began building when he joined MGM. The anti-war film *The Big Parade* (1925) established him. *The Crowd* (1928), *Hallelujah* (1929), *Street Scene* (1932) and *Our Daily Bread* (1934) had an equally humanistic, if sentimental, tone; in individual scenes he manipulated camera and sound brilliantly. From 1935 to the late fifties his work was more commercial: *Duel in the Sun* (1947) is the high point of this period. He wrote an autobiography, *A Tree is a Tree* (1953).

Walton, Ernest Thomas Sinton 1903–

Irish physicist. A physics graduate from Trinity College, Dublin, he won a scholarship to Cambridge to work in the Cavendish Laboratory under Ernest Rutherford. There, in 1932, he took part with J.D. Cockcroft in a classic experiment in which atoms of lithium and boron were split by bombardment with protons. For this, the two men were jointly awarded a Nobel prize in 1951. Meanwhile Walton had returned to Dublin as fellow of Trinity College (1934–74) and professor of natural and experimental philosophy (1947–74). His later research was on hydrodynamics, nuclear physics and microwaves.

Warner, Jack L. 1892–1978

Canadian-born film executive. With his three brothers, he dabbled in film distribution and production before setting up the Warner Bros studio in 1923 and later expanding into distribution. The breakthrough came in 1927 when they launched the first sound film, *The Jazz Singer*. Their thirties' pictures – gangster movies, social dramas, biographies and musicals – reflected the mood of the Depression years.

Wells, H. G. 1861–1946

British novelist, journalist, historian, prophet and one of the founders of science fiction, Wells was a major figure in the spread of the new ideas at the start of this century. After studying biology and working as a journalist, he published scientific fantasies, such as *The War of the Worlds* (1898). Wells, initially believing that science could create a perfect world, subsequently realized it could also work for evil and felt that human civilization was likely to destroy itself. He outlined his socialist, internationalist and Utopian solutions to the ills of modern society in books such as *The Shape of Things to Come* (1933). Predicting modern technological achievements, such as the atomic bomb, he advised the public on the dangers of such progress. Wells also dealt with social issues, influencing contemporary public opinion. A strong advocate of world unity, he criticized the League of Nations and was involved in the Shankey declaration of the Rights of Man.

Whiteman, Paul 1890–1967

US bandleader and violinist. His major contributions were to publicize jazz, to make it "respectable" and to popularize it; indeed he promoted the first prestige jazz concert – the première of Gershwin's *Rhapsody in Blue* – at New York's Aeolian Hall. He devised the band show and his own band presented spectacular, bowdlerized versions of jazz typified in the Universal film *The King of Jazz* (1930).

Williams, William Carlos 1883–1963

US poet. Williams studied medicine at the University of Pennsylvania until 1906 and in Leipzig until 1910, when he returned to the USA where he practiced medicine and wrote poetry in his hometown, Rutherford, New Jersey. Williams found his own poetic voice with *Al Que Quiere!* "To Him Who Wants It!" (1917), a voice that celebrated the world of the senses with directness, simplicity and startlingly clear imagery – see "Red Wheelbarrow". In Williams' finest work, the five-volume *Paterson* (1946–58), he uses the metaphor of a city on the Passaic River in New Jersey to explore the soul of America and of modern man. Williams also produced a great deal of prose – historical essays, a novel-trilogy, many fine short stories and a play *A Dream of Love*

▲ Virginia Woolf

▲ William Butler Yeats

▲ Emiliano Zapata

(1948). His autobiography appeared in 1951, and his final collection *Pictures from Brueghel and Other Poems* (1962) won him the 1963 Pulitzer Prize (awarded posthumously).

Wills, Helen 1905–

US tennis player. She was the world's top woman player from 1927 to 1935, with powerful serves and overhead shots which compensated for her lack of speed. Indeed, between 1927 and 1932 she did not drop a set as a singles player. A deeply committed competitor, she was nicknamed "Little Miss Polar Face". She won Wimbledon eight times (1927–30, 1932–33, 1935 and 1938), the US singles seven times (1923–25, 1927–29 and 1931) and four French singles and 12 US, Wimbledon and French doubles titles between 1923 and 1939. She also won the singles and doubles titles at the 1924 Olympics.

Wilson, (Thomas) Woodrow 1856–1924

28th US president. Wilson rose to prominence as the reforming Democratic governor of New Jersey, and in 1913 became president. He immediately embarked upon a program of radical domestic legislation, to achieve what he had described as the New Freedom. He passed the Underwood Tariff Act, and, to regulate the currency, the Federal Reserve Act. In 1914 the Federal Trade Commission was established to promote competition, and later the same year came the Clayton Anti-Trust Act. Abroad, Wilson abolished US exemption from Panama Canal tolls. The Mexican situation presented him with a longstanding problem, and he failed to end the civil war there. Adopting a neutral stance in World War I, he offered to mediate. In 1916 he issued an ultimatum to Germany over the dangers their submarines posed to American shipping, and a short time later Germany promised the abandonment of submarine warfare. However in 1917 they reneged on this, and a proposal for an antiAmerican alliance of Germany, Mexico and Japan was revealed. Wilson declared war later in the same year. This year also saw the passing of the 18th amendment, the beginning of the "Prohibition" legislation fully enforced in 1920. In 1918 Wilson listed his Fourteen Points necessary to a lasting peace. In 1919 he attended the Paris Peace Conference, which undertook notably the establishment of the League of Nations on his recommendation. He was a signatory to the Treaty of Versailles, and was awarded the 1919 Nobel Peace Prize. He left office in 1921.

Woolf, Virginia 1882–1941

British novelist and critic. Daughter of the eminent literary man Sir Leslie Stephen, Woolf was the central figure in the Bloomsbury Group. She was subject all her life to fits of intense depression and mental illness. In 1917, she and her husband, Leonard Woolf, founded the Hogarth Press.

After two "ordinary" novels, she produced the innovative *Jacob's Room* (1922). *Mrs Dalloway* (1925) and *To The Lighthouse* (1927) – brilliant novels, exhibiting a poetic, near-musical, formalism, and exploring the current beneath the surface, in individuals and relationships. *Orlando* (1928) scandalized some readers; its main character's life spans four centuries, and includes a change of sex. *The Waves* (1931) is a stream-of-consciousness tour de force. She was a literary critic – see, for instance, *The Common Reader* (1925), and social commentator, especially in the field of women's rights – as in *A Room of One's Own* (1929). Woolf's work is extraordinary in its poetic and personal sensitivity, limpidity of mind, and commitment to the representation of the natural flow of consciousness, which does not observe seriality, or follow the reason imposed by convention, or ordinary language.

Yeats, William Butler 1865–1939

Irish poet. Yeats, as an art student in London, cofounded the Rhymer's Club, and took up writing poetry seriously, using Celtic myth and occult symbolism. In 1889 he met Maud Gonne, for whom he had an unrequited passion. In Dublin in 1899, with Lady Gregory, he set up the Irish Literary Theatre, which became, in 1904, the Abbey Theatre. He wrote many plays for it. His collected works of 1908 contain all his mythic lyrics, including "The Lake Isle of Innisfree" and "Down by the Sally Gardens". *Responsibilities* (1914), is a collection on socio-political themes. It was written in the period of Ezra Pound's influence on him. In 1922 Yeats entered the Irish Senate; in 1923 he was awarded the Nobel Prize. *A Vision* (1925) is an occult-based and esoteric text inspired by Blake. As well as the Gaelic folk tradition, he was influenced by Japanese and Chinese art and philosophy – see "Lapis Lazuli". Yeats' penetrating and uncompromising vision, coupled with an intensity of feeling matched by the lyrical beauty of his language and musicality of his phrasing, and his drawing on his ethnic roots, make him a master poet.

Young, Owen D. 1874–1962

US lawyer and businessman. Young practiced law until 1912 when he was appointed general counsel for the General Electric Company, also serving as chairman (1922–39). He organized the Radio Corporation of America in 1919, becoming honorary chairman of its board of directors (1919–29) and chairman of the executive committee (1929–33). A member of the first committee of experts appointed to advise the Reparations Commission over currency stabilization in post World War I Germany, he chaired the second international committee of experts in 1929. The plan, which became known as the Young Plan, proposed a new settlement for reparations.

Revising the Dawes Plan of 1924, it reduced the amount of reparations due from Germany, established the Bank for International Settlements to handle the transfer of funds and ended Allied control over German economic life. Before the plan got underway the Depression of the 1930s began and after Hitler came to power in 1933 German obligations made under the Treaty of Versailles were not kept.

Zapata, Emiliano 1879–1919

Mexican leader of agrarian revolutionaries during the Great Revolution (1910–17) whose agrarian reforms were eventually included in the constitution and implemented by subsequent leaders. Zapata opposed the practice of landowners expanding their holdings at the expense of village lands in his native Morelos and became leader of a growing peasant movement. Under president Madero, Zapata became leader in Morelos (1911). However, Madero failed to restore land under the old Indian communal system of the *ejidos* and Zapata proclaimed the "Plan of Ayala", which called for radical land reforms and condemned Madero as inadequate to the task. Adopting the slogan "Land and Liberty", he continued his campaign against subsequent governments and dictatorships whilst maintaining control in Morelos, where he carried out his own reforms. He drove out the rich landowners, divided the lands of their estates among the peasants, and established schools, social services, and agricultural credit organizations. The reforms were reproduced in the 1917 constitution and implemented under subsequent governments. Although his methods were controversial, Zapata became a national hero.

Zetkin (Eissner), Clara 185–1933

German feminist and communist leader. Zetkin became a prominent and influential socialist theoretician on women's issues. She maintained that women's oppression originated from economic dependence on men and lack of employment. Recognizing the different roles of men and women and their equal importance, she also believed that women should be able to carry out meaningful work as well as function as wives and mothers. However, she did not advocate women's rights for their own sake but for the good of the working class as a whole. Her achievements included helping to found the Second Socialist International (1889); editing the socialist women's paper *Equality* (1892–1917); cofounding the International Socialist Women's Congress (1907) and the radical Spartacus Group (1916); serving the Reichstag (1920–33) as a member of the German Communist Party; and serving in the Russian communist regime increasingly after 1921, in which year she joined the Presidium of the Third International.

ACKNOWLEDGEMENTS

Picture credits
1 Charlie Chaplin CPI
2–3 Constructing the Empire State Building International Museum of Photography at George Eastman House
4–5 Crowds at Cubs Parks, 1922 Chicago Historical Society
6–7 New York's financial district c.1917 CPI
8–9 The Stars celebrate Hollywood's export achievement Museum of Modern Art, New York/Film Stills Archive
10–11 Battle of Passchendale IWM
46–47 German weapons captured in 1918 IWM
82–83 Soviet members of a collective farm PF
120–121 The Beach at Deauville JH

15 HDC 17t IWM 17b The Tank Museum, Bovington 18 Bibliothèque de Documentation Internationale Contemporaine, Paris 19 National Museum, Dresden 21 IWM 22t National Museum of Ireland, Dublin 22b PF 23t DKC 23c New York Public Library 23b RV 24l Lenin Library, Moscow 24r DKC 26t, 26c AA 26b Mayakovsky, 20 years of work, Museum of Modern Art, Oxford 27t DKC 27c JH/Marc Riboud 27b Universidad Autónoma de Chapingo, Chapel 29l National Museum, Washington D.C. 29r, 30 IWM 31t David Low 31b UB 32–33 HDC 33 HDC Bettmann Archive 34t HDC 34b TPS 35 PF 36t Collection of the Heckscher Museum, Huntington, New York © DACS, 1990 36b AA 36–37 Galleria Schwarz © ADAGP, Paris and DACS London, 1990 37t M/David Seymour 37b M/Bruno Barbey 39, 40 DKC 41 Alexander Meledin 42 HDC 43 AA 44–45 Alexander Meledin 44 inset t International Museum of Photography at George Eastman House, N.Y. 45t RV 45c IKON 45b M/Robert Capa 51 UB 52t MEPL 52b PF 53 TPS 54t ETArchive/IWM 54b RV 55t AA 55b HDC 56t TPS 56b RV 57 MEPL 58b, 58–59 RV 59 UB 60t TPS 60b PF 61 International Museum of Photography at George Eastman House, NY 62b MEPL 62t PF 63t Arkady Siskir 63b Max Alpert 64t Harry Ransom Humanities Research Center, University of Texas 64t CP 64b Mark Edwards/Still Pictures 64–65 PF 65t Barnaby's Picture Library 65b Network 67 National Archives, Washington D.C. 68t, 68b, 68–69 KC 69b Science Museum London 70 HDC 71t Ann Ronan Picture Library 71b David Sarnoff Research Center Archives 73 IWM 74b PF 74–75 The Rockefeller Archive Center 76 Greater London Photo Library 77 RV 78t, 78b Eli Lily and Company 79 Tate Gallery London 80t, 80c PF 80b Deutsche Afrika Linien 81t TPS 81c Peter Inglis 81b CP 87 Jürgens Photo 88, 89t, 89b RV 90t Beryl Williams, University of Sussex 90b Jürgens Photo 91 RV 92t Jürgens Photo 92b, 93 Beryl Williams 93t MEPL 94, 95 AA 96t, 96c, 96–97 HDC 96b Private Collection 97t PF 97b Frank Spooner Pictures 98t, 98–99 British Museum (Natural History) 98b PF 99t HDC 99b SPL 101 RV 102t AA 102b, 103t HDC 103b RV 104–105 Bournville Village Trust 105 HDC 106 LC 107t Brown Brothers, Pennsylvania 107b HDC 108t Advertising Archives 108b, 109 SV 110t Robert Opie Collection 110b Bettmann Archive 111t Barnaby's Picture Library 111b Angelo Hornak 112t Shirley Baker 112b Museum of Childhood, Edinburgh 112–113 Robert Opie Collection 112–113 inset Brown Brothers 113t PF 113b IKON 115 IWM 116 Barnaby's Picture Library 117 HDC 118, 119 SV 124–125 The National Motor Museum, Beaulieu 126l FP 126cr Olivetti, Milan 126br AGE Fotostock, Barcelona 127l AA 127r Time Inc, New York 128t MEPL 128c Geffrye Museum, London 129 John Frost Collection 130 Brown Brothers 130–131, 131r The National Motor Musuem, Beaulieu 131tl, 132b HDC 132t RV 132–133 Chicago Historical Society 133c FPG International 133t CP 134t, 134–135 HPC/The Bettmann Archive 134b UP/Bettmann Newsphotos 135t CPI 135b RV 137t, 137b CPI 138–139 Ramsey Archive 139l, 139cl, 139r AA 139cr CPI 139t SV 140b AA 141t Mander and Mitchenson 141b RV 142, 143t MEPL 143c SV 143b Barnaby's Picture Library 144 MEPL 145l, 145br Bridgeman Art Library 145tr, 145cr Angelo Hornak 147 CPI 148 AA 148–149 Novosti Press Agency 149t KC 150t, 150c CPI 150b NFA, London 150t KC 150b

Barnaby's Picture Library 152–153 Dick Busher 152t KC 152b Museum of Modern Art, New York/Film Stills Archive 153tl APL 153r CPI 154l PF 154c, 154r HDC 155l World Health Organization 155c CPI 155r, 156l, 156c PF 156r Syndication International 157l HDC 157c PF 157r HDC 158l Novosti Press Agency 158c HDC 158r PF 159l CPI 159c, 159r, 160l PF 160c HDC 160r Henry Huntington Library 161l KC 161r HDC 162l Jürgens Photo 162c PF 162r HDC 163l RV 163c AA 163r, 164l, 164c HDC 164r CP 165l, 165c HDC 165r PF 166l Halsman/Magnum 166r AIP Niels Bohr Library 167l, 167c PF 167r HDC 168l, 168t CPI 168c Österreichisches Nationalbibliothek 169l HDC 169c PF 169r KC 170l HDC 170c APL 170r PF 171l, 171c HDC 171r PF

Abbreviations
APL Aquarius Picture Library, Kent
AA Andromeda Archive
BPK Bildarchiv Preussischer Kulturbesitz, Berlin
CP Camera Press, London
CPI Culver Pictures Inc, New York
DKC David King Collection, London
FP The Futile Press, Brighton
HDC Hulton Deutsch Collection, London
IWM Imperial War Museum, London
JH John Hillelson Agency, London
KC Kobal Collection
LC Library of Congress, Washington D.C.
M Magnum Photos, London
MEPL Mary Evans Picture Library, London
NFA National Film Archive, London
PF Popperfoto, Northampton
RF Rex Features, London
RV Roger-Viollet, Paris
SPL Science Photo Library, London
SV Süddeutscher Verlag, Munich
TPS Topham Picture Source, Kent, UK
UB Ullstein Bilderdienst, Berlin

t = top, tl = top left, tr = top right, c = center, b = bottom etc

Editorial and Research Assistance
Steven Chapman, Mary Davies, Jackie Gaff, Jane Higgins, John Horgan, Louise Jones, Nick Law, Andy Overs, Mike Pincombe, Maria Quantrill, Graham Speake, Michelle von Ahn

Artists
Alan Hllingberry, Ayala Kingsley, Kevin Maddison, Colin Salmon, Dave Smith, Del Tolton

Design Assistance
Cyndy Gossert, Nicholas Rous, Dave Smith, Del Tolton, Michelle Von Ahn

Photographs
Shirley Jamieson, David Pratt

Typesetting
Brian Blackmore, Catherine Boyd, Anita Wright

Production
Stephen Elliott, Clive Sparling

Cartography
Maps drafted by Euromap, Pangbourne; Alan Mais (Hornchurch); Sarah Rhodes

Color Origination
J. Film Process, Bangkok; Scantrans, Singapore

INDEX